*f*P

IN THE SHADOW OF THE DAM

The Aftermath of the Mill River Flood of 1874

Elizabeth M. Sharpe

Free Press

New York   London   Toronto   Sydney

*f*P

FREE PRESS
A Division of Simon & Schuster, Inc.
1230 Avenue of the Americas
New York, NY 10020

For information regarding special discounts for bulk purchases,
please contact Simon & Schuster Special Sales at
1-800-456-6798 or business@simonandschuster.com

Designed by Karolina Harris

Map on page xiii copyright Jeff Ward

Manufactured in the United States of America

10   9   8   7   6   5   4   3   2   1

Library of Congress Cataloging-in-Publication Data
Sharpe, Elizabeth M.
In the shadow of the dam : the aftermath of the Mill River flood of 1874 /
Elizabeth M. Sharpe.
   p. cm.
Includes bibliographical references and index.
1. Floods—Massachusetts—Mill River Valley (Hampshire County)—History—19th century.
2. Dams—Massachusetts—Mill River Valley (HampshireCounty)—History—19th century.
3. Mill River Valley (Hampshire County, Mass.)—History—19th century. 4. Mill River
Valley (Hampshire County, Mass.)—History, local.   I. Title.
   F72.H3+ 2004
   2004043308

ISBN 0-7432-2357-8

Cover: Williamsburg Reservoir showing break in west wall.
Back cover: View at Haydenville near the depot showing boardinghouse.
Frontispiece: The William Quigly house in Leeds, after the flood.

ACKNOWLEDGMENTS

I N all the years it has taken me to complete this book, not a day has gone by that I have not shuddered when I thought about the horrible fate the victims of the Mill River flood met and the terrible future the survivors beheld without them. I hope this book honors them.

My first thanks go to my dissertation committee at the University of Delaware who encouraged me to write on the Mill River flood and challenged me to think broadly about the causes of the disaster and the nature of the aftermath. They are: Bernard Herman, J. Ritchie Garrison, Richard Bushman, and Gary Kulik.

I have used the resources of many libraries and historical societies, and I am grateful to their staffs for their assistance: the Library of Congress; the National Archives; the National Museum of American History, Smithsonian Institution; the Massachusetts Archives; the Williamsburg Historical Society; the Sophia Smith Collection at Smith College; the Connecticut Valley Historical Museum; the Wistariahurst Museum; and the Hampshire Law Library. Special thanks go to those staff members at the following institutions who took particular interest in this study and provided special assistance: Brian Tabor and Elise Feeley at Forbes Library in Northampton; Lisa Wenner at the Meekins Library in Williamsburg; Marie Panik at Historic Northampton; and Michael Milewski at the University of Massachusetts Library, Special Collections. I would also like to thank the staffs of the Williamsburg and Northampton town offices as well as the Hampshire County offices, including superior court, probate, registry of deeds, and county commissioners, who have made their records available to me.

Experts in many fields have advised me. Richard Delmar, Mark Gelfand, and David Wall have helped with legal issues. Reverend Kenneth Fuller and Reverend Dit Talley advised on the religious response to the disaster.

William Sharpe and Heather Henderson consulted on literary interpretations of the flood and its heroes. Historians Steven Lubar, Kevin Sweeney, Jeffrey Stine, Donald Jackson, Donald Meyer, and Janet Hutchison suggested paths for research. For technical help on how the Williamsburg dam was constructed, why it failed, and how the flood moved down the valley, I have received very generous assistance from Tom Famulari in the Division of Water Resources of the state of Massachusetts, and James Dall, an engineer in New York state. Both reviewed the entire manuscript and offered much technical information about the forces of nature, dams, and the materials used to construct them. Robert Finney, Robert King, and Rawl Silva provided engineering advice early on. My heartfelt thanks to Joanne Gernstein London, David C. Smith, Mark Gelfand, and Elise Feeley who also read the manuscript.

Over the years, I have had assistance from Jared Cohen, Alan Freeman, Brigid Brown, and Barbara Gilmartin in gathering resources for the study. Nathaniel Drummond deserves special mention for his excellent research abilities. Professional encouragement came from Brian Ogilvie and Sheila MacDonald.

I have benefited from, and thoroughly enjoyed, the local enthusiasm for the study of the flood. Early on, Phyllis Beals, Marilyn Everett, and Gertrude Ronk of the Williamsburg Historical Society, and Jeanne Hemenway and Anne Johnson of the Williamsburg Historical Commission, aided my research. In the past few years, I have come to know Ralmon Black, one of the curators of the Williamsburg Historical Society, who has offered his vast knowledge of local history and his understanding of how the dam builders used local materials. Mary Bisbee has graciously made available newspaper accounts of the flood she had typed into the computer. Eric Weber has generously shared his extensive knowledge of Williamsburg genealogy and the local landscape, and has provided access to the three hundred images of the flood, which he has gathered for study. Eric and Ralmon know more about the path of the flood and its effect on the Mill Valley landscape than anyone. They have introduced me to Sarah Skinner Kilborne and I have benefited from her interest in the Skinner family and the flood. In Leeds, James Parsons has been a valuable source for information on Leeds, yesterday and today; he knows more about the flood in Leeds than anyone. I am forever indebted to him for sharing Fred Howard's letters on the disaster. Ralmon Black, Eric Weber, and James Parsons provided numerous corrections and suggestions to the manuscript. The enthusiasm, knowledge, and untiring support of these local historians has nourished me and made this study more complete than it would have been without them.

The contributions of these people have made this a better book. Any errors of fact or interpretation are mine alone.

My writing group, James Doyle and Linda Wolfe Keister, read countless versions of parts of the book and offered sound advice on the craft of story-telling and encouragement on the project. My literary agent Nina Graybill's unfailing efforts turned an idea into a book. My editor Andrea Au has dispensed expert guidance with patience and good cheer through the entire project. Every minute of working with her has been a delight. I also offer my gratitude to Eric Fuentecilla in the art department and Patty Romanowski and Ted Landry in the copyediting department of Simon & Schuster who have worked to turn a manuscript into a handsome book.

Writing a book is a long-term project that requires the help and support of friends and family. For their favors, interest, and encouragement, I thank loyal friends Nancy McCoy, Clare Cuddy, Jan Majewski, Elizabeth McCullough Johnston, and Carol Gabranski, who has accompanied me on more research expeditions in western Massachusetts than she would care to remember. I could not have written this book without Sarah Gallant's help.

Finally, for help in thousands of ways, I thank my family and particularly my mother, Marie Sharpe, and my husband, Christopher Kostas, who has made it all possible. My final thanks are for my children, Franklin and James Kostas, who have never known a time when I wasn't writing this book. We are all glad this process has come to an end.

To my mother, Marie Chapman Sharpe
and to the memory of my father, George Ezbon Sharpe

Contents

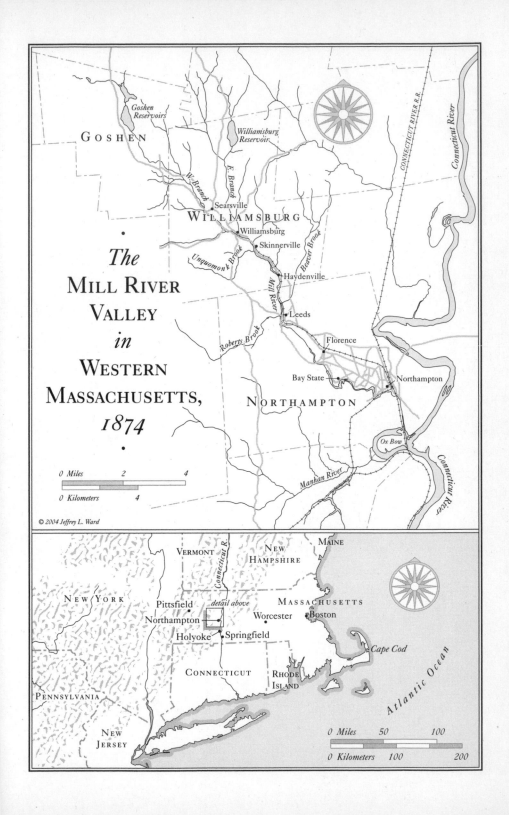

The
MILL RIVER
VALLEY
in
WESTERN
MASSACHUSETTS,
1874

GOSHEN

Goshen Reservoirs

Williamsburg Reservoir

W. Branch

E. Branch

Searsville

WILLIAMSBURG

Williamsburg

Skinnerville

Unquomonk Brook

Beaver Brook

Haydenville

Mill River

Leeds

Roberts Brook

Florence

Bay State

Northampton

NORTHAMPTON

Ox Bow

Manhan River

Connecticut River

CONNECTICUT RIVER R.R.

Connecticut River

| 0 Miles | 2 | 4 |
| 0 Kilometers | 4 | |

© 2004 Jeffrey L. Ward

VERMONT

Connecticut R.

NEW HAMPSHIRE

MAINE

NEW YORK

Pittsfield

detail above

MASSACHUSETTS

Northampton

Worcester

Boston

Holyoke

Springfield

CONNECTICUT

RHODE ISLAND

Cape Cod

PENNSYLVANIA

NEW JERSEY

Atlantic Ocean

| 0 Miles | 50 | 100 |
| 0 Kilometers | 100 | 200 |

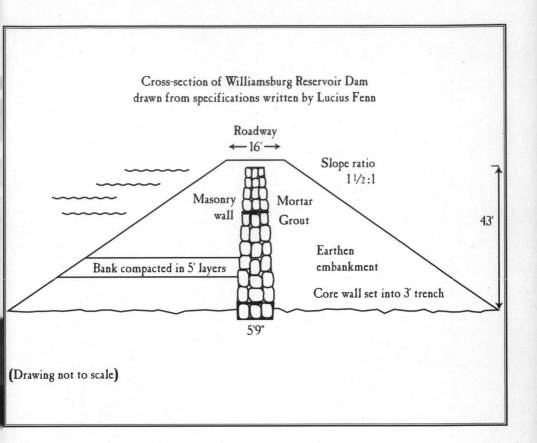

Cross-section of Williamsburg Reservoir Dam
drawn from specifications written by Lucius Fenn

Roadway
← 16' →

Slope ratio
1 1/2 :1

Masonry
wall

Mortar
Grout

Earthen
embankment

Bank compacted in 5' layers

Core wall set into 3' trench

43'

5'9"

(Drawing not to scale)

IN THE SHADOW
OF THE DAM

PROLOGUE

O N the last day of the coroner's inquest into the cause of the Mill
River flood deaths, Joel Hayden Jr. was the morning's first witness.
Two weeks earlier, on May 16, 1874, three of his factories had
been destroyed when the Williamsburg reservoir dam broke, sending an
avalanche of water over five factory villages that lined the Mill Valley in
western Massachusetts. When the flood reached Haydenville, the mill village his father had built, it picked up a house and slammed it into his brass
factory with such force that the three-story brick structure collapsed, ends
folding over the middle as though it were a cardboard box. Brass goods, the
company safe, and even the granite columns that had framed the entrance
to the office building were found hundreds of yards downstream amid heaps
of debris so dense and tangled that men used crowbars to pry the items
apart. Twenty-seven of the 139 people killed were from Haydenville.

Coroner Ansel Wright offered Hayden the opportunity to make a statement before questioning. He accepted. For the record, he said, he wanted
to correct a report by the *New York Herald* that in earlier times his father
had instructed workers to leave the brass factory as soon as they heard the
cry "reservoir" in the streets. There was no such warning system, Hayden
insisted, because there was no thought that the dam would ever break.
Hayden's father, who had died six months earlier, had been partners with
his son for more than a decade in the brass and cotton factories. At thirty-
nine, Young Joel (as everyone still called him) had grown to look like his
father, a successful manufacturer and former Massachusetts lieutenant
governor. They shared the same handsome face with finely chiseled features, a long straight nose, thick, wavy gray hair, and a dignified, energetic
manner. A *Springfield Republican* reporter observed that Joel Jr. "reminds

one forcibly of his father, who especially in his old age, was a man of rarely fine presence."

Ansel Wright turned the questioning over to Charles Delano, a prominent local attorney and a former U.S. congressman, who had been appointed assistant coroner for the inquest. Delano knew Young Joel from Northampton civic affairs and his father from Republican party politics. As Hayden testified, reporters from the Springfield, Boston, and New York papers scribbled furiously, summarizing the proceedings that they would telegraph to their newspapers, or to a wire service, so that Hayden's testimony could be served up that evening or with tomorrow morning's breakfast. According to the newspaper summaries, their dialogue went like this:

Delano asked: What was your father's opinion of the Williamsburg dam?

Hayden said he had no personal knowledge of what his father thought about the dam.

Delano must have thought that Hayden would hold back. The other mill owners, sitting with their attorney at the front table, watching Young Joel, were all partners in the reservoir company that owned the failed dam. Few had willingly offered any information about the dam. Delano picked up a copy of the *Hampshire Gazette*, a Northampton newspaper, and read aloud what purported to be Joel Hayden Jr.'s own statement:

> Mr. Hayden says that "his father was always in fear of this reservoir dam." He believed it to be weak and dangerous, and "a thousand times" says Mr. Hayden "have I heard him express such fears." It worried him and when there was a heavy rain he could not sleep at night, so great was his apprehension that the dam would break away. Several times I have known him to get up in the night and drive up to the reservoir to examine it, so as to personally satisfy himself that it was all right.

Delano asked, did you talk with Henry Gere, the newspaper's editor, about your father's fear of the Williamsburg dam? Young Joel knew Gere well. Twenty-nine years earlier, in 1845, young Joel's father had begun publishing the *Hampshire Herald*, the first newspaper in the county to call for the abolition of slavery, and had hired seventeen-year-old Gere as an apprentice printer and later as editor.

Yes, his father had talked to Mr. Gere, but his words were misunderstood. His father in his later years was timid, especially in the springtime with the threat of flash floods. He was concerned about all the reservoir dams, but not the Williamsburg dam more than the others.

Why did he go up to the Williamsburg reservoir?

Hayden supposed that he went for the same reasons he would sometimes go over to the brass works, to make sure it wasn't on fire.

But the brass factory was across the street from your father's home, while the reservoir was five miles up in the hills. It was "no child's play to drive up there in the night," Delano countered.

No, but it was only on rainy nights that he went, and only to see that it was all right. He was old and frightened easily. He didn't think it would ever go off.

How long would he be gone on these trips to the reservoir?

Hayden didn't know. He never personally saw him go to the Williamsburg reservoir at night. He had only heard from family members that he had gone about a dozen times.

Did your father ever go to one of the Goshen reservoirs at night? The reservoir company owned two reservoirs in the town of Goshen, northwest of Williamsburg, on the West Branch of the Mill River, which supplied power to their factories.

No, Young Joel never knew of him doing that and was under the impression that he never did.

Delano and the jurors asked no more questions. "He [Hayden] gave his testimony with reluctance," the *Springfield Republican* reported.

When Joel Hayden Jr. stepped down, his future was uncertain. The day after the flood he had posted notices promising to rebuild the brass works in the same location in Haydenville. Thrilled, his employees eagerly took jobs with him digging the riverbed with picks and shovels to uncover manufacturing patterns and finished brass goods washed out of the factory. Their wives and children followed behind scooping up the salvage, finding some still packed in their original boxes. But a week after the flood, business leaders from larger manufacturing centers like Chicopee and Holyoke on the Connecticut River, and Norwich, Connecticut, on the Thames River, offered Hayden vast quantities of cheap waterpower from their large rivers to entice him to move his business. If Hayden had changed his mind about rebuilding his father's village, he hadn't made any announcements yet. His employees fished bricks out of the mud to use in building the new factory, and waited.

CHAPTER 1

THE MILL VALLEY

THE Mill River that Joel Hayden Sr. knew was a slim, rocky stream, just fifteen miles long, that tumbled down the east slope of the foothills of the Berkshires to its outlet in the Connecticut River. In its upper reaches, the Mill River was shallow, a ten-foot-wide mountain stream that one could easily step across on rocks protruding through the quick water. For most of its run, the river broadened to forty feet as it raced southeast through the towns of Williamsburg and Northampton. Only when it meandered across the silty floodplain of the Connecticut River on the outskirts of Northampton did it widen to sixty feet. Along its course, it collected water from smaller streams with names like Beaver Brook, Potash Brook, Unquomonk Brook, and Roberts Meadow Brook. Usually the Mill River murmured and gurgled, but when it rushed over several natural waterfalls, it thundered. In the springtime, it roared down in powerful freshets, flash floods fed by snowmelt and spring rains. It shrank and quieted during the dry summer months.

The river basin was shaped like the letter Y. Two large tributaries, the arms of the Y, united in the center of Williamsburg to form the river's main trunk. The Y's left arm, known as the West Branch, sometimes called the Mill Brook, was the longer of the two. It reached up seven miles to the northwest through the high hills of western Williamsburg and into the town of Goshen. The right arm, called the East Branch, stretched three miles straight north from the center of Williamsburg to the town's northern border. The West Branch, the East Branch, and the smaller network of brooks and rills spread through the hills like veins on a leaf to catch the rain and snowmelt and deliver it to the Mill River.

With its rocky base, strong flow, and steep slope, the Mill River made excellent waterpower, typical of New England. Throughout the region, long strings of factories clustered into villages, and villages congregated into small industrial centers on rivers like the Swift River, the Westfield River, the Ware River, and so on. In Massachusetts in the early 1870s, all but a dozen towns had some commercial manufacturing drawn from river power. By 1880 the six states of New England possessed one third of the developed waterpower of the United States, even though New England represented only 2 percent of the nation's land area.

Industrialists like Joel Hayden Sr. knew that the steeper the slope the greater the waterpower, and the Mill River's descent was steeper than most. The West Branch fell seven hundred feet in elevation along its downhill course from Goshen to Williamsburg, while the East Branch dropped three hundred feet as it flowed to Williamsburg. From the confluence where the two branches formed the Mill River, they tumbled another four hundred feet before reaching the Connecticut River. With such a steep slope, the fast-moving water packed sufficient force to turn water wheels and turbines. Mill owners like Hayden channeled water out of the river at as high a level as possible and allowed it to drop to as low a level as possible. The higher the fall, the less water required to produce power. During its drop, it filled buckets in waterwheels to drive the wheel around. Falling water turned the more efficient turbine by weight as well as by pressure.

If speed was the virtue of New England rivers, extreme variability in flow caused by the fickle New England climate was the downside. Rainy springs and dry summers and falls left mill owners with too much water in the spring months—sometimes so much that it flooded the waterpower equipment—and not enough flow midsummer through early fall. (Just 12 percent of annual rainfall came in June, July, August, and September.) The occasions when factories operated with sufficient water were such newsworthy events that the *Hampshire Gazette* cheered when factories could "run the machinery full time."

In the spring and summer of 1864, several manufacturers who shared the power of the Mill River talked about the need to maintain a more steady water flow to their factories. Business was booming, but they wanted to scale up production to meet consumer demand and keen competition, brought on by a nationwide system of railroads. Over the years, the mill owners had enlarged their factories, but larger mills with more machinery required more power. Fifty years earlier, the river's first grist- and sawmills were small and pulled one or two horsepower (550 foot-pounds per second equal one horsepower) from the river. But in 1864, the power demands of the new larger factories—sometimes with two or more waterwheels side by side—

was as much as 70 or 100 horsepower, and the power was needed all year long, not seasonally.

Other New England manufacturers had addressed the problem by creating upstream reservoirs that acted like giant holding tanks. To construct a reservoir, mill owners could erect a dam across a river's headwaters so that the water backed up behind the dam, creating an artificial pond or lake. With a long iron pipe through the reservoir dam, they could tap the water whenever they needed it.

The challenges of waterpower were a perennial topic of conversation for New England mill owners, who were responsible for designing, building, and regulating waterpower resources, along with their other duties. With the sciences of geology, meteorology, and hydraulics not developed enough to provide accurate information about stream flow, they acted on instinct and experience. They watched the weather and tinkered with their machinery and wheels, adjusted the levels of their mill dams and the size of their mill pond storage, trying to find the best proportions. They improved their systems by purchasing more efficient wheels or turbines. They supplemented with steam engines, but transporting coal made them expensive to operate. Many discovered that as the nineteenth century wore on, their water supply actually decreased as New England farmers upriver turned forests and watersheds into tillage, pasture, and orchards. With few trees to hold water and soil, rain and snowmelt rushed down hillsides carrying silt that clogged waterwheels and turbines and lined mill ponds, decreasing water storage capacity at the mills. Over time, mill owners spent less effort improving their factory waterpower systems and more on upstream solutions, like reservoirs.

By the 1830s, reservoirs began to fill pockets in the hills of New England, upstate New York, and the upper Mississippi Valley. Reservoirs dotted the upper reaches of the Saco and Penobscot Rivers in Maine, the Housatonic River in far western Massachusetts, the Salmon Falls River in New Hampshire, the Pawcatuck and Blackstone Rivers in Rhode Island, and the Hoosic, Willimantic, and Naugatuck Rivers in Connecticut, to name a few. One geologist later estimated that as much as 10 percent of the floodwaters of New England and New York were held in artificial storage reservoirs and ponds.

In the Mill Valley, by 1864, Hayden and other mill owners had already built a reservoir at the tip of the West Branch, which captured runoff from the Goshen hills. A new reservoir at the headwaters of the East Branch would double the amount of water they controlled. Over the next year, a group of eleven Mill Valley manufacturers, including Hayden, would form the Williamsburg Reservoir Company and receive a charter from the state to build the Williamsburg dam.

On a July day in 1864, Joel Hayden Sr. scouted the headwaters of the East Branch in search of the most advantageous site for the new reservoir and dam. At sixty-six years old, he was serving as lieutenant governor of Massachusetts under Governor John Andrew, and he had been manufacturing on the Mill River for forty years. Hayden stepped through farmer Simeon Bartlett's pastures and over his stone walls and fences as he surveyed the land to find the best location for the dam. He found the ideal place where three ridges converged around a low flat plain of about one hundred acres. In the center of this natural basin, two brooks, one running south from the town of Conway and another from the west, joined a seasonal stream which carried water from the east in a heavy rain. Here, the water caught from rain and snow mingled with natural underground springs before flowing south as the East Branch. Hayden knew that if a dam plugged the outlet to the oval-shaped basin, the reservoir would hold the headwaters plus the drainage from a three-square-mile area.

If Hayden had climbed the tallest of the three peaks, High Ridge, which loomed 600 feet above the river, to gain a better perspective on the dam, he would have seen one of the most spectacular panoramas in western Massachusetts from the open rocky pasture at its peak. To the east lay the entire Connecticut Valley in Massachusetts, a seventy-mile span dotted with the steeples of eleven village churches. The hills and valleys were dressed with hay fields, broad pastures dotted with trees to shade cows and sheep, corn fields, apple and pear orchards, groves of sugar maples, and woodlots. It was an agrarian patchwork yielding the mix of crops and livestock raised by valley farmers that they sold regionally to village and city dwellers. Mount Holyoke and Mount Tom in the distance overlooked the oxbow, the bow-shaped bend in the Connecticut River where the Mill River spilled. Along the Connecticut ran the railroad that linked the Mill Valley's factories to the sources of their raw materials and to markets in Springfield, Boston, New York, and the world.

From High Ridge, Hayden could have traced the ragged southeasterly course of the Mill River, obscured in spots by lower hills. Like nodes on a branch, sixty-four mills beaded along both riverbanks positioned at the base of natural falls, rapids, or below a dip in the terrain to take advantage of a sudden drop in the river's elevation. The river swelled artificially at a dozen spots where mill dams backed up the water into ponds which held the river's nighttime flow to produce the next day's power. The excess slid over the mill dams, downstream to another mill. At each mill, a canal, or head-race, diverted the flow to a waterwheel or turbine before sending it out another canal, or tailrace, to rejoin the river. Every mile or two a village hugged the river, each with rows of small white houses and shops, a few farmhouses, a boardinghouse or two, one or two white church steeples, and wooden and brick mill buildings in a factory yard. One nineteenth-century writer quipped that if you've seen one tidy New England mill village you've seen them all.

And while the Mill Valley villages did have a similar appearance, they had distinct personalities, shaped by the men whose businesses and person-al interests dominated them as Hayden dominated Haydenville. Because their power source was used serially, one after the other, the mill owners had to subordinate individualistic tendencies to make the stream flow work for everyone. For example, an upstream mill owner couldn't hoard so much water in a mill pond that it took days to reach the factories below, nor could he raise his dam so high that it overfilled his mill pond and spilled onto adjacent farms (without compensating the farmer) or backed up to the upstream mill inundating that factory's waterpower system. The relation-ship of mill owners to each other and to the community with respect to water was subject to legal doctrine derived from medieval England and amended by statutes and court rulings. As a harmonious group who pri-vately negotiated to solve disputes, the Mill River manufacturers didn't chal-lenge each other legally. The Mill River was their conduit, their canal, their power system, and their source of power in the valley.

The first bead in the string of mills was in the village of Williamsburg, a hamlet within the town of the same name. Onslow Spelman's small button mill sat at the head of the village and Lewis Bodman's wool mill at the foot. A mile below Skinnerville was home to William Skinner's silk factory; two miles downstream, Haydenville stretched along the river with the brass works, iron foundry, tobacco mill, and cotton factory. The river crossed into Northampton and coursed a mile further to Leeds where the Nonotuck Silk Company, managed by Lucius Dimock, stood a few hundred yards upstream from Alfred Critchlow's button factory. In Florence stood the Greenville Manufacturing Company cotton mill, owned by Hayden and John Payson Williston, and the Nonotuck Silk Company's Florence mill, run by Samuel Hill and Alfred Lilly. Nearby factories made sewing machines, brushes, and baskets. Downstream, in the village of Bay State, William Clement manufactured hoes and rakes and—since the Civil War began—bayonets and rifle barrels. Next came Paper Mill Village where

William Clark's paper mill stood. The Mill River skirted Northampton's commercial center and then meandered through the broad alluvial plain before entering the Connecticut River.

Compared to other large Massachusetts manufacturing centers, like Lowell and Lawrence on the wide Merrimack River, Mill River manufacturing was small-scale. Even with all that Northampton and Williamsburg produced, Hampshire County—which also included the manufacturing town of Ware—ranked only tenth in value of goods produced of the fourteen counties in Massachusetts, one of the nation's leaders in manufacturing. In 1870, Hampshire County employed 7,575 workers in 433 establishments while Middlesex County in northeastern Massachusetts, where Lowell was located, employed more than 47,000. None of the Mill Valley factories employed more than a few hundred workers, 1,500 in the entire valley, and the owners knew them by name. Unlike the wealthy absentee investors who owned Lowell's mills, Mill Valley manufacturers were technically minded men of humble beginnings. Some were local, others came from New England towns to make Williamsburg or Northampton their permanent home, and two immigrated to the valley from England as young men. As a small tight-knit group, they invested in each other's companies and served on each other's boards of directors. In 1860, seven companies offered fifty-four directorships. These were held by twenty-eight men, with four or five men—Samuel Hill, Alfred Lilly, and Joel Hayden among them—holding five or more posts. The manufacturers held in common their ideal of using profits to improve their industries and to shape educationally and culturally rich communities for themselves and their workers.

If you had lived in Haydenville between the 1830s and the 1870s, you couldn't have worked, worshiped, banked, belonged to a club, or voted in an election without encountering Joel Hayden Sr., his money, or his politics. Hayden was the richest man, largest employer, biggest landlord, and greatest contributor to charity. He owned a brass factory, a cotton factory, a foundry, and a gas works, which illuminated the factories, streets, and a few dozen homes. He was the Haydenville Bank president, a director of the railroad, the leader of the Masonic lodge, the head of the cemetery association, and a member of Hope Engine Company, the local firefighting squad. The only club he didn't belong to was the cornet band. He lived in the grandest house—a white-columned Greek Revival mansion—across the street from the brass factory. His political career as selectman, county commissioner, and state legislator culminated with three terms as lieutenant governor, as a Free-Soiler and, later, as a Republican.

Hayden was born into a deeply religious farm family in Williamsburg, a wilderness town on the upland rim of the Connecticut Valley; his grandfather Josiah had been one of the original settlers in the 1760s. When Joel was born in 1798, John Adams was president and George Washington was still alive. Hayden's generation came of age after the American Revolution, a time of great economic promise. Extensive turnpikes built in the 1790s integrated rural and urban markets, and colonial restrictions placed by England on American manufacturing were removed. Starting a factory didn't require a huge capital outlay. With personal ambition, a can-do attitude, and a technical mind, Hayden fit the era.

Hayden learned about waterpower at an early age. When he was eleven, in 1809, his uncles David and Daniel Hayden built a cotton mill along the Mill River in Williamsburg, the first cotton factory in western Massachusetts. A few years later his father opened a cotton mill in 1812, on the Swift River in nearby Cummington. New England was undergoing a spurt of textile manufacture as imports from Britain were cut off during the War of 1812. Besides his father's and uncles' mills, he would have seen woolen mills on the Mill River in what would become Leeds.

But when it came time for him to choose a profession, most nearby textile factories had closed in the post-war depression as finer English imports came back on the market. He had only a few years of study at local schools, and farming in Massachusetts offered meager rewards. And, with no promise of professional training with a doctor or lawyer, Joel entered a trade—gunmaking.

Later in life, Joel liked to say that his early ambition had been to be a singing teacher. He had noticed that the soloist at Sunday services was more popular among the younger members of the congregation than the long-winded minister whose fiery sermons admonished them against youthful follies. Joel was teasing by gently deriding the ministers and lay preachers he knew, including his father, who was a lay Baptist minister. Joking or not, his father saw no monetary future for Joel as a singing teacher and sent him to Pittsfield, twenty miles away, to apprentice to Lemuel Pomeroy, a locksmith and arms maker known for his inventiveness. Pomeroy was one of a dozen or more arms contractors working in close enough proximity to the Springfield

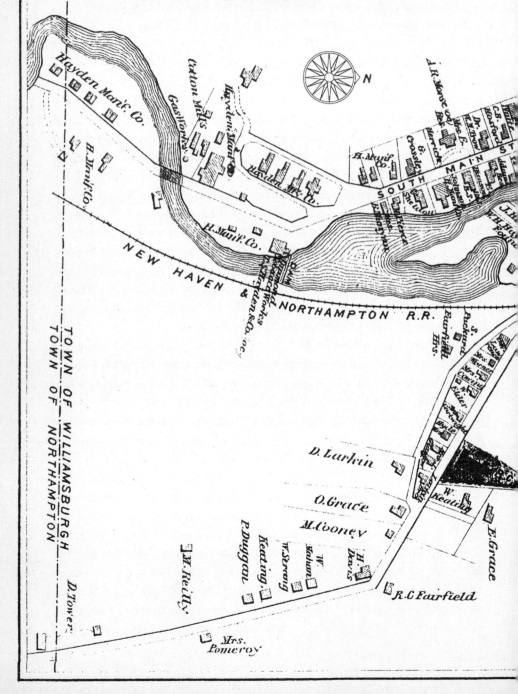

HAYDENVILLE, 1873

TOWN OF WILLIAMSBURGH

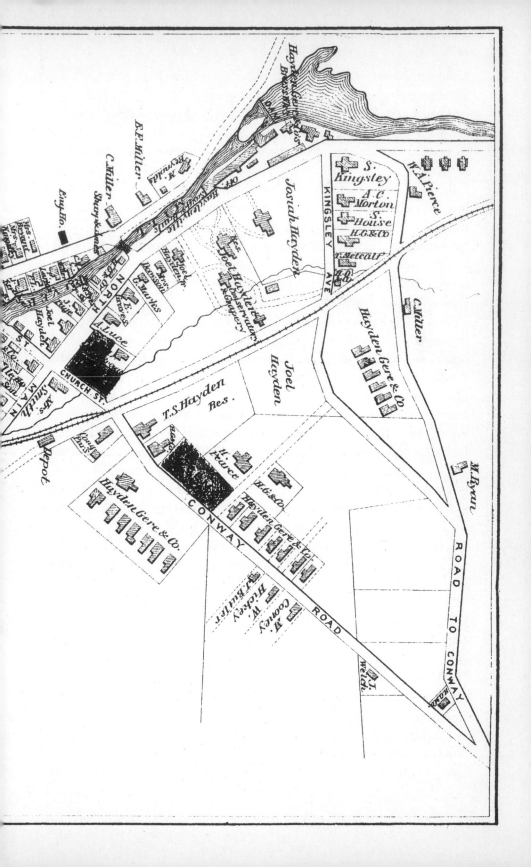

Armory to share tools, patterns, labor-saving improvements, and new manufacturing techniques. It was the best possible apprenticeship for Joel.

The hardest part of the apprenticeship was separation from his close family. A few mornings after Joel left for Pittsfield, his younger brother Josiah III woke to find Joel sleeping in the front room, having walked home twenty miles over the dark hilly country roads from Pittsfield to Cummington. Either his father ordered him to walk back to Pittsfield or drove him, but Joel did not return home again until his apprenticeship was done three years later. He never forgot the pain of that first separation from his family but became very good at controlling it. Years later, he counseled one of his daughters as he returned her to boarding school after an unexpected trip home, "When your heart gets up in your throat so you can't speak and it chokes you, you may come home."

Three years after his apprenticeship ended, in 1822, he bought his uncles' idle cotton factory in what was already called Haydenville. With a capital investment of fifteen hundred dollars, Hayden and a partner repaired the factory, rebuilt the dam, dug a new canal, and began to manufacture power looms for the small textile mills that had sprung up on the Mill River and other fast-moving New England streams in a resurgence of the textile industry. Three years later, with the loom market slackening, Joel, with his brother Josiah as partner, operated a "jobbing" machine shop and iron foundry where they made everyday objects and machines needed by locals, such as door locks, harness trimmings, and cast buttons. His reputation for thoroughness, ingenuity, and inventiveness brought businessman Samuel Williston to his door to ask him to perfect a machine for manufacturing covered buttons. With Williston's money and Joel Hayden's technical knowledge, they forged a business partnership that lasted twenty years and a friendship that lasted a lifetime.

As well as being an age of entrepreneurship, the early nineteenth century was an era of reform. Reformers, like Hayden, believed that society, however flawed it might be, could be changed by its citizens. Hayden's first cause was temperance; he led the local temperance society in trying to banish alcohol in social settings. Next was abolition. When the tide of abolition swept across the north in the 1830s, Hayden was among the seventy-six founding members of the Old Hampshire Anti-Slavery Society in Northampton. With John Payson Williston, Samuel's brother, he founded Northampton's first abolitionist newspaper, the *Hampshire Herald*, the voice of the Liberty Party. The *Herald* captured the reform spirit of

Northampton and included articles on education, temperance, and women's rights. Hayden's religious thinking grew more liberal as he aged. He funded Methodist, Congregational, and Catholic churches. Toward the end of his life he followed no single creed.

One could take in Haydenville in a glance. By 1870, it consisted of one hundred white-washed buildings, one and two stories in height, that lined two main streets stretching along both sides of the Mill River. The village was squeezed onto the narrow river plain that lay between green hills. At the downstream end of the village stood the four-story brick cotton mill with a store house, office, and two barns in the yard. His son Joel Jr. was part owner. The workers lived in the neighboring houses, some single-family and some multi-family. A nearby brick building housed the gas works. A hundred yards upstream, fifteen people worked in the three-story wooden tobacco company, managed by another son, Thomas. On the other side of the tobacco works' mill pond, next to the railroad track, was a foundry, managed by another son William, which turned out steam heaters.

At the top of the village, across from Joel Hayden's house, stood the brass works that made plumber's supplies—faucets, pipes, and valves for city systems, bathroom fixtures for upper-class Americans, and water pumps for middle-class homes. The factory was frequently referred to as "the largest and most extensive of its kind in the country," with markets in the United States, Cuba, and Canada. Even if the claim was based on local pride, it wasn't far off. Its string of nine brick buildings stretched nearly six hundred feet, the length of two football fields. At one end stood the office building that held the company offices, the Haydenville Savings Bank, and the Masonic hall, all appointed with inlaid marble floors and mahogany and rosewood cabinetry. The buildings showed such elegant architectural details that if a visitor hadn't seen the smokestack rising up from the back, he or she might have imagined this to be a block in an urban center.

Haydenville was considered a model mill village, and Hayden easily attracted workers. By 1860, the four-story brick cotton mill employed twenty-five men and sixty women who managed 4,000 spindles and one hundred looms on which they wove 20,000 yards of sheeting per week. Most were New Englanders from nearby farms, but before the Civil War, Irish immigrants added to the ranks, and after the war, French Canadians joined the workforce. No matter where they were born, women made half the wages of men who performed identical tasks. Workers went to their jobs six days per week at five in the morning and worked eleven or twelve hours with two half-hour breaks, one for breakfast and one at mid-day for dinner. The noise and vibration of the weaving room was fierce; weavers, mostly women, tended a half dozen looms and carefully avoided misfired shuttles or uncovered gears, pulleys, and drive belts, which connected their machinery to the overhead lineshaft turned by the waterwheel. A worker could be badly injured or killed by any of these exposed fast-moving parts if they brushed their body or clothing against them. They strained their eyesight as they tied up broken ends of warp yarn in dim light. In the weaving rooms, children as young as ten kept looms supplied with bobbins and performed other menial tasks.

For the brass works, Hayden recruited skilled metal workers from Ireland. They were among the highest paid workers in the valley and many bought their own homes, while others rented one-story cottages that Hayden had erected around the village in clusters, forming neighborhoods of skilled workers. By 1860, one hundred employees produced goods valued at $90,000, which were sold from a warehouse and showroom in New York City. Workers cast brass parts singly. In wooden pattern molds, they made a wax cast of the item. They buried the wax cast in sand and poured in molten brass, an alloy of copper and zinc and other metals. The wax vaporized as the brass took its place in the sand. When the item cooled, a worker removed it. A brass finisher ground, bored, threaded, polished, and assembled the pieces. Some of the factory's mechanics were so capable that they received patents for their inventions.

The year after Hayden began manufacturing brass works, in 1852, Isabella Weir Hayden, his wife of twenty-nine years, died at age fifty-two; the youngest of their ten children was ten years old (three others had died before age four). By then Hayden was a very wealthy man. That year, he was listed in *The Rich Men of Massachusetts*, a small book published to be an inspiration to young men and as an inducement to the rich to be generous with their money. That year Hayden had $150,000, accumulated during the past eighteen years. Hayden's entry read: "Began poor . . . A very public-spirited and benevolent man. Gives much to poor people. A man of whom a town might well say, 'Wish we had *more* such.'"

Above Haydenville, the village of Williamsburg, a hamlet at the center of the town of Williamsburg, consisted of several streets lined with boxy white houses that wound back and forth across the Mill River as they circled a gristmill, two sawmills, a tannery, woolen mill, and two button mills. The din of creaking waterwheels and the thumping and grinding of machinery provided a relentless background beat to the comings and goings of villagers visiting the grocer, butcher, shoemaker, wheelwright, harness maker, or tailor. An ever-present gathering of men could be found outside the mills, exchanging news as they watched water spill off the turning wheels.

The cluster of buildings around the confluence of the East and West Branches had been the center of village life only since the 1830s. Before that, farmers had settled on Williamsburg's hills, away from the alder-covered swamp that bordered the river and out of reach of its annual floods. As mills started using the river, houses and shops soon sprang up nearby. Bogs were drained and a river wall was built to confine and channel the water. By 1832, the new village of Williamsburg was firmly established when Joel Hayden erected a Methodist church there (previously services had been held in his button mill). Four years later, when it was time to replace the Williamsburg Congregational church, the new one was built in the riverside village. It was no accident that mills resembled nearby churches—both were the same general size and shape and were topped with a cupola and bell. The mills' design was intended to provide a civic presence and to equate capitalism with Protestantism: working hard and making money were reflections of a healthy spiritual life and of a strong community.

Two men who would become shareholders of the Williamsburg Reservoir Company lived in Williamsburg. The first was Onslow Spelman, who owned a large new house in the fashionable Second Empire style in the center of the village. Born in Granville, Massachusetts, he had been a farm laborer and a broom maker before he came to Haydenville to work as a Hayden factory employee and then as a clerk in Joel and Josiah Hayden's store. Afterward, he managed a local button factory and soon purchased a share of the business. By 1860, Spelman had a small shop in which four men and fifteen women produced $8,000 worth of suspender buttons and button molds. His factory was located above the confluence of the Mill River and depended solely on the East Branch for power. A nervous but likable fellow, Spelman was eager to help in the process of constructing the reservoir.

The second was Lewis Bodman, a woolen-mill owner, who lived in a large white house across the street from Spelman. Like Hayden, Bodman was a Williamsburg son from one of the oldest and most respected families. Twelve years younger than Hayden, he was tall and erect, with shaggy eyebrows shadowing vivid blue eyes and a prominent hooked nose. He was known for being honest, direct, reliable, and approachable. Bodman got his

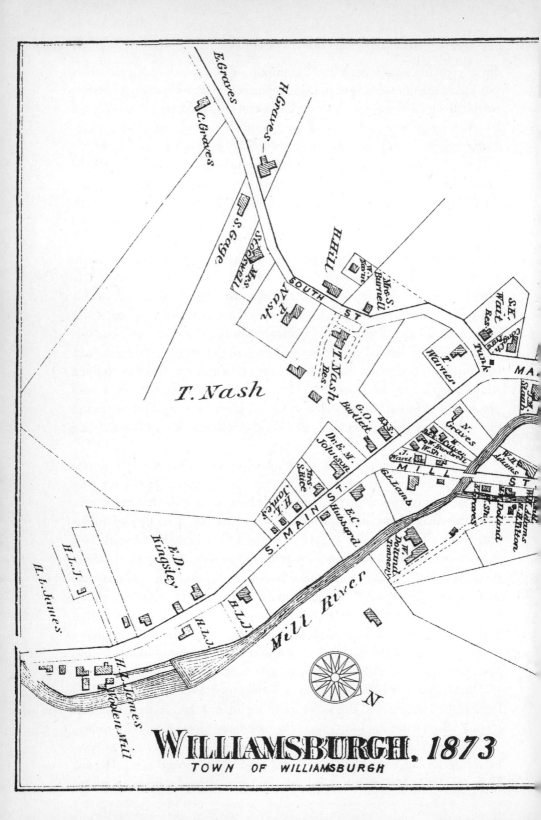

WILLIAMSBURGH, 1873

TOWN OF WILLIAMSBURGH

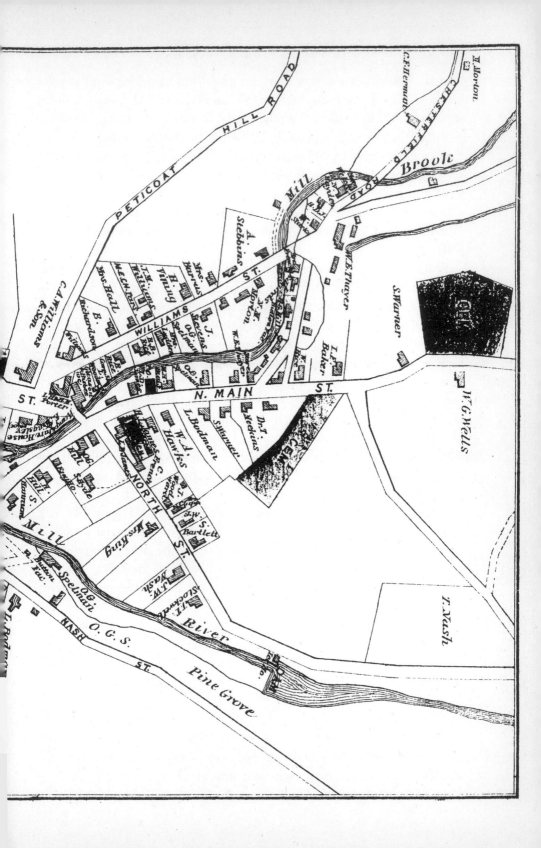

start as a postmaster and store manager who distributed long strips of palm leaves to local families for braiding and assembling into broad-brimmed straw hats worn by farmers. With the capital he earned, he bought a woolen mill at the bottom of the village. By the 1860s, in a factory heated with wood stoves and lighted with oil lamps, three dozen men and women spun wool yarn that they wove through sturdy cotton warps, tough enough to with-stand the rough motion of the power looms, into an inexpensive fabric called satinet. Some of the workers occupied the five houses that Bodman owned, while others lived in the village with their own families, or boarded with another.

At the other end of the village, Mary Hill lived in a house near the Hill family button mill on the West Branch. Like most of the 80 percent of Williamsburg women who didn't work in a factory, Mary Hill kept house for a husband and child and managed a network of other relationships. She described in her diary how her life revolved around home, her parents' farm, temperance meetings, and the Williamsburg Congregational Church. Every spring she cleaned the house from top to bottom, even tacking net-ting over the pantry windows to keep out flies. In between chores, she exchanged favors and acts of kindness with other women—a cake sent over to a neighbor on the best hand-painted plate, for instance, and returned with another treat. When Mary passed time with visits by friends, such as her childhood companion Emma Wood, they brought sewing and watched the children together, laughing when Emma's baby crawled away into the potato bin. For more formal calls from women of stature, like Mrs. Henry James, whose husband had purchased Lewis Bodman's mill in 1868, or Mrs. Joel Hayden Jr., Mary served tea in the sitting room. Sitting and talking bored industrious Mary, who hated idle moments, and she complained that her callers "talked too long" and "hindered my work greatly." Mary rarely missed church, except for the time she and her hus-band had traveled to Saratoga Springs, New York, and sent their trunks after them. But the trunks returned late and without their best clothes to wear, they stayed home. Williamsburg was a small town, but its members still observed Victorian protocol.

From the woolen mill at the bottom of the village of Williamsburg, the Mill River bent southeasterly and gathered water from two brooks before it entered Skinnerville, a half-mile-long strip of thirty-five buildings strung along a single street parallel to the river's east bank. In 1844, nineteen-year-old William Skinner left his father's London silk mill, where he had trained as a dyer, for a Northampton dye works and silk mill. A decade later, he began manufacturing upstream on the Mill River, replacing the old mill in 1857. Skinner was taller than other men, with a broad frame, snow-white hair, and rosy cheeks. He was known for being impeccably dressed, favoring embroidered English silk vests. By 1860 he was employing forty or fifty workers making sewing silks. He would become a shareholder of the Williamsburg Reservoir Company.

Skinner's children grew up in the Mill Valley, where young adults and teenagers took great advantage of the wide range of community activities, which allowed them the freedom to play, flirt, and court out of the watchful eyes of parents. No one knew the young people's social scene better than Skinner's son, William Cobbett Skinner, called Will, who divulged his goings-on to his diary in 1874 when he was sixteen years old, providing a portrait of valley life.

Each Saturday afternoon after classes let out at Williston Seminary, a boarding school for boys founded in Easthampton by button manufacturer Samuel Williston, Will Skinner took the train home to the Williamsburg depot, walking a few hundred yards down to his house and up the long circular driveway that set it back from the river road. It was the largest, most expensive house in Williamsburg and looked like a grand hotel among cabins. Its bulky three-story frame dwarfed the surrounding one- and two-story farmhouses, and its curved mansard roof contrasted sharply with the straight pitched roofs of the neighbors' homes. The house, which was built in 1868, was home to the large Skinner family: Will's father; his mother, Sarah Allen Skinner, a native of Northampton; his half sisters Nina and Nellie from his father's first wife, who died young; and his four younger siblings. In 1874, Libby was fifteen, Joey twelve, Belle eight, and Kate was a baby.

Skinnerville, Haydenville, and Williamsburg were Will's world of fun: "Nothing happens of any account. Except on Saturday and Sunday." As soon as he arrived home he walked or rode horseback down to the Haydenville brass shop to find his best friend and neighbor, eighteen-year-old Dick Hills, who worked there along with his father. Dick and Will walked or rode between the villages "looking for anyone of any account." They attended church services, Sunday school, benefit concerts, dramatic readings, card parties, skating on the brass works mill pond—anyplace they might see other young people. Will attended the Williamsburg Dramatic Club reading, which raised forty dollars for the church's new piano, and the

1873
SKINNERVILLE
TOWN OF WILLIAMSBURGH

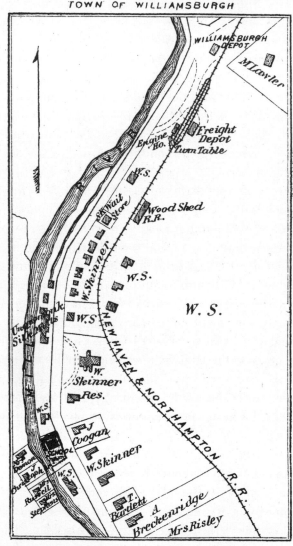

Haydenville high school evening of music and readings, the profits of which enabled them to buy a set of encyclopedias. He took Ida Simpson, the niece of Henry James, to a Christmas supper in Haydenville and signed her autograph book. Lewis Bodman's daughter, Minnie, came by Will's house in her father's carriage to look for Dick Hills; since he wasn't there, Will was happy to chat with her instead. Another evening, Will's older sister Nina gave a sleigh-ride party in which twelve young people piled into a box sled filled with straw and set up on sleigh runners. They rode into Northampton, the Skinner's servant holding the reins. Will confided that "Dick and I had a good time. We had a bottle of hard cider."

Having just passed childhood himself, Will fretted over deaths of children. He recorded the death of Henry James's six-year-old daughter Bertha and mourned on the shared birthdays of his two little sisters who had died years earlier. "Today is May & Louise birthday. May would have been 6 and Louise 2 years old." He mentioned his sister Belle's measles.

Most of Will's social life centered around Haydenville Church, where he and Dick socialized with the other children of Williamsburg's upper crust: the sons and daughters of well-to-do farmers, mill owners, and skilled brass-factory workers and managers. One week Will and his "fellows" rocked their seat so hard that an old woman sitting on the end of the bench jumped up and had to "hold on for dear life." Another week Will "had a pair of eye-glasses which I put on in church. Made a fool as usual of myself." In church, Will struck a deal with his pal Nat Luce, whose father was a brass-mill superintendent, that if Nat went home with Gerty Hayden, Joel Hayden Sr.'s niece, then Will would write to Mattie Dickinson, a relative of a farm family. Will had been smitten since he met Mattie at his sister's sleigh party. Several weeks later Will wrote: "In the eve after church I and Luce took Mattie Dickinson and Gerty Hayden to walk." The next week he escorted Mattie to a card party given by the daughter of Williamsburg farmer and politician Hiram Nash.

One Sunday evening at the Haydenville Church service, weeks after he had been escorting Mattie around town, Will and "a few of us boys" sat in the Skinner children's pew while "some boardinghouse girls" occupied the other Skinner family seat. The mill owner was responsible for protecting the moral standards of his workers, and Skinner probably paid an annual fee for the girls' pew as many mill owners did, placing it next to his own so that the mill girls could worship like members of his own family. Their reputations as churchgoers reflected well on him and his village, assuring New England farm parents that it was respectable to allow their unmarried daughters to live and work in Skinnerville. Will reached over his pew and "got hold of one of their hands" and "kept it until church was over."

The mill girl didn't withdraw her hand, though she may have wanted to. She may have feared showing disrespect to the Skinner family by calling attention to Will's antics, or maybe she thought it would jeopardize her job. Or, perhaps she was flattered by the attention of the fun-loving, educated son of the mill owner and played along to give herself something to whisper with her friends about, delighting in the improbability of their association. It was an out-of-bounds act on Will's part, but it wasn't scandalous. Their world was divided by wealth and opportunity, and they both knew it. The code permitted Will to tease a mill girl but not to marry one.

The young women who worked at the silk mill were on average in their late teens and early twenties, mostly from other New England towns, although some were Irish, a few French Canadian. Most of the mill girls came and worked a few months or years before returning home to marry; they weren't there to make a new life in the community. Many said that it was the happiest times of their life, a time of great independence and a rare chance to spend long days with their peers. They could not have shared such camaraderie if they had stayed on the farm or had taken a job as a domestic servant or a seamstress, other typical occupations for unmarried women. While the factory offered long, tedious, sometimes dangerous work, it was also a social institution.

If Will's parents had found out that he had spent a church service teasing a mill girl, they would likely have scolded him as they did regularly for his wild behavior at school. Will's father and mother worried about their son's future. This was his last year at Williston Seminary and he was barely passing. He was so bored with school he wrote on January 1, 1874, that "this year will probably bring my career at Williston to a close and, oh, how glad am I." When Will asked his mother what she wanted for her birthday, she replied that "the best present she could get would be a good report." He had already been caught out of his room without permission four times, was nearly failing Greek, Latin, and geometry, and was in danger of not getting a diploma. If his father had expected him to attend Amherst or Yale after graduation and had entertained thoughts about Will entering the business, then he knew that Will had a great deal of maturing to do.

For all his capers, Will was a keen observer of his father's business world. He noted that his father traveled to the silk manufacturing center in Paterson, New Jersey, to confer with others in the silk business and that his future brother-in-law Fred Warner, at age twenty-five, went to work for Will's father in New York. He mentioned that a son of brass works superintendent Samuel Wentworth told him there had been a brief strike at the brass works. But Will never mentioned the river or the reservoir dams. He didn't write about his father's mill dam, turbines, canal, or the fierce sound of the machinery and the steam engine that supplemented water power when the river was low. For people in the valley, these were the everyday sights and sounds of the landscape.

Three miles below Skinnerville lay Leeds, the small village in the northern corner of Northampton. First called Shepherd's Hollow, then named Leeds after Leeds, England, the postmaster's home town, the village boasted the first ivory nut button shop in the country. It was founded in 1858 by Alfred Critchlow, who would become a shareholder of the Williamsburg Reservoir Company. Josiah Hayden, Joel Sr.'s brother, had induced Critchlow to emigrate from England in 1843, with a button-turning lathe so that he could begin manufacturing horn buttons (actually made of animal hooves) in Haydenville, but soon Critchlow went out on his own. An unschooled "practical chemist," he invented a chemical composition of shellac, wood fiber, and lampblack. An early form of plastic, "Florence compound" could be molded and dyed to fashion buttons, daguerreotype cases, and hairbrush handles. He made a success of the business by running the machinery night and day when the water was high, sometimes sleeping in the mill where he could be available to attend to any emergency. After he sold that business, he turned to making vegetable ivory buttons in Leeds.

Critchlow was not as interested as Hayden in community social activities or in building churches. As a result, Leeds had the reputation for being less inviting, and a little dirtier, than the other mill villages along the river. The road down the middle of the village was a dusty or muddy path, depending upon the season, lined with houses whose front doors opened on to the street. There were no sidewalks, fences, or granite horse-mounting blocks as there were in Haydenville and Williamsburg. But Critchlow shared with Hayden the belief that all men were born equal and free, and so participated in abolition activities in Florence. His abhorrence of monarchical government was one of the reasons he left England.

Critchlow's old wooden colonial house overlooked the tiny village from the river's east bank. A set of wooden steps built into the hillside took him to the depot and the railroad tracks. If he walked along the railroad tracks a couple of hundred yards and down another steep flight of wooden stairs he would enter the rear of the button factory. Workers would look up when they saw this very short man with a trim gray beard walk in. In 1864, he was fifty years old.

Critchlow imported several hundred tons of a particular species of palm nut from Panama and South America. The fruit of the palm, about the size of a man's head, contained leathery pouches that held triangular-shaped nuts almost the size of a hen's egg. Inside the nut was the ivorylike kernel used for buttons. In the boiler house, roaring fires produced steam heat, which shrank the hard shell so that the kernel could be easily removed. In the brick mill, which took its power from the river, men wielded small circular saws to cut slices off the kernel's exterior. They tossed away the insides or burned them for fuel. Other skilled men turned the slices on lathes, shaping them into round buttons, which they sent to the dye house.

In the dye house, workers dunked the buttons in huge vats—some in white to brighten their natural color and others in darker colors. Dyers sent some colored buttons back to lathe operators who removed a stripe of color to reveal a decorative band or two of natural white "ivory." Some buttons made many trips between the lathe operators and dyers, who colored each newly added white strip a progressively lighter shade until the buttons achieved a variegated effect.

Once dyed, polished, and drilled for sewing, someone brought the finished buttons from the brick mill to the smaller wooden building where they were prepared for shipping. On the second floor, young women with the job of "looking over" sorted them by quality and color. Female sewers, or carders, applied two dozen to a card and packers placed one gross in each box. Packers wrapped five one-gross boxes in a carton to be sent to the sales room in New York. The factory could complete fifteen thousand gross a day, or 216,000 buttons, ranging in size from tiny buttons for baby clothes to large coat buttons two inches in diameter. They met a ready market in an expanding nation interested in fashionable garments and in need of buttons to fasten them.

Next door to Critchlow lived Lucius Dimock, who managed the Leeds mill of the Nonotuck Silk Company at the top of the village. Dimock came to Northampton from Connecticut in the early 1850s to work at the Nonotuck Silk Company at its headquarters in Florence. Silk was all the rage in nineteenth-century America. After 1865, so much silk was produced in the United States that most middle-class women owned one silk dress, while upper-class women, like the Skinners and the Haydens, might have

LEEDS
TOWN OF NORTHAMPTON

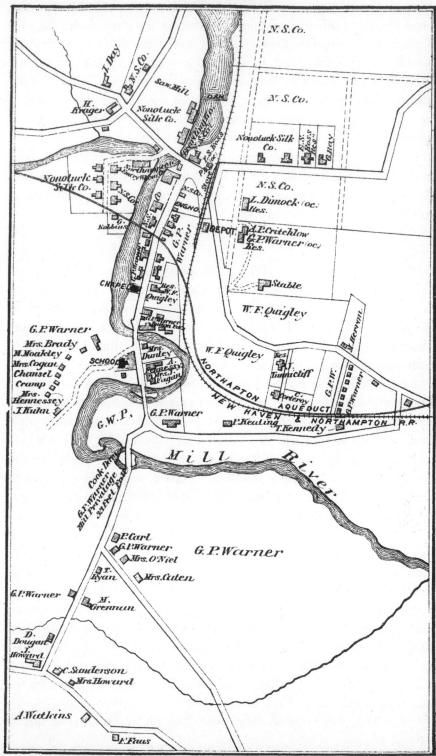

N. S. Co.

J. Day

N. S. Co.

Saw Mill

N. S. Co.

H. Krager

Nonotuck Silk Co.

Nonotuck Silk Co.

E. S. Brass Co.

C. Gray

Nonotuck S. Co.

Northampton Emery Wheel Co.

N. S. Co.

N. S. Co.

L. Dimock (oc.) Res.

G. Robbins

G. P. Warner

DEPOT

A. P. Critchlow
G. P. Warner (oc) Res.

CHAPEL

Res.
W. F. Quigley

Stable

W. F. Quigley

G. P. Warner

Mrs. Brady
M. Moakley
Mrs. Cogan
Chansel
Cramp
Mrs. Hennessey
T. Kuhn

SCHOOL

Mrs. Dunley
A. Hennessy
Mrs. J. Fagan

W. F. Quigley

NORTHAMPTON

Res.
Tunnicliff

E. Heron

G. P. W.

A. P. Warner

C. Pordevoy

G. W. P.

G. P. Warner

NEW HAVEN & NORTHAMPTON R.R.

AQUEDUCT

F. Kealing
T. Kennedy

Mill River

Cook Bro.
G. P. Warner
Mill Privalage
33 Feet head

P. Carl
G. P. Warner
Mrs. O'Niel

G. P. Warner

T. Ryan

Mrs. Caten

G. P. Warner

M. Grennan

D. Dougan
J. Howard

C. Sanderson
Mrs. Howard

A. Watkins

F. Faus

worn silk dresses every day and dressed their daughters in silk. A factory girl might be able to afford silk ribbons for a bonnet or a silk dress for the centerpiece of her trousseau. Dimock rose steadily through the ranks until he became manager of the Leeds factory. At thirty-eight in 1864, he was known for his mechanical skills and knowledge of waterpower. As a member of the reservoir company, he would be heavily relied upon in the construction of the dam. When the reservoir company met, they usually gathered at Critchlow's factory offices, the midpoint along the river.

The river left Leeds with a long, noisy rush over Cook's dam, and then through a gorge that opened out on to the broad, flat stretch of Leeds and Florence meadows. Florence, a community of sixteen hundred, spread from the riverside factories up a gentle rise to the village center.

Florence was known for three things: silk, abolitionism, and free thought—interests shared by several of Florence's business leaders. Two of them—Samuel L. Hill and Alfred T. Lilly—would become members of the reservoir company. Samuel Hill was president of the Nonotuck Silk Company, one of the largest silk companies in the country, and Alfred Lilly superintended the Florence mill and served as treasurer of the corporation.

A carpenter by training, Samuel Hill came to Northampton in 1841 at the age of thirty-five as a founding member of a utopian community, formally named the Northampton Association of Education and Industry, but locally referred to simply as the Community. Appalled by the social and economic inequities resulting from industrialization, the founders of the Community believed in goods shared in common, wages paid according to need, complete religious tolerance, the right of individuals to express their thoughts, a shorter working day (eleven hours instead of the customary twelve), and equal rights regardless of sex, race, disability, and religion. Several former slaves, including Sojourner Truth, lived as Community members. Peddlers and abolitionists sold the Community's silk thread all over New England as an alternative to slave-tainted cotton. When the Community dissolved in economic disarray in 1846, Hill agreed to assume all Community debts if he could carry on the silk business under his own rules, which were the customary work patterns of the day. He abandoned the shorter working day, paid wages according to work performed, and set unequal pay scales for men and women. Prudence, not reform, guided his business interests.

Under Hill, the company flourished. The silk machine twist thread invented there in the early 1850s was the first on the market compatible with sewing machines, and was heavily promoted by the newly formed Singer Sewing Machine Company. Hill rode the silk boom to prosperity, expanding the company's products to include spool silk, crochet, embroidery, knitting, and lace thread, rope sashes, and buttonhole twist. The company imported raw silk from Asia and traded its finished products through Boston and New York, under the brand names Nonotuck and later Corticelli. Sewing silk was sold in envelopes on which was printed "Giovanni Lapamo Monticelli, a Firenze" a fanciful Italian translation of "Samuel Lapham Hill of Florence" (the village was named for Florence, Italy). The silk was thought to have more marketable value if buyers thought it was Italian. In 1860, the Nonotuck Company operated both the Florence and Leeds mills with $65,000 worth of capital, forty-six male workers, and ninety females.

Alfred T. Lilly joined the Nonotuck Company in 1853 in the early growth period, having been a silk mill superintendent in Connecticut. Strictly temperate, Lilly used neither tobacco nor alcohol and often counseled young men on their habits. When he advised one young man to give up tobacco, the youth replied that it was an addiction he couldn't stop. Lilly lectured him, "Then if I were in your situation, I would go out and hang myself; if I had come to the condition that I could not control my own conduct I would put an end to my life." He was an atheist, a farmer known for high hay yields, and a drummer who established a youth drum corps.

Hill was seven years older, but Lilly and Hill looked alike as they aged. In a late 1860s photograph of the board of directors of the silk company, they are seated next to each other, both slender of medium stature, with long serious, thin faces, pale eyes, thinning gray hair, and moustaches so long they blend with full gray beards. Lilly and Hill thought alike on moral issues and supported many of the same causes, including the evening school for those who worked in the mills. In the corner of Hill's office, below a bookshelf stacked with reform-minded periodicals, pamphlets, and papers, was a sign that read, "For free distribution; help yourself." He encouraged female employees to save money, invested it for them, and paid interest. When a man saved five hundred dollars toward the price of a home lot, Hill loaned him money toward building a house worth from two to three thousand dollars. His policy created a neat village of white cottages, each on its own fenced plot, inhabited by factory-loyal homeowners firmly rooted in the community.

Hill and Lilly were passionate abolitionists. Hill was reputed to have participated in Underground Railroad activities in Florence, as was Alfred Critchlow in Leeds. Lilly's strong, unbending opinions and no-rest-until-victory policies irritated many of his neighbors. Hill and Lilly were equally intense about free thought and free speech. Some members of the defunct Community remained in Florence and formed in 1863 the Free Congregational Society of Florence "for the promotion of general intelligence, good morals, and liberal religious sentiment." That same year, when the town of Northampton voted to give Florence a sum of $2,000 to build a schoolhouse, Hill thought the amount insufficient and received permission to do what he thought best with the money. On his own lot he built a school and added rooms for the Free Congregational Society on the second floor, including a hall that could hold 600 persons—at a cost to him of $30,000. In addition to nondenominational worship, frequent visiting speakers were Elizabeth Cady Stanton, William Lloyd Garrison, Ralph Waldo Emerson, and Lucy Stone. Each Sunday, the Society held a morning and evening service and in the afternoon the Catholic mill hands used it for a service for their children.

In 1864 at the Christmas party in the newly completed hall, Hill found out how grateful his community was. As a surprise, his workers took up a collection and bought him a sleigh worth $800, which they secretly hoisted up to the second-floor vestibule so that it would be visible from the hall when the doors were open. After Hill had distributed the gifts to his workers and while the Christmas tree was still candlelit, Charles Burleigh, the resident speaker of the Free Congregational Society, stepped up and spoke on behalf of the workers about a good, kind, and true friend that they wanted to honor. Hill, who thought he knew everything about the Christmas festivities, drew forward filled with curiosity about who the recipient might be, but when he realized they were talking about him he shrank back, eyes welling with tears. When Burleigh was finished, the doors to the vestibule were thrown open to reveal the sleigh as three cheers were raised for Hill. Once he composed himself, he handed a paper to Mr. Burleigh, who leaped upon one of the benches to read it by gaslit chandelier. It was a deed from Hill to the town of Florence for the building they were assembled in and a pledge of $1,000 per year for its upkeep. Six men carried the sleigh on their shoulders to Hill's house. That year his taxable income was $12,463, while the average silk worker made a little over $200.

Another Florence man, John Payson Williston, an old friend of Joel Hayden Sr., became a shareholder in the reservoir company. He invented

Payson's indelible ink and became its largest manufacturer. In 1865, he earned $51,633, making him the third wealthiest person in Hampshire County that year. Soon after, he pledged to donate all but $500 each year for ten years to charity, but later changed his pledge to ten percent of his annual income. In addition to his abolition activities with Hayden, he helped settle former slaves in Florence; about 3 percent of the village's population was African-American. When the Community broke up, he and Joel Hayden purchased the silk mill on the Community's property and outfitted it as a cotton factory where they turned slave-grown cotton into cloth.

Below Florence, the river rushed past Bay State Village, where William Clement, a practical mechanic from Shelburne Falls, Massachusetts, owned the Bay State Hardware Company, a hoe and rake factory, which sold most of its planter's hoes to Southern cotton growers for use by slaves. He received a patent for a screw-socket hoe in which screw threads were cut into the metal hoe and the wooden handle so that they wouldn't come apart. During the Civil War, the factory was retooled to manufacture gun barrels, ramrods, and bayonets, which were shipped to Springfield Armory. Clement was a private man, known for his business acumen and his technical abilities. He would become one of the prime movers in building the Williamsburg dam.

Paper Mill Village was the last factory village on the river. There, William Clark Jr. superintended his father's paper mill, where twenty-five men and seventy-five women produced two hundred tons of writing paper a year. The Clark family ran a large boardinghouse and store, which they supplied with meat from the cattle, hogs, and chickens raised on their nearby farms. Like Clement, Clark would become a driving force in constructing the Williamsburg dam.

On its way to the Connecticut the Mill River skirted Northampton's commercial center and the county seat, where shops covering eight square blocks sold everything from window sashes and blinds to crockery, clothing, and wallets. Northampton had been a trade and market center since its founding in 1654. By 1870, one could visit a hotel and saloon, restaurants with waiters and waitresses, and offices of professionals such as an architect, lawyer, civil engineer, insurance agent, and photographer. One quarter of the population was foreign-born, mostly Irish, and French Canadian, with many Germans and English. Northampton attracted artists, writers, and freethinkers throughout the nineteenth century, such as Thomas Cole,

Sylvester Graham, and Lydia Maria Child. Jenny Lind, who spent a three-month honeymoon there in 1852, dubbed Northampton "the Paradise of America."

Joel Hayden knew every inch of the Mill Valley and all its manufacturers as well as he knew Boston and state politics. Since the mid-1850s, the Republican party had monopolized Northampton and the state. By the Civil War, besides a Republican governor, Massachusetts had two Republican senators, Charles Sumner and Henry Wilson, who were among the Senate leaders. Abraham Lincoln had easily carried the state. Massachusetts Republicans were closely allied with the economic elite— manufacturers, professionals, clergymen, teachers at Harvard—those who were comfortable, responsible, and high-minded. Hayden fit right in. As lieutenant governor, besides standing ready to fill the governor's seat if he left office, his only official duty was to serve as a nonvoting member on the governor's council and as council president in the governor's absence. Hayden's record was one of quiet diplomacy and strong convictions, especially on the issues of slavery. Although politically astute and extremely tactful, he was soft-spoken and not a good orator; if he had been, he might have been governor himself. Just before he took office, in 1862, Joel married for a third time (his second wife, Lydia Graves, had died in 1859) to Anna Elizabeth Hall, age thirty-seven to his sixty-four. Six years later, they had a daughter together. Little Eliza was forty-four years younger than her father's oldest child.

In the middle of his second term as lieutenant governor, in 1864, Hayden would like to have supervised the design and building of the Williamsburg dam, as he had done with the Goshen dam in 1852, but he was in Boston frequently and would have to settle for siting it and looking over the shoulders of those more involved. On a July day in 1864, he determined that the new dam would start on the west side of High Ridge and extend across the ravine to the next hill. He drove stakes into the ground and piled rocks around them to mark both ends of the embankment. The reservoir would cover one hundred acres. His job done, Hayden rode home. If villagers saw him, they might have wondered what he was up to; if they had asked, he would have told them. Governor Hayden, as they called him, was approachable with a warm smile, extremely courteous and at ease talking with people at all levels of society. The villagers had always gone along with his plans to develop manufacturing and waterpower in the valley and they would have approved of the new "resevoy" as they pronounced it. They felt, like most Americans, a complacent satisfaction that factories were good; their owners accumulated wealth, which, in some measure, was shared with all. Reservoirs were part of the chain of progress.

CHAPTER 2

BUILDING THE
WILLIAMSBURG DAM

A F T E R Hayden staked the location of the dam, in midsummer 1864, Onslow Spelman, the good-natured Williamsburg button manufacturer who years earlier had become accustomed to working under Hayden's direction as his store clerk, began escorting small groups of Mill Valley manufacturers to the reservoir site. With two or three men at his side, Spelman likely walked along the river and pointed out Hayden's stakes, which marked the ends of the dam on slopes that rose up on either side of the river. The manufacturers agreed that this was an ideal spot for the new reservoir and that they should apply to the Massachusetts Legislature for a charter to incorporate themselves as the Williamsburg Reservoir Company to raise the money to build the dam. They estimated that they needed $30,000 in capital to be divided into shares purchased among themselves. Since it would be months before they received the charter, the group urged Spelman, in the meantime, to acquire the necessary land from the farmers who owned it; the reservoir company would reimburse him once it was officially formed.

At the beginning of August, for $1,500, Spelman secured an easement from Simeon Bartlett for the right to erect a permanent dam and reservoir on his farm and to take stone, earth, and gravel to build it. The easement document shows that Bartlett coaxed several concessions from the reservoir company to enable him to farm around the dam and reservoir. He required access roads on both sides of the dam leading to a sixteen-foot-wide road across the dam's crest with good railings on both sides so he could drive cattle and wagons across it to his pastures and woodlots on the east side. He compelled the company to build a stone wall along the north line of his property, in what would become the reservoir bed, so that when the water was drawn down, his cattle could not walk across the dry reservoir bed and damage other people's property. Finally, Bartlett required gates and bars along the county road to the dam to be kept in good repair.

Bartlett added one more condition: that the dam and reservoir be located at such a place and height as a competent engineer considered safe. In an era when engineers weren't licensed, and most were trained on the job, "competent engineer" was the usual designation for someone knowledgeable of engineering practices. Whether he trusted Hayden's judgment on the dam's location or not, he required that an engineer check it.

Later that month, Spelman bought adjoining acreage for the reservoir— thirteen acres for $400 from farmer Obed Hemenway and a tract worth $1,400 from Alonzo Pomeroy. Hemenway retained his fences and stone walls to contain his livestock when the reservoir was drawn down. Besides his crops and wood, Pomeroy reserved the right to dig and cart away muck and earth from what would become the silted-in reservoir bottom to fertilize his crops.

That fall, still unincorporated, the manufacturers moved ahead to satisfy Bartlett's stipulation that an engineer determine the size and location of the dam. It was probably at Hayden's suggestion that Spelman contacted the civil engineering firm of A. D. Briggs and Company in Springfield; Albert Dwight Briggs, the principal in the firm, was Hayden's friend, a well-known engineer who had constructed the railroad bridge across the Connecticut River at Springfield. Spelman brought two of Briggs's associates, engineers John R. Smith and George Raymond, to survey the reservoir site. The engineers first tackled the question of how high the dam should be. They calculated that a 32-foot-high dam would create a 93-acre reservoir with a capacity of 332 million gallons, while a 40-foot-high dam would flood 104 acres and hold nearly 600 million gallons, 80 percent more. "True economy," Smith and Raymond advised, seemed to "point to the erection of a dam not less than forty feet in height." Next, the engineers took up the question of exact location of the dam. They evaluated two sites in the vicinity of Hayden's stakes, and recommended one over the other because it would require a smaller dam made of less material.

In November, farmer Simeon Bartlett accepted Smith and Raymond's proposal for the dam's location, and stipulated in an agreement attached to the easement that the height and location they determined was "to be final and never altered or raised higher."

The next step for the manufacturers was to select a dam design. Hayden liked to have plans for everything he built, and so he urged Spelman to request several designs. Smith and Raymond presented the first plan, and

Spelman gathered the mill owners at Alfred Critchlow's office in Leeds to evaluate it. The three mill owners who would become the building committee—Lucius Dimock, William Clement, and William Clark Jr.—looked it over most carefully.

As the manufacturers had expected, Smith and Raymond proposed an embankment dam, the most common design for reservoir dams in New England and the oldest and simplest type of dam. An embankment dam has broad sloping banks on both the upstream and downstream side, and a flat top for a roadbed, which gives the structure a trapezoidal profile. Constructed of a huge mass of material—rock, earth, wood, concrete, or any combination—it is too heavy and bulky for the water to dislodge or overturn. As water presses against the dam's sloping banks, the dam's weight, pushing into the ground, easily resists displacement. Since water pressure increases with depth, an embankment dam is thicker at its base than at its top.

If the earth or stone on the dam's banks is loose enough for water to filter through, as was the case with most New England dams made from on-site materials, the dam had to be built with a core impervious to water to ensure that the structure was essentially watertight. Typically, core walls, running inside the length of the dam, were fashioned of masonry, wood planks, or puddled earth made of a mix of clay, sand, or gravel that had been compacted while wet. As the upstream slope of a reservoir saturated with water, a strong core wall, set deep into a trench of bedrock or hardpan (a layer of granules of sand fused together under pressure until it was impervious to water), prevented reservoir water from seeping through to the downstream side and kept animals such as eels and muskrats from burrowing holes through the structure. In other words, the core wall was the most important structural part of the dam, which the embankments protected and supported through their massive weight. Hayden was familiar with embankment dams. In 1852, he had built one in Goshen on the West Branch of the Mill River with a core of wooden planks sandwiched between two stone walls, surrounded by earthen banks sixty feet thick at the bottom and forty feet thick at the top.

Smith and Raymond's plan called for a forty-feet high core wall, of cut stone and other stones fit tightly together and laid dry, without cement between them. On the reservoir side, timbers set lengthwise were to cover the wall over which would be spiked two-inch-thick chestnut planks that had been tongued and grooved together. This masonry and wood core would be covered with a gently sloping gravel embankment three feet at its base for every foot of vertical height, providing a gentle slope of 18 degrees to absorb the water pressure. Smith and Raymond explained that a reservoir with property and people below it had to be as substantial as possible and that the watertight masonry wall they proposed would keep water out of the interior of the dam. But the manufacturers gasped at their cost—an estimate of $96,764 that could climb as high as $106,441 with contingencies. The manufacturers wanted to keep their cost well under the $30,000 for which they would be chartered and so rejected the proposal. They assumed a wall of cut stone on the interior of a dam to be decorative, unnecessary, and wasteful. A stone dam, as they called Smith and Raymond's design, was an expense they could not consider, so they asked Raymond to design an earthen dam. When he came back with a plan that cost $75,000, the manufacturers rejected that, too.

Next, Spelman contacted Stewart Chase, the engineer of the Holyoke Water Power Company, which regulated the Connecticut River, its dam, and canals for Holyoke's extensive mills. His plan called for an earthen embankment dam with a core wall made of brick, a common method of building a watertight center. "What you want is to construct a wall that will not wash," he wrote in an accompanying letter, "then pack dirt over it." At $24,000 it was affordable, but the reservoir company rejected his plan as well. Although it is not clear why, it may have been that they wanted to design the dam themselves.

As the mill owners evaluated the plans, they argued about the utility of the core wall, challenging the engineers' notions of what made a safe dam. Some, like John Payson Williston and Lewis Bodman, contended that a center wall was unnecessary. Another said that wood pilings alone would make a sufficient wall to keep out burrowing animals. William Clement agreed, reasoning that muskrats, the real enemies of dams, were not interested in reservoirs because the water level was not constant, and therefore no center wall was necessary. Conservatives among the group, like Hayden, wanted the strongest wall possible.

The mill owners thought their opinions as valid as the engineers'. In the 1860s, there were no standards for dam construction. Members of the emerging engineering profession were inventing techniques as they tried them out on projects, and few had expertise in reservoir dam construction. Most engineers—perhaps Smith, Raymond, and Chase were among them—were "practical engineers" who had begun their careers building railroads or canals and who transferred their skills to other projects or had spent years training with an experienced engineer. The manufacturers were practical mechanics who had learned on the job and believed that their firsthand experience and observations with waterpower and mill dams made them knowledgeable about building a reservoir dam, making them reluctant to grant control to engineers who, like Smith, Raymond, and Chase, had well-formed ideas that clashed with their own.

The winter of 1864–65 passed with no plan for the Williamsburg dam. By April 1865, the Legislature chartered the Williamsburg Reservoir Company "for the purpose of constructing and maintaining a reservoir of water on the East Branch of Mill River . . . for the supply of mills." The company could hold property up to $30,000 and divide the capital expense into 300 shares of $100 each to be purchased by members. Since the nation's beginnings, charters like this were a common way for legislatures to encourage economic development without levying taxes. Cash-poor states such as Massachusetts had few funds with which to construct transportation infrastructure or public works, so they granted charters and franchises to private investors to develop roads, canals, railroads, and reservoir dams. The private enterprises then owned the public improvements and assessed fees to users. Because the development of waterpower aided industry, the Massachusetts Legislature regularly granted charters for reservoirs, including one in 1840 for the Mill River Reservoir Company (composed of Joel Hayden and Northampton woolen manufacturers Stephen Brewer and Luther Clark) for the purpose of constructing a reservoir on the West Branch of the Mill River in the town of Goshen. They enlarged a sawmill dam that year, and built a larger dam on the same site in 1852.

A month after the Williamsburg Reservoir Company was chartered, on Monday, May 8, 1865, the company held its first meeting at the Mansion House hotel in downtown Northampton with eight of the Mill River manufacturers present: Joel Hayden, Lewis Bodman, William Skinner, Onslow Spelman, Alfred Lilly, Lucius Dimock, William Clark Jr., and William Clement. John Payson Williston and Alfred Critchlow did not attend. Lilly and Dimock from the Nonotuck Silk Company represented Samuel Hill as they would at all the reservoir company meetings. A month earlier, the Civil War had ended and the manufacturers hoped to have sufficient waterpower to take advantage of postwar economic expansion.

Lewis Bodman ran the meeting. The members accepted the act of incorporation, adopted the bylaws, and allotted the shares of stock. Joel Hayden purchased the most—50 shares—Spelman the fewest, 10. Critchlow took 33, Clement 25, Clark 25, Bodman 22, Williston 20, Skinner 15, and

Nonotuck Silk Company bought 50 (25 each for their Leeds and Florence factories). Requiring an investment of $1,000 to $5,000 per board member, the reservoir was a moderately priced improvement—a new home for a factory manager might cost $2,000. At a follow-up meeting ten days later, William Clark Jr., Lucius Dimock, and William Clement were chosen directors of the corporation, since they had already been acting in that capacity. Clement was named president, and Spelman would later be made clerk, as he had already assumed that role.

The main topic of conversation during their May meetings was the design of the dam. Dissatisfied with the proposals submitted by Smith and Raymond and by Chase, Clark suggested they ask his friend Lucius Fenn for a design. Fenn was a practical engineer surveying for the Williamsburg link to the Northampton and New Haven Railroad, and although he had never built a dam before, the building committee felt confident that he could write up specifications with their input; they would require no drawings. The company wanted an adaptable, flexible design that could be fixed later if it wasn't adequate. Like many other nineteenth-century builders, they wanted to experiment, improve, and modify throughout construction, as they had done when they built their own waterpower systems, and to fine-tune the design as they went along to prevent overbuilding and overspending.

Fenn proposed an earthen embankment dam with a masonry core wall built into a five-foot trench (or shallower if hardpan was reached) or a trench of sufficient depth to give a firm, hard, and secure bottom for the masonry to rest upon. Notching or "keying" the wall into soil or hardpan would help the wall resist the reservoir. Fearing high costs, the building committee told him to reduce the depth of the trench to three feet to minimize digging. He conceded. Fenn advocated that the angle of the upstream and downstream banks be a ratio of two feet at the horizontal base for every one foot of vertical height (2:1), giving the bank an angle of 27 degrees. But the mill owners thought such a slope was more gradual and costly than necessary. Clark wondered if an earthen slope with a 45-degree angle, or 1:1, on the upstream side would hold. When Fenn said it would not, the mill owners asked if a dam with a grade of 1½:1, an angle of 34 degrees, would "fill" with water without the earth sliding off. Fenn responded that he thought it would, and one of the mill owners replied, "We can fix it afterward," implying that they could increase the slope by dumping on more dirt if it did not hold, or if it wasn't sufficient to resist the weight of the water. They expected the reservoir to be full for short durations during the fall and spring so the walls wouldn't have to resist the full weight of the reservoir for long. Again, Fenn took the mill owners' suggestions and wrote the specifications their way.

By the time Fenn and the mill owners finished designing the structure, the specifications called for an earthen embankment dam, forty-three feet high at the highest point in the center (they may not have consulted Bartlett when they raised the height to forty-three feet) and diminishing to nothing at the ends. The bank was to be sixteen feet wide at the top and level enough for a roadway, with steep slopes at an angle of 34 degrees. For a distance of five feet on each side of the wall, the earth was to be placed in thin layers and puddled. The whole embankment was to be made in five-foot-thick layers of compacted earth, all free of any organic material. A rubble wall, set in a three-foot trench, would form the core of the dam. The core wall was to be two feet thick at the top and sloped one inch per foot, so that its base would measure five feet and nine inches. Through the center of the embankment was to be a low masonry wall for an iron gate pipe, eighteen inches in diameter, to rest on. The whole structure was to be constructed "in a substantial and workmanlike manner." Clement presided over the meeting of the full board when Fenn's plan was adopted.

In 1865, Massachusetts laws were mute on the subject of dam construction. The state required no plans to be drawn up or approved by engineers, no oversight of the work, and no inspection by experts. As one *Springfield Republican* editorial later put it, the company was "free to build a dam of sawdust, if it liked." The Mill and Reservoir Dams Act, passed in 1854, allowed only for elected county commissioners, who had no special engineering knowledge, to review the work if petitioned by either the reservoir company or by concerned local citizens. Upon review, county commissioners could recommend repairs to be made at the owner's expense. Noncompliant owners would have to pay to have their dam repaired or removed. In an effort to discourage citizens from making frivolous requests for inspections, the individual who called for the inspection would be required to pay all fees if the dam was deemed safe by the county commissioners.

Fenn's design in hand, the building committee placed an ad in the *Hampshire Gazette* for contractors to bid on the dam's construction. When partners Emory B. Wells of Northampton and Joel L. Bassett of Easthampton responded, they came with a favorable recommendation from Samuel Williston, Hayden's old business partner, for whom they had built two mill dams in Easthampton. Wells's contracting career was short (previously he had run a livery business in Northampton), but Joel Bassett had been in the construction business for several years. Neither had built a reservoir dam.

Clement and Clark gave Bassett and Wells a copy of Fenn's specifications and sent them to examine the reservoir site, telling them that the materials in the immediate vicinity would make as good a dam as they expected to build. On site, Bassett and Wells found stones and boulders for the wall and gravel deposits for the embankment. They bored test holes to determine the kind of soil the dam would rest on. Upon their return, they estimated they could do the job for $22,000. The building committee liked their price. In late June, Clement, Clark, Dimock, Bassett, and Wells met to discuss the contract, but Fenn was still adjusting the specifications. On a handshake, both parties agreed to proceed. They could sign a contract later.

On July 15, 1865, Wells and Bassett began construction. It would take six months during which they would supervise the work of up to seventy men. For the first two weeks Henry Bush of Westhampton cleared the site for thirty feet on each side of the center of the dam. He and his crew removed logs and rocks, pulled out bushes, and used cattle to extract alders rooted near the streambed. They plowed the land to loosen it, then scraped off the dirt, roots, muck, and stones, which they dumped beyond the site of the embankment where another man separated roots and stones so that the "cleaned" dirt could be laid on the dam embankments and the stones could be placed in the wall. Roots cut off by the plow were left in the ground. As they cleared the land, Wells and Bassett noticed two natural streams bubbling up on the east side, one on the upstream side beyond where the wall was to be and one on the downstream side, fifty feet below where the wall was to be erected. At first they were concerned that the flow of water from the springs might harm the bank that would be built over them, but then decided they were small and harmless enough that they left them there, although they watched them carefully in case they enlarged. When Spelman, Clement, Clark, and Dimock visited the site, they saw the springs but didn't tell Wells and Bassett to divert them.

When the ground was cleared, Wells and Bassett started to construct the long, low masonry wall through the middle of the dam and on which the gate pipe would rest. During construction, they would channel the river, which was ten feet wide, along winged walls, to funnel it into the gate pipe so that it could be released below the construction site.

When they finished the wall, Clement, Clark, and Dimock came to the work site to present Wells and Bassett with a contract. It called for a 16-inch pipe instead of the 18-inch pipe they were expecting because Dimock, who was in charge of purchasing the pipe, had reduced its size. Wells and Bassett protested that the smaller pipe did not have sufficient capacity to carry off the river water. A good brisk shower, Bassett argued, could wipe out their work. The contractors considered quitting, but with a month of work behind them and $8,000 invested in the project, they decided to continue the job with the 16-inch pipe. The committee presented no more contracts and none was ever signed.

For weeks during the summer of 1865, Bassett's crew dug the trench for the base of the stone wall that was to rest on a firm foundation. In the vicinity of the river, hardpan was a few feet below the surface. On the east side, they shoveled through soft and springy ground before they hit a hard rocky layer of soil. On the west side of the dam, at about the midpoint, they shoveled ten feet through layers of dirt and gravel without finding firm soil or hardpan. They kept digging until Spelman told them to stop because he thought they were digging too deep. He summoned Clement, Clark, and Dimock and told them he didn't think they could afford the additional expense of reaching hardpan, perhaps $150 added to the cost of the dam. The building committee asked Bassett if the dam would leak if it rested on gravel, a mix of sand and tiny pebbles. Bassett said yes, but they could patch the leaks. Clark spoke for the committee when he told Bassett to lay the wall on gravel. Go ahead and "risk it" were the words someone would recall later. Driving home that day, Bassett confided to a coworker his concerns about a dam built on gravel. If the reservoir company used it, he said he "wouldn't give a dollar for all the property in the valley."

Throughout the fall, workers erected the core wall. Beginning on the east side, Franklin Bush of Westfield laid the bottom stones in an unlined trench. On the west side, where the land rose up steeply, he set the bottom stones in steps to compensate for the change in elevation. When Bush was about one third complete, another crew followed behind to build up the wall. They brought pegmatite quarried a half mile away, which they split to square up the sides and cobblestones found on Bartlett's farm. As they erected the wall, they didn't match the rocks' size and shape so that often larger boulders stuck out above cobblestones, producing a ragged-faced rubble wall with a great variety of sizes and shapes. When the wall was three to five feet high, Ebeneezer Burnham, a mason from Easthampton, dug sand from a nearby bank to mix with lime for the grout and added water from the spring that flowed from the upstream side of the east bank. He supervised a small team as they poured grout on the top of the wall for a length of 15 to

20 feet and let it slide down into the vacant spaces between stones, expecting it would fill every crevice and void and maintain its consistency as it flowed. The top 10 to 15 feet were laid in mortar, which was less impervious to water than grout and less costly. They plastered grout over the upstream face of the wall.

Crews formed the embankments as the wall was built up, so that the wall was never four feet higher than the banks. Men shoveled gravel, loam, sand, and any other material they could find from nearby banks, carving out an acre from the upstream side of High Ridge beyond the east end of the embankment. With a bail scoop they loaded two or three cubic yards of fill into a cart, which horses pulled to the bank. Once the load was dropped, men spread it into location. Five feet from the wall, in two-foot-thick layers, workers puddled the earth. For the rest of the bank they smoothed the earth in layers five to ten feet thick. They assumed running over the earth with horses and carts was as good as tamping it down, but in reality, it only compacted the top foot of the layer. In all, they dumped 24,000 cubic yards of earth, the equivalent of 1,300 full loads in one of today's dump trucks, which holds about 18 yards of earth. When Bassett and Wells told Hayden that they thought the slope was too steep—that it ought to be a ratio of 3:1 on the upstream side—Hayden replied that they intended to dump more earth on it the following year. On October 30, 1865, when they had finished the east bank, Wells wrote an entry in his project journal to show his partner: "W. T. Clement and William Clark, Jr., two of the directors of the Williamsburg reservoir, expressed their entire satisfaction with the work, and said it was better than they expected we should build it."

On the west end of the embankment, the contractors left a notch for a thirty-foot spillway, or wasteway as they called it in the nineteenth century, which protected the dam from overtopping if the reservoir was filled beyond capacity. December's weather turned so cold that some of the laborers' ears were frozen and work had to be suspended. Clement questioned Bassett about using grout in such cold conditions. Knowing that no cement-like material should be installed in cold temperatures because it will not bind, Bassett reassured him that the wall was protected by earth on each side as it progressed upward and that they laid brush over it on cold days. Finally, workers covered the top of the wall with two feet of earth and smoothed the top to form a roadway.

On January 11, 1866, Clement, Clark, Dimock, Spelman, and Hayden traveled up the dam, accepted the work, and paid Wells and Bassett $23,600 for 24,000 yards of earthwork and 1,600 to 2,000 cubic yards of stone laid.

The dam stood 43 feet high, as tall as a four-story building, and almost 600 feet long, nearly the length of two football fields end to end.

Throughout the six months of construction, villagers watched the daily parade of men, horses, and wagons up and down the valley road. The cast iron pipe—160 feet long—was carted up to the site in sections on perhaps as many as sixteen or twenty ox carts. If villagers were keeping track of who was traveling up to the dam to supervise the contractors, they would have had no clear picture of what was going on. Villagers would have seen Lucius Fenn, whom they knew from his railroad work, ride up August 1 when he staked the trench for the core wall, but they wouldn't have seen him again. He had moved out west.

Before he left, Fenn had told his friend William Clark about his doubts of the dam's design and that he "would not trust this work to any contractors, even if they were his most intimate friends." He further urged Clark "to have the work looked over carefully" by a competent engineer. In the nineteenth century, it was customary for an engineer who was allied with the owners' interests to be hired to act as an inspector over the work of contractors as protection against contractors who might take advantage of the owners' ignorance. In a cost-cutting measure, the building committee hired a part-time superintendent, Eugene Gardner, and established no regular schedule of site visits. Gardner was a native of Florence and an architect who had built a large and stylish residence for William Clark Jr. and a foundry at Hayden's brass works. He was designing a new factory for William Clement.

But Gardner rarely went to the dam. From the end of August to October, he was ill with typhoid fever. In November he visited a few times until there was sickness and death in his family that caused him to be absent for two weeks. While Gardner was away, villagers would have seen carriages bringing the mill owners—singly or in small groups—to the dam several times per week to inspect the work. According to the contract, if there were no superintendent, the mill owners were in charge. With all the comings and goings of contractors, work crews, and manufacturers, word about how the construction was going drifted down to the villages.

In the spring of 1866, a few months after the dam was completed, the reservoir company closed the gate pipe. For this first season they planned to fill the reservoir slowly and keep the water level at ten or twelve feet to test the strength of the structure, then add more dirt to the banks if needed. But one Sunday, as rain and melting snow began to fill the reservoir, workers who had been watching the dam raced down the valley to find Bodman and

Hayden to tell them that water was quickly climbing up the banks, which looked like they were about to crumble. Bodman and Hayden arrived to see the water high on the banks, which were so saturated they were beginning to slump. The sixteen-inch gate pipe couldn't discharge fast enough, and the wasteway, an unlined dirt trench, was in danger of washing away, threatening the embankment. Bodman would later say that both he and Hayden had expected to see the dam break that day.

Faced with a near disaster, the reservoir company board members did as they had planned—they modified the dam. Hayden and Bodman directed laborers as they cut hemlock trees and stretched them across the dam, piled brush on the upstream bank to protect it, and laid more brush across the lower portion of the downstream bank where it was wet and slushy. A few days later, they hired some of the men working on the local railroad project to begin more serious repairs. In an effort to secure the west end bank, workers prepared timbers and drove them down into the bank to stabilize it. As the water receded, they dumped thousands of loads of earth on the banks to decrease the slope to an angle of 27 degrees from the steeply pitched 34-degree angle it had been. That May, with his term as lieutenant governor over, Hayden became president of the reservoir company.

In the summer when the water was out of the reservoir, Hayden and Dimock directed John Belcher, a local livery keeper who owned horses and probably vehicles and equipment for moving earth, to alter the dam. Belcher lengthened the dam six or eight feet by extending it near the wasteway, and he attempted to stop leaks on both the east and west downstream banks by digging down to the hardpan along the slope where the natural and artificial banks met and by puddling the trenches. But this did not stop the leaks, which ran mostly at the bottom below the level of the pipe all along the bank, nor did it stop an especially large one about thirty feet east of the gate pipe. Someone dug trenches to channel the flow from the leaks back into the river. Despite repairs, the west bank on the downstream side became so soggy that no one could walk on it. Even after Belcher put logs and stone on the bank to prop it up, so much water ran out that men watered their horses there. Finally, the bank was fenced off to keep cattle out so they wouldn't get mired in the mud.

The condition of the Williamsburg dam was a regular topic of conversation for locals. A year after it was put into service, a mass of earth slid off the dam—eight feet thick, forty feet wide, and two-thirds the height of the slope. Although the slide was repaired, the dam could no longer be ignored. Otis Hill, a prosperous Williamsburg farmer known for his conservative, careful judgment, wrote in his diary for April 11, 1867: "Men and horses sent to work on new reserv. Looked upn [sic] as unsafe." Hill never mentioned the dam again in his diary, but he and his neighbors must have talked a great deal about it since the reservoir was three miles above their heads. A month later, the reservoir company voted a special assessment for more repairs and to build a house at the dam for the gatekeeper to live in so he could always watch it.

Villagers regularly asked Bodman and Hayden what they thought of the dam. Despite reassurances from the mill owners, some vowed to petition the county commissioners to inspect it. (Without a petition, the commissioners had no authority to examine the dam.) To quiet public opinion, the mill owners called for an inspection themselves. In October 1867, three commissioners examined the dam with the mill owners, who explained how the dam was built; none of the contractors were called. Seeing the leaks, the commissioners refused the dam. The next spring, the reservoir company spent $5–10,000 on improvements. John Belcher was hired to stop a leak on the west side near the wasteway by digging ten to twelve feet to a bed of coarse gravel through which water could be seen coming through. He puddled the earth below the gravel bed to stem the flow, and laid stones on the upstream bank to prevent erosion. The commissioners returned in October 1868 and accepted the dam.

Talk about the dam never stopped. One day in 1869 or 1870, after the dam had been in use for three or four years, Hayden's friend Albert Dwight Briggs, whose civil engineering firm had conducted the initial site survey, had been fishing in the reservoir when he saw water oozing out of the dam. He called Hayden's attention to the leaks, warning him that if the dam broke, it would "sweep everyone on its way into the Connecticut River." Hayden warned William Skinner, who adopted the habit of moving his raw silk from his storehouses near the river to higher ground when it looked like rain might last for days.

For seven years, Hayden, the immediate supervisor of the reservoir, kept the water level low. He never allowed it to be filled until after danger from a spring freshet was over. Then he cautiously raised it and observed how the banks were holding before he let it rise again. He didn't push the dam too hard, but let it fill just enough to get by. By reacting to its cues and relying on his own intuition about the dam's limits, he made the dam work, well enough. A half-full reservoir holding 300 million gallons of water was better than no reservoir. Coaxing and coddling a lame dam was less costly than removing it and building a new one.

On rainy nights in the late 1860s and early 1870s, as villagers lay in bed after having spent the evening at a prayer meeting, a Sunday school concert, a card game, or a fire company drill, Hayden's thoughts turned to the dam. He couldn't sleep. To allay his fears, he crept down his carpeted stairway, walked through heavily draped rooms filled with carved furniture, and out the door. On his way to the stable, he passed the greenhouse, the gardener's cottage, and the ornamental fish pond. Every inch of his home and property was decorated or landscaped in a show of civilized refinement, a demonstration of man's triumph over nature. In his late sixties and early seventies at the time, Hayden headed out into the dark, rainy night and rode horseback or drove a carriage alone from Haydenville through Skinnerville to Williamsburg village. He turned off the road that lead to Goshen and headed up toward the Williamsburg dam. For three miles on a muddy road, the river rushed to his right. He followed the narrow lane leading to the dam and crossing the top. Perhaps he sat in his carriage or on his horse and listened to the waves lapping the bank or to the overflow running down the wasteway. Most likely, however, he walked along the top looking for leaks by lantern light. In the last years of his life, when he was ill and his fears got the better of him on rainy nights, he called for his son Thomas, then a nearly fifty-year-old man with seven children of his own, and asked him to ride up to the dam. Each time, Hayden Sr. or his son Thomas returned, satisfied that the dam was holding.

Hayden became ill in the summer of 1872, but the seventy-four-year-old recovered enough to pay attention to waterpower. In need of more water to compensate for the reduced amount the Williamsburg reservoir held, Hayden and the other mill owners decided to build a third reservoir dam on the Mill River—the new one to be on the West Branch in Goshen, a mile above the reservoir Hayden had built in 1852. To finance the new dam, the members of the Mill River Reservoir Company, which owned the Goshen dam, consolidated with the Williamsburg Reservoir Company to form the Mill River and Williamsburg Reservoir Company. In 1872, the new company was chartered by the Legislature for $100,000. The directors of the new company were Joel Hayden, William Clement, and Lucius Dimock, who had charge of building the new Goshen dam. They hired a well-known Northampton engineer, Emory C. Davis, to design the dam. By the next year, the new fourteen-foot-tall earthen dam would extend 528 feet and flood seventy-five acres.

On a spring day in 1873, Hayden, his son Thomas, and William Clement traveled up to the Williamsburg dam for their annual inspection. After an hour's observation, Hayden declared that he was better satisfied with the dam than he had ever been. For seven years he had coddled it, gently filled it, watched it in storms; now he finally believed it was safe. He never offered any reasons for his change of heart and nothing was different about the dam. Perhaps he believed that the dam grew stronger the longer it stood, though any of the engineers he knew—Briggs, Smith, Raymond, or Davis—could have told him that a structure degrades the longer it stands. Or, perhaps he was just feigning optimism for his colleagues. When the valley mill owners learned that Hayden believed the dam was safe, they were relieved and did not question his rationale. William Skinner stopped moving his silk when there was a danger of a freshet. When villagers asked Lewis Bodman if the dam was safe, he reassured them with new confidence. The old fears about the reservoir became a joke. When someone asked William Skinner what they did up in the Mill Valley for excitement, he quipped, "We occasionally have a freshet; then there is a general alarm that the reservoir has broken loose."

That spring Hayden's health failed, and with it his attention to the dam. Late in the summer, Hayden suffered an attack of acute rheumatism from which he improved enough by November to travel by train to New York City, attended by his youngest son, Samuel Williston Hayden. From his hotel he walked down and back to the headquarters of his brass firm on Beekman Street. That evening his daughter Jenny, who lived in New York, visited him at the hotel and left him feeling comfortable. Later that night he was seized by stomach and chest pains. A doctor was called and found Hayden's heartbeat normal. Hayden slept some during the night, but the next morning the same pain returned. After breakfast he sank into a chair and slumped forward into his son's arms. Reaching for his heart, he murmured "I am gone" and died. It was November 10, 1873. Three days later, two hundred mourners attended his funeral at the Haydenville Church. Brass-shop workers carried his casket around the corner to the village cemetery. Henry Gere's obituary in the *Hampshire Gazette* said he was "like a father to his village," a man who would be sorely missed.

As the weather turned colder and fall became winter, the foot-deep puddles in the reservoir froze and were covered with snow. Although the reservoir company didn't formally appoint him, Onslow Spelman became the dam's overseer; he lived the nearest and had served as secretary-treasurer of the Williamsburg Reservoir Company for seven years. Spring 1874 arrived late. During the last two weeks of April, four big storms dumped so much snow that Williamsburg residents took sleighs to church the last Sunday in April. On May 1, Mary Hill remarked in her diary, "It doesn't seem much like the first of May. The hills are all covered with snow and it is cold." When warm weather finally came a week later, as if to make up for lost time, Spelman instructed gatekeeper George Cheney to close the gate pipe to fill the reservoir, and keep it closed. Cheney complied. The reservoir seemed to fill all at once. Within a week, 600 million gallons of water pressed against the earthen dam, from the base to within a few feet of the crest.

Two weeks later, on Friday, May 15, 1874, the officers of the reservoir company drove up to Goshen for their annual inspection of the dams there. In the hills, new green leaves colored the branches of maples and oaks as apple blossoms pinked the orchards. The officers had planned to continue on to view the Williamsburg dam once they finished in Goshen, but they spent too long there and couldn't make it to Williamsburg before nightfall. So Spelman and Cheney inspected the dam by themselves. Finding no new leaks, they were satisfied that the dam was in its usual condition and they pronounced it in working order for the season. Cheney and Spelman went home, Cheney to his unpainted cabin by the dam and Spelman to his large ornate house in town. The sun would be up at four-thirty the next morning, after which workers would fill the riverside factories.

CHAPTER 3

THE FLOOD

WHEN George Cheney awoke on the morning of Saturday, May 16, 1874, he heard the sound of rushing water. The reservoir was full, and the excess was slipping down the wasteway that ran past the cabin door. Cheney couldn't help but constantly watch the dam. The three- or four-room house had been built into the hillside to which the west end of the dam was attached, about 150 feet downstream from the crest. It sat on a wooden platform, supported by posts, so that the first floor was almost level with the top of the embankment. Through the windows on the north and east sides, he could see the reservoir and the entire downstream slope. From the front door, he could cross a footbridge over the wasteway and walk onto the road that crossed the dam. From the back door, he could step down the hill and climb up onto the embankment. It was like he was living on a mountain—a mountain with a lake pressing against it, reaching almost to its peak. The lake weighed two and a half million tons.

At six o'clock, Cheney went out to check on the condition of the dam, as he did every morning. Dark clouds rolled overhead, pelting him with rain that promised to continue all day. At twenty-nine, he was lanky with a long, thin face and a goatee that accentuated his pointed chin. His dark, thin hair fell limply in one straight lock to the tops of his ears. It was his job to open and close the gate, keep an eye on the reservoir, inspect the dam twice daily, and tell Spelman if he saw anything unusual. The job paid $200 per year, about what a male cotton-mill worker in Haydenville made. But instead of working eleven- to twelve-hour days, six days a week, he had only a few duties and was able to supplement his income by working as a day laborer on nearby farms. Like the hundred other farm laborers in Williamsburg, he could earn $1.50 or $2.00 a day. When he was away, his wife watched the dam. The reservoir company gave him a half acre to farm for his own use.

Cheney's only real possession was a horse—a poor one used for transportation, not farm work, worth only $75 when most were valued at twice that amount. He had stretched to buy the twelve-year-old mare, taking out a $50 loan to complete the transaction. Even though he owned no home, land, farm animals, or trade tools, and had no money invested in a bank or company, he was better off than almost half the men who headed households in Williamsburg. He saw himself as a member of the community so he paid the $2 poll tax each year to vote.

Cheney expected this summer to be like the last two. He would keep the gate pipe closed until the river level dropped, then release enough to keep the flow in the river uniform, allowing the water to refill the factory storage ponds. Depending on rainfall, he would open and close the gate many times during the summer and fall.

Cheney walked the embankment, leaning forward into the steep slope to keep his balance. From the top of the dam, Cheney could see up and down the valley. To the north, the reservoir covered one hundred acres, filling a basin shaped by the green hills. Because the shoreline rose and fell dramatically, it had few of the reeds, cattails, or grass that marked the shoreline of natural lakes or ponds. It was an open-topped vessel, a gravelly banked holding tank, filling and emptying upon demand.

The dam, and Cheney, were inside the valley, hemmed in by hills that rose up on both ends of the structure. The west end joined a smooth knoll of pastures that stood one hundred feet taller than the dam. Over the brow of the hill were his nearest neighbors, three quarters of a mile away, in a cluster of half a dozen farms, a cider mill, a maple sugar house, and a one-room school. The east end of the dam met the lower slopes of High Ridge, a hill that jutted several hundred feet above the dam. Across the top of the dam, which spanned almost six hundred feet, was a smooth road with a sturdy fence, built at farmer Simeon Bartlett's insistence to connect his pasture on the west side to his woodlot on the east. From the center of the dam, the river ran forty-three feet below.

Cheney walked up and down the embankment but saw nothing peculiar. The dam was in the same condition it had been in when he took the job two and a half years ago. The usual row of leaks, which ran all year long, dotted near the base of the dam along its entire length. Now that the reservoir was full, they ran heavily. A trench drained their flow back to the river. Cheney had been especially concerned about the largest of them, the diameter of a man's arm, which spouted from the east bank about thirty feet from the center. A year earlier, he had told reservoir company member Lucius

Dimock about it and they had examined it together. But when they saw that the discharge was clear, indicating to them that it was not carrying away any bits of the inside of the bank, Dimock attributed the flow to a harmless spring bubbling up from the riverbank. Another leak that bothered Cheney ran on the west side near the wasteway at the bottom. The previous spring Dimock and Isaac Stone, a mill manager in Florence and the clerk of the consolidated Mill River and Williamsburg Reservoir Company, examined it by digging in with a shovel to see if the flow had created a cavity by washing out the inside of the dam. They saw mud and dirt and concluded nothing was wrong. The hole they dug was still there a year later.

At the side of the gate house, a small enclosure built into the bank at the center of the dam, Cheney noticed the muddy patch where a chunk of soaked earth, about as much as a wagon load or two, had fallen away a year ago. Neither Dimock nor Spelman had asked him to repair it. Inside the gate house, the wheel Cheney turned to open and close the gate pipe was locked as he had left it when he filled the reservoir.

As he walked back to his cabin near the west end of the dam, Cheney passed the fence he had repaired the day before. It marked off a parcel of wet, slushy land where water seeping from the dam had combined with underground springs to create earth so marshy that cattle wandering off neighboring farms had sometimes gotten mired in the mud. This spring, like many springs, the water in the wasteway washed away hunks of dirt from the wasteway banks, turning the overflow muddy.

Satisfied that the dam was in its usual condition, Cheney went home to a house crowded with family. In addition to his baby daughter, four young sons, and his wife, who was pregnant with their sixth child, he now shared the cabin with his parents, who had moved in three weeks earlier. Nine occupants made the little house even smaller.

About seven-fifteen, when Cheney sat down to breakfast with his family, the villages along the Mill River were full of life. Five thousand people lived and worked along the river. In Williamsburg, milkman Collins Graves had already started his deliveries, as had John B. Gleason, the butcher. Jerome Hillman was headed from Skinnerville to Haydenville to collect the village's mail. In Haydenville, Jimmy Ryan was returning home after having driven his father and brother to the brass works. Downstream in Leeds, Fred Howard took his place in the box-making room at the Mill River Button Company. Myron Day hitched his horse to his wagon to visit his sister Laura Birmingham and his three nieces in Williamsburg. Mill River manufacturers Onslow Spelman, William Skinner, Joel Hayden Jr., and

Lucius Dimock were at their residences. If they had gone to their respective factories first thing in the morning to unlock their factory doors, they were home again by now.

When breakfast was over, Cheney's wife cleared away the dishes as George pushed back from the table. His father, who had already stood up from the table, gazed out the window. He suddenly tensed up. "For God's sake, George, look there," he called. Cheney looked out in time to see a mass of earth—about forty feet wide and twenty-five feet high—slide off the bank's east side beyond the gate and shoot downstream. The bank had been so saturated with water from leaks that it could no longer stand.

George called for someone to bring him the key to the gate, which hung at the head of the bed. He ran to the gatehouse, unlocked the wheel, and turned it to open the gate that blocked the pipe. He was both brave and foolhardy to go to the downstream side of a failing dam. Reservoir water rushed through the pipe into the riverbed. He hoped to relieve enough pressure to prevent a break, but knew that his effort was futile. Dozens of streams of water, as thick as his wrist, spurted from the spot where the slab had fallen. Every moment, new rivulets popped through. The bank was becoming a muddy mush. He thought that in minutes the wall would burst.

Cheney dashed to the house to tell his father he was riding to Spelman's in the village. At the barn he bridled his horse as his father cut him a switch. Cheney climbed on his barebacked mare and headed her down the trail to the river road, the old horse at a gallop. His father ran for Hemenway's farm to warn him to get his cows off the riverside pasture.

Cheney must have feared Spelman's reaction. Twice in the past year, Spelman had reprimanded him for alarming the valley needlessly by spreading news that the dam was breaking. He didn't think this would be a third false alarm because he had never seen such a big chunk slide all at once and so many new streamlets popping through the dam.

Cheney's ride along the river was a straight, steep, hurried descent, just like the water's. The water rolled straight downhill, making only slight turns with no stops to pool. It didn't pause and neither did he. From the dam to the village, it traveled three miles and descended three hundred feet in elevation. The downhill grade urged Cheney's horse on.

On the trail, Cheney could hear the river, but he couldn't see it. The streambed was sunken into a deep gorge, seventy-five feet below his left side. Before the dam was built, the mile-long stretch of river between the dam and the spot where Bradford Brook entered was ten feet wide, wider in the spring, and the rocky bottom was visible. It had teemed with plant and animal life, but since the dam had been built, this stretch was often silent and dry. Like the reservoir, it no longer had the natural rhythms of spring floods and summer shallows, and its natural edges had been erased by the artificial fluctuations of water.

After almost a half mile on the trail, Cheney turned onto the river road, which had been built for the construction of the dam. He crossed over Bradford Brook, which added its spring flow to the river. Cheney rode hard along the wet road as it dropped through a series of gorges. He passed the back of Obed Hemenway's farm and saw his cows in their riverside pasture on the slope above his right shoulder. Behind Hemenway's stood a rolling ridge lined with farms, a mile away but several hundred feet higher in elevation. If farmer Robert Loud, who was busy with morning chores, had looked down at that moment, he would have seen Cheney racing toward the village and might have suspected something was wrong with the dam. But he didn't happen to look in that direction.

Halfway to the village, rough pasture land turned to a soft green bank, ankle-deep with strawberries. Oliver Everett, a fruit grower, was in the midst of spring planting. Within the last two weeks he had set out rows of crab apple and pear trees and had repaired the fences that kept livestock out of his orchards. In another week or two, he would plant raspberries. Everett didn't notice Cheney either.

A half mile above the village, Cheney passed John Gleason's slaughter-house, which stood next to the river. Gleason was already in the village selling meat. A quarter mile below, outside the village, Cheney raced past a small house sandwiched between the road and the river. Cheney had to know that if the dam broke, this house would be the first one hit. If Sarah Cowing Bartlett, who was inside with her three-year-old daughter, Viola Colyer, heard the horse galloping past her door, she thought nothing of it. Cheney pressed on.

When he saw the river widen and smooth over, he knew he was at the top of the village at the millpond that fed Spelman's button factory. He followed the road as it bent to the right, turning away from the river. Within seconds he was in the heart of the village, headed for Spelman's house.

The village of Williamsburg was a short, thin braid of streams and house-lined streets, looping around each other. In the center of the village, the West Branch and the East Branch met to form the Mill River. Above their confluence, streams were easily diverted into winding canals that led to the gristmills and sawmills and the handful of factories that made buttons and hardware. Williamsburg's broad streets were lined with large old trees, side-

walks, and whitewashed clapboarded houses—one hundred twenty in number—arranged in neat rows with ample yards between.

When Cheney reached the bottom of North Street, he turned right onto
North Main, past the Congregational Church and the house where Henry
James, who had bought Lewis Bodman's woolen mill, lived. James and his
wife were in New York City, packed and ready to sail to Europe that night.
He had left Henry Birmingham, the superintendent, in charge of the woolen
mill. Cheney crossed the street and stopped briefly at Lyman James's store
and post office. The broad front porch was a good place to pass time and
gather news. Cheney told someone out front that the dam was breaking.
Cheney didn't wait to hear their reaction; he continued down the street to
Spelman's. Ten minutes had passed since he left the reservoir.

Cheney's exhausted horse faltered up Spelman's drive. The house was the
largest and most fashionable in the village, built a decade earlier with profits
from button sales. A bay window protruded from one side while round windows peeked through a curved mansard roof. Cheney saw John Gleason, the
butcher, in the yard with his meat wagon and shouted at him to tell Spelman
to come out right away. When Gleason called to him, Spelman was already
walking out the door. His daughter Lizzie had been looking out the window
and told her father that Cheney was riding in on horseback. Spelman asked
what the matter was. For a few moments Cheney was so agitated he couldn't
speak. Gleason remembered Cheney and Spelman's exchange:

"The dam's breaking away!"

"It can't be! Which part?"

"The east part," Cheney replied.

"No, you don't mean the east part; you mean the west part, near the
[wasteway]."

"No, I mean the east part."

Spelman asked, "Have you raised the gate?"

"Yes."

Spelman and Cheney argued. Over and over again, Spelman asked, "Are
you sure the dam is breaking away? It can't be possible." Cheney repeatedly insisted that it was and that something had to be done—someone had to
go through to Haydenville. Spelman didn't want to be made a fool if
Cheney was wrong, again. After a discussion of several minutes—which
some later said was as long as fifteen minutes and Spelman would claim was
two minutes—Spelman ordered Cheney to warn Haydenville. When
Cheney protested that he needed a fresh horse, Spelman sent him to
Belcher's livery stable, two hundred yards way.

Cheney banged on John Belcher's door. It seemed like it took a few minutes for Belcher, who was still dressing, to come out into the yard. He asked Cheney repeatedly if he was sure. Belcher knew the dam well. The reservoir company had paid him to make repairs. While Cheney explained, Collins Graves, the milkman on his morning route, drove into the yard. He had seen the frightened expression on Cheney's face as he passed him and that Cheney had been pushing his horse hard, so he followed him to Belcher's. He asked: "George, what's the matter?"

Cheney answered, "The reservoir's giving way."

"Do you mean it?"

"Yes, I do."

"Well if that's so, someone's got to let them know it. You, George, alarm the folks here, and I'll drive down the river."

Graves started off. It had been about twenty-five minutes since the dam first slumped. Two minutes later, Cheney galloped away on a fresh horse. Graves was nowhere in sight and he would not see him again that day. As Cheney raced by the Williams House Hotel, he saw Theodore Hitchcock, the miller, come out. He had heard what he thought was thunder. Cheney called, "The flood! The flood! The reservoir is broken!" Hitchcock ran into the hotel, told everyone there and dashed to the mill a few blocks away to retrieve his business records. In another two hundred yards, Cheney was cut off by high water. For a few minutes, Cheney warned villagers, but then afraid for the safety of his family, he turned around and headed home. It had taken Cheney ten minutes to reach the village and fifteen minutes for him to convince Spelman and Belcher that the dam was breaking.

Back at the gatekeeper's cabin after George Cheney left, his wife, Elizabeth, positioned a chair on the porch where she could watch the dam. About twenty minutes after the slide of the east bank, Elizabeth saw and heard the eastern half of the dam explode upward. She would later say that it "seemed to burst all at once, from the bottom, where the earth seemed to be lifted up," as though someone had inserted a giant shovel under the base and thrown the dirt skyward. As the ground heaved, a column of dirt and rock rose in the air, but instead of falling back to earth, it was pushed forward by the great surge of reservoir water, suddenly free of the dam. It "made an awful noise, like an earthquake," she said.

A convulsive boom echoed through the Williamsburg hills, and was heard as far away as Goshen. Elias Cheney, George's father, heard it as he ran to Hemenway's to tell him to remove his cows from the river pasture. Elias later said it was "louder than the biggest clap of thunder" he had ever heard.

Elizabeth Cheney couldn't take her eyes off the sight. She watched the water rush through the gap, biting hunks out of the edges of the hole and widening the gap to two hundred fifty feet, nearly half the width of the dam. When the gap broke through the west side of the gate, she sent the children across the footbridge and up the hill to safety. Her mother-in-law refused her invitation to join her on the porch, saying the sight sickened her, and so stood with her back to the reservoir, taking an occasional whiff of camphor to revive herself. For twenty minutes, the water leaped down the valley in a muddy floodwave that pushed forward at a rate of 60,000 cubic feet per second. There were 600 million gallons to let out. It would take one hour for all the water to leave the reservoir. Some of the water that came through the gap first slid down the valley ahead of the floodwave, free of debris. This was the water that Cheney and others saw washing over the streets.

Standing in his hillside orchard three quarters of a mile below the dam, Oliver Everett heard a roar, which he would later describe as like that of a train of railroad cars passing by or the falling of a heavy wall. He looked up and saw, somewhat indistinctly through the trees, water running over the dam. After he warned his parents, who lived on the farm with him, he started running down the valley through the pastures along the bank above the road. He saw a group of people on the road and shouted at them that the reservoir was coming and to get away. Although he started a half to three quarters of a mile ahead of it, he had run only another three quarters of a mile when the flood passed him. He calculated that it took twenty minutes for the flood to reach the village. It was traveling at nine miles per hour.

At the moment the dam broke, Robert Loud happened to step into his farmhouse doorway high on Merritt's Hill, and look out at the valley and the dam below. He knew instantly what had happened and took off on foot on the high road and ran two and a half miles to the village, turning left onto Village Hill Road. He stopped at Lewis Porter's store just long enough to ask a boy who was out front on horseback to warn the village. When he reached William Adams's gristmill on the near side of the river, he was so winded he couldn't shout and threw a stick at Adams to get his attention. Adams looked up to see Loud waving wildly, pointing at the rising stream. Years later, a local history would say that although Loud had survived Civil War battles, he never recovered from the effects of the run. Adams and his employee Henry Tilton ran to their homes to warn their families and everyone they saw along the way.

Up to this point the word had passed quietly between a few men: Cheney to Spelman and then to Belcher, whose conversation was overheard by Graves, and from Cheney to Hitchcock and the others in the Williams

House Hotel. By the time Loud reached the town, the warnings became noisy, panicked, urgent. The few who had heard the warning ran and yelled as they sought out family members. But the warning was one-to-one. The only formal alarm system that could reach the hundreds of people in the village quickly was the church bell, which no one had yet rung.

After leaving Spelman's yard, meat peddler Gleason went across the street to Lewis Bodman's, the former owner of the woolen mill, to tell him. Then he headed for the bridge to cross the river to his home on Nash Street, near Spelman's mill, but the first wave had swelled the river so high he couldn't get across.

Meanwhile, Spelman went inside for his hat, and when he came out again, Cheney was gone. In a moment, Gaius Wood, who had been in Lyman James's store when Cheney came by, entered the yard to ask Spelman about Cheney's warning. Spelman said he didn't know what to make of it. For four or five minutes, Spelman calmly explained why he thought the reservoir would never break. Not reassured, Wood, who was the bookkeeper at the James woolen mill, left to drive there.

Spelman retraced the route Cheney had used to enter the village: down North Main Street, past the homes of other mill owners and the Congregational Church, across the gristmill bridge and up the east side of the river to his button factory, where he told his workers to flee to higher ground. Despite his misgivings, he didn't take any chances. Upon crossing back over the river, he returned to the village to look for the sexton to ring the bell at the Congregational Church, but the first wave had reached the village and was overrunning the riverbanks. Spelman climbed up the hill behind the houses on North Street, where he held a commanding view of the river as it exited the gorge and entered the village. He heard the roar. He waited and watched. Belcher rang the bell once or twice.

With only Cheney's word that the dam was about to break to spur him on, Collins Graves snapped the reins and turned his milk wagon out of Belcher's livery stable and onto Main Street, confident that Cheney and others would warn the rest of the village. He shot past the Methodist Church, the town hall, and the school. When he reached the watering trough for horses that stood in the middle of the road, he took the left fork, ignoring the road that would have taken him up to his farm, high above the Mill River. He steered onto South Main Street, which hugged the river all the way to Haydenville. He knew this road, like all of those in

Williamsburg, like the back of his hand. He had seen every house, shop, bend in the road, and turn in the river a thousand times before. He knew everyone who lived along the route and they knew him.

Collins Graves was a fourth-generation Williamsburg son, a dairy farmer and milkman who sold milk, cream, and butter that he stored in a stone icehouse at the base of Spelman's button mill dam. On this morning, his icehouse was packed with milk cans surrounded by blocks of ice cut from Spelman's millpond. He lived a mile from the village with his wife Ellen and three children, ages one to eight, in a big house diagonally across from his brother's on one side and his father's on the other. Both his father's sisters had married manufacturers: Lydia had been Joel Hayden Sr.'s second wife, and Emily was married to Samuel Williston. At thirty-three, Collins Graves was slender with a boyish face, big, dark, sad eyes, and short straight brown hair. A long moustache hid his mouth. Quiet and likeable, he had been named Daniel Collins Graves after a colorful and beloved village doctor named Daniel Collins, who promoted the education of local young men he thought showed promise.

Graves knew firsthand the power of the Mill River. In the 1860s, he and his older brother Henry had owned the gristmill that William Adams operated at the confluence of the East and West Branches. In all their time working on the river, the highest the Graves brothers had ever seen the river was sixteen feet above its normal height, the result of a torrential rain in October 1869.

Reflexively, Graves headed for the factories where he knew the largest concentration of people to be: 50 men and women at Henry James's woolen mill at the bottom of Williamsburg village, 100 at Skinner's silk mill in Skinnerville, 300 at the Haydenville brass works, and 125 at the cotton mill in Haydenville. He hoped that people in homes along the route—mostly mothers, children, sick and elderly men and women, servants—would hear his own cries as he rode by.

Graves urged his mare to a dead run down the river road. Even pulling a light wagon with a half dozen milk cans, she moved fast—ten or twelve miles per hour—on the half-mile run along the flat meadow to Henry James's wool mill. He met no one along the road and saw no one outside the twenty houses he passed. He shouted, "The reservoir's here! Head for the hills!" and hoped that those inside heard him. In the patter of the rain and the din of factory machinery, no one did. Even if it had been quiet, most of those at home were in their kitchens at the rear of the house, serving breakfast or doing chores.

Almost halfway to the woolen mill, Graves cried out his warning as he passed the home of Dr. Elbridge Johnson, the village doctor. Home recovering from an illness, the doctor was inside with his wife, eight-year-old son, six-year-old and four-year-old daughters, and his mother. A surgeon in the Civil War, Johnson had moved his family to Williamsburg five years earlier with the intention of practicing medicine in a quiet setting, but he had become so ill that he was planning to go to New York City later that day for treatment. His house was silent, and Graves raced on.

Graves just missed Sophia Hubbard, who lived across the street. Minutes earlier, she had left her house to go to a neighbor's for milk, leaving her husband, a farmer, at home with their daughter, Emma Wood, who was visiting from Chicopee with her one-year-old son Harold.

From the Hubbards' to the James woolen mill, Graves passed twelve houses owned by Henry James. James had built half of them for his workers and purchased the others from farmers, providing the bigger ones to his managers. The largest belonged to Henry Birmingham, the mill's superintendent. Birmingham had arrived in Williamsburg the previous year to make a new start. His own woolen mill in Hinsdale, Massachusetts, had failed in the depression and downturn of wool prices the previous year, and he needed to earn wages to pay his debts. Graves assumed Birmingham was at the mill. He saw no one else, not Birmingham's wife Laura nor their three daughters, including Mary, the eldest at twenty, who had arrived home the night before from Northampton where she taught school.

Graves rode past the house where Dwight Adams, the carding room foreman, lived. He was in the mill; his wife and seven-year-old son were at home. Across the street, the Kingsley houses were quiet. The Kingsley men, father and son, were house carpenters who shared a carpenter shop that stood between their two homes. For the past few days, the elder Elbridge Kingsley had been away in another town constructing a building. That morning, he had come home, helped his wife clean house, and played with his little granddaughter, three-year-old Nellie. Then, while his son was at work in the village, he started for the shoemaker's shop to get his shoes repaired. His wife Elizabeth, a lifelong Williamsburg resident, stayed home; her daughter-in-law, Annie, was in the other house with Nellie and one-year-old Lyman.

Graves saw the swell of the woolen mill's pond and heard the rush of water over the mill dam. He tracked alongside the canal and pulled up to the three-story mill, which stood ahead of the small office building, the wood house, and a dye house. The woolen mill vibrated with the motion of the waterwheel, carding machines, spinning machines, and power looms. A machinist tinkered in the basement shop, below the level of the river.

Graves recognized Thomas Brazel, a wool spinner, standing in the doorway looking out into the rain. Brazel, about Graves's age, was an Irish immigrant who had been in town at least four years. Graves told Brazel the reservoir had broken away and instructed him to alarm the workers and inform superintendent Birmingham. Without waiting to see whether Brazel had done what he'd asked, he pulled out to the river road and headed down to Skinnerville.

It was between seven-thirty and seven-forty-five. As Graves raced downstream, Onslow Spelman stood waiting on the hill. Within a minute after reaching his vantage point, he heard the water's roar announcing the floodwave's arrival at the village. More than twenty feet tall, it struck Sarah Bartlett's house as it carried away Sarah and her four-year-old daughter Viola Colyer, making them the flood's first victims. Sarah's husband, who was painting houses in the village, survived.

It next hit Spelman's factory. It tore down the dam and ripped away Collins Graves's icehouse from beneath it, then gouged out the long canal that brought water from the pond to the mill. Next, the torrent pounded the mill building with such force that it swept the mill out from under the roof, which floated four hundred feet downstream. All that remained was the rocky ledge the factory had sat on and two wooden sheds that had stood on higher ground back from the river. The site was so completely cleared that it looked as if someone had swept their arm over a game board to clear the pieces. Spelman's workers had escaped unharmed. His house in the village was untouched, his wife and daughter safe.

Below Spelman's factory, the gorge opened up and the wave jumped upon the village, spreading one hundred fifty feet beyond the banks on both sides of the river and enveloping the structures that stood there. It surged up to Spencer Hannum's house, clipped off its rear rooms, removed the sitting room's exterior wall, and cleared away the furniture. The Hannums had sought refuge across the street at the home of button manufacturer Hiram Hill, directly in the flood's path at the corner of East Main and Mill Streets. The Hannums and the Hills were lucky. Some of the wooden beams from Spelman's mill and some uprooted trees caught on the two large apple trees in front of the Hill house, interlacing and thatching themselves so tightly that they formed a timber barrier the width of Hill's house. The breakwater, plus the elevation of the house lot, divided the current around the house, shielding it and the two families huddled inside.

The breakwater forced a section of current next door to the home of Lewis Warner, who had been standing in the doorway idly watching the river rise. When he saw the floodwave approach he called to his wife, tucked his child under his arm like a football, and ran to a neighbor's house. By the time he and his wife reached safety, their house was swept away.

Witnesses saw a wall of water, between twenty and forty feet high and three hundred feet wide, the length of a football field. As it passed down the narrow streambed, it formed a huge rolling wave that grew and intensified, like a snowball tumbling downhill. As it advanced, the water scraping the riverbed and banks was slowed by friction and overtaken by the waters on top of it, which, in turn, were forced to the bottom and sides, where they slowed only to be overtaken by more water. The leapfrogging of waters over each other gave a rolling effect. As it tumbled, the flood gathered up rocks, earth, and trees, turning them over and incorporating them into its mass the way a cook folds ingredients into a batter. By the time the torrent reached the village it was so completely filled with material that no water was visible. A cloud of brown spray, caused by the violent agitation of waters, surrounded the wave and added ten feet to its height.

Years later, a man who saw the flood as a boy tried to put into words what he saw as the flood approached:

A great mass of brush, trees, and trash was rolling rapidly toward me. I have tried many times to describe how this appeared; perhaps the best simile is that of hay rolling over and over as a hayrake moves along the field, only this roll seemed twenty feet high, and the spears of grass in the hayrake enlarged to limbs and trunks of trees mixed with boards and timbers; at this time I saw no water.

One quarter of what the wave carried was sediment from the bottom of the reservoir and river, a deep layer of rotting organic matter that emitted such a terrible odor that people as far as a mile away smelled it.

At five minutes to eight, the main torrent plowed onto William Adams's sawmill and gristmill, two buildings that sat on opposite sides of the river like saddlebags—the gristmill on the west bank and the sawmill on the east. After Robert Loud ran down to the mill from his farm overlooking the dam to warn him, Adams and his two workers ran home. Adams crossed Mill Street and found his wife and two sons, ages sixteen and twelve, to be safe. When he attempted to cross the river to get back to the sawmill, the water knocked him down and carried his body a mile downstream where it was covered so deeply with sand that only two fingers protruded.

Meanwhile, Adams's assistant, Theodore Hitchcock, had learned of the flood at the Williams House Hotel and raced to the mill to get the mill's books after warning his wife. Someone saw him gathered into the swell as he tried to reach the mill.

Adams's other employee, Henry Tilton, lived about one hundred yards below the sawmill. He hurried home to find his wife and four of their five children safely upstairs, but his three-year-old son Willie and his mother-in-law were not with them. Tilton soon located his wife's mother, Sarah Snow, near the house. As he tried to carry her to safety, the water hit them; she slipped from his grasp and fell into the current. Tilton grabbed hold of a cherry tree limb, climbed the tree, and clung there for twenty minutes until the churning water a few feet below subsided. From his unsteady perch he could see the torrent scour the yard and take away the barn where Willie had been playing. Tilton's house was protected by the widening of the valley, which allowed the water to spread out around his house so that family members who remained upstairs survived.

The wave crashed into the properties across the river from Tilton's house on Mill Street, destroying them all: a house rented to a watchman at James's woolen mill, Nathan Graves's carriage shop, and the tenements of two Irish families. In one, Eliza Downing, her one-year-old son, and her mother-in-law were killed. In another, Patrick Scully's family met the same fate. Earlier that morning, Scully had walked up the South Street hill to work at Thomas Nash's farm. Startled by the roar, Scully looked out over the village in time to see his house go down. He must have known that his wife Mary and their two small children—three-year-old Mary and eight-month-old John—and her mother, Mary Brennan, had perished.

By this time the wave had collected great masses of things that people had grown, made, shaped, or bought, as well as pieces of the natural landscape. It contained trees, shrubbery, and boulders; timbers from houses and barns; fences and sheds; rakes, carriages, and harnesses. It conveyed the tools of technology: waterwheels, millstones, lathes, and anvils. It held the products of industry—button molds, wool blankets, and sacks of flour—and the fruits of agriculture—baled hay, grain, and seeds. It brought the contents of houses: furniture, stoves, dishes, toys, books, clothing, and bedding. It bore cows, horses, pigs, and chickens. And, most horrifying, the deluge contained the bodies of human beings, a few alive but most dead.

The torrent moved with such momentum that it ignored the southeasterly turn in the river's course and charged directly south, cutting a new channel through the lower half of Mill Street until it slammed into the South Street hill on which Nash's farm sat, forcing the torrent to the southeast down South Main Street. On this new path it ground up four houses along the lower half of Mill Street. The first belonged to Edgar Chandler, a railroad conductor who had left the house at six that morning on his daily trip to New Haven, while his family was asleep. When he arrived there four hours later he learned that his house was gone and his wife, Caroline, and their eight-year-old daughter Mary were dead. They would be found in their nightclothes.

Next door, railroad engineer Alexander Roberts and his family lived on the first floor. Dewey Williams, who had been wallpapering their home earlier that morning, had just left to go to Lyman James's store in the village of Williamsburg for more bordering. On his way, Williams saw the flood and escaped, but the Roberts family was caught unawares. Roberts, his wife Caroline, daughters Nettie and Olivet, and son George, had just sat down to breakfast when the water picked up the house and carried it away. The family and their servant, fourteen-year-old Mary Ann McGee, clung together inside until the structure broke apart as if it had been made of kindling. Ten-year-old George lost sight of the others as he grabbed hold of a timber and floated away. He survived a harrowing journey during which he was badly battered, but the others were swept further downstream and died. On the second floor of the house, Susan Lamb and her sixteen-year-old nephew, who had been visiting from Leverett, Massachusetts, drowned. Her husband, George, was at his horse barn in the village hitching up his team and was not injured.

Jeremiah Ward, a seventy-one-year-old stone mason, lived across Mill Street from the Robertses and Lambs. Ward and his wife, Sarah, got out of the house safely, but when Ward went back for Electa Knight, his wife's sister, his luck ran out. As Ward and Knight reached the sidewalk, the water overtook them and they were both swept away. Ward's wife survived.

West of Ward's, William Bardwell had been at work in his carriage shop next to his house on Main Street when he left to go back to the house for some thread. Returning to the shop, he saw Collins Graves drive by at a dead run, but thought nothing of it; Graves always drove fast. Bardwell then looked up the valley and saw the wave approaching. He warned his family at the house, and they all ran two hundred yards to a hill, their house skidding along behind them. If they had left the house a half minute later, they would not have survived. As the water pushed the house down the street, it carved two front rooms from the first floor, leaving the painted walls exposed and the upstairs rooms jutting out over empty space. One commentator who toured the wreckage said that the rooms were removed as neatly as if the house had been made of cheese.

When the torrent crashed into the home of farmer Spencer Bartlett, a lifelong resident in his seventies and in poor health, he and his wife, Saloma, tried to leave the house but were swept up and killed. Their daughter, who remained inside, survived. The structure was lifted off its foundation and floated about two hundred feet, but it was only partially wrecked. Like most of the victims of the flood, the Bartletts had only a second to think. Was it better to leave the house and try to cross the rising water to make it to higher ground, or to stay in the house and hope that the structure withstood the force? Most people were better off leaving their houses because of the danger of structural collapse. However, as the Bartletts' situation showed, there was no right or wrong way to act; sometimes it was just luck. As one newspaper eloquently put it, in its [the flood's] presence reason was too slow a guide and instinct missed as often as it hit."

As the torrent turned down South Main Street, it headed for houses that Collins Graves had shouted to a few minutes earlier. As it moved, it carved two new channels: one centered on the row of houses on the north side of the street, and the other channel centered on the homes that lined the south side. The channels converged again just above the James woolen mill but not before they left the flat a rock-strewn wasteland with a few partially wrecked structures standing in the middle. Someone on the riverbank saw Dr. Elbridge Johnson running out of his house carrying two of his children, his wife holding the other until the torrent swooped down and gobbled them all together. The house was so completely destroyed that afterward it was impossible to tell exactly where it had stood. Across the street, the wave demolished the home of farmer Epaphro Hubbard, who was killed along with his daughter, Emma Wood, and her one-year-old son, Harold. Sophia Hubbard, his wife, was spared. A few minutes before the flood struck, she had gone to a neighbor's, out of the flood's path, to get milk. The wave cleared the rest of the Hubbards' property, taking an unoccupied house and then reaching across the street to gather up the home and barn of Willard Williams, who managed to escape. When it slammed into the Kingsley houses, it killed both Kingsley women and the young Kingsley children. Across the street, it swept away Mary Josephine Adams and her seven-year-old son William. Mary's husband Dwight, foreman of the carding room, was working at the James mill and survived.

Graves had left his warning with Tom Brazel at the James woolen mill, who alerted the workers and superintendent Birmingham. Brazel believed Graves, whom he knew to be a working man like himself; he respected him and his family and knew Graves had no reason to exaggerate. The wool sorters, spinners, and weavers emptied the mill fast. Henry Birmingham's only thought was to get home. Looking up the road, he could see that his house had been destroyed and probably assumed his family was dead, but still he challenged the water by walking upstream, powerless against the current. One observer later described how the water rose around him and how he threw his arms above his head as if to surrender to the same fate as his family. It was a terrifying prospect to know that once the wave gathered you up you couldn't escape—you would either be drowned or beaten to death by its load. When the head machinist at the mill, Sanford Gage, got the word, he climbed up from the basement in time to see about twenty mill workers run across the bridge to the hill, about one hundred fifty feet away. Just one second after they had passed over it, the bridge lifted off its piers. He escaped. Another employee, Mr. Raymond, saw his house sail by and assumed his family was in it, but they had fled to a knoll behind their house.

Floodwaters circled the James mill and rose to the second story. It surged through the basement, toppling the iron carding engines, weighing several tons each, that combed the wool in preparation for spinning. The water overturned vats of dye as it wiped away the dye house and swept up a storehouse that held a $15,000 supply of raw wool meant to supply the mill all summer. The wooden mill building survived, but the torrent destroyed the mill's power by filling in the millpond and cutting a new river channel on the opposite side of the mill from where it had been.

Eight of the houses belonging to the James mill were destroyed, and fourteen employees and family members perished. Michael Burke lost his home along with his three young grandchildren, Michael, Jennie, and Annie Burke, ages nine, eight, and five. Upon seeing the flood, seven mill workers dashed to their boardinghouse. Once there, three of them decided it would be safer to leave the building. Despite the pleas of the others, the trio left, and with the water rising, saw no alternative but to climb a nearby apple tree. The water uprooted the tree, drowning all three, while those who remained in the boardinghouse survived.

One of the houses that stood next to the river between the wool mill and Skinnerville belonged to a brass-factory worker named Thomas Ryan. That morning his twelve-year-old son, Jimmy, had driven his father and a brother to the factory, as he did every morning. When Jimmy got back home, he was about to put the horse in the barn when his mother came out and asked him to go into the village for groceries. Jimmy rode as far as the horse watering trough when he met Dewey Williams, the wallpaper hanger, who told him to go home and get his folks out of the house at once because "the reservoir has gone out." Jimmy wheeled around and raced home as fast as he could, so excited that he stood up in the buggy and shouted warnings to the houses he passed. When he arrived home he warned his mother and younger brothers. Before they started for higher ground, his mother instructed him to dash down to the brass shop.

The last house before Skinnerville belonged to a carriage painter named Lester Carr. Through a rear door he saw the flood approach. The water swelled to thirty feet high but loomed taller with trees and sticks poking through the crest like a spiked crown. He, his wife, and son ran up a hill and watched the torrent march steadily downstream until it suddenly halted fifty feet below their house. Temporarily held up by a dam of dropped debris that spanned the front of the wave, the rear piled up against the stalled front end. Seconds later, a section split off and leapt sideways up Joe Wright's Brook, which ran along the back of Carr's house. A tree speared Carr's porch, the tip toppling one post while its roots wrapped around another. The wave lapped a few feet up the side of the house, but left it undamaged. For an eighth of a mile up the brook, the offshoot of the torrent pushed its load, then dropped it. In one pile, the battered bodies of mother and daughter Caroline and Mary Chandler, plucked from their Mill Street home, were entombed. Stretched across another pile lay the iron bridge that twenty wool-mill workers had crossed to safety a minute earlier, unbroken as though someone had gently set it down.

It took three minutes for the torrent to rip and grind its way through the center village of Williamsburg, rolling quickly and steadily at nine miles per hour. In one single, crushing motion it killed fifty-seven people, including twenty-two children under the age of sixteen. Many were saved because they were standing in doorways or looking out windows, but most had not a moment's warning before they were caught up in it. The *Springfield Union*, searching for comparisons of the swiftness of the disaster, could only recall the suddenness of the destruction of Pompeii and Herculaneum.

Skinnerville was next. The village, part of the town of Williamsburg, was a half-mile-long string of about thirty-five buildings, home to 200 people, most of whom worked at William Skinner's Unquomonk Silk Mills as reel-ers, spinners, and dyers. From the dam, a long canal brought river water to turbines that powered the machinery. A steam engine supplemented when the river was low.

On the morning of May 16, Skinner had sent Jerome Hillman on his horse to ride down to Haydenville to pick up the mail for the silk mill and the village of Skinnerville. After breakfast, Skinner probably would have a chance to read it before going over to the mill. He sat down to eat, perhaps with his wife, Sarah, and his youngest children. He expected his errant sixteen-year-old son Will, who had been studying at Williston Seminary all week, to arrive home from school on the two o'clock train for the weekend. The future looked bright for the Skinners. The silk business was recovering from a sluggish market caused by the financial panic the previous year, which Skinner had survived by reducing his workforce and by holding on to a large supply of raw silk. He had recently erected a building in which he planned to manufacture silk cloth and was producing $300,000 in business each year. Bullish on silk, in another six weeks he would announce at the American Silk Products banquet in New York City that "in ten years we shall be shipping silk to China," and he intended to be one of the pioneering exporters. That day, the largest amount of silk he had ever held—$60,000 worth—was packed in a storehouse next to the river.

When Graves bolted from the wool mill, he headed straight for Skinnerville, not stopping along the mile-long route. As he pulled up to the silk factory, he recognized Nash Hubbard, the bookkeeper, standing in the doorway and someone, perhaps Hubbard, ran over to Skinner's house to tell him. In less than a minute, Graves took off for Haydenville. Along the way he yelled the warning to four people—three men and a boy—who relayed the word to nearby homes. Graves didn't stop until he reached the brass works nearly a mile below.

The order to leave was given quietly, and the workers at first took it to be a joke. But they hesitated only briefly before they started emptying the factory, thundering down the wooden stairs of the three-story building and out the doors. The wave of men and women flowed across the road and up over the railroad tracks, about twenty-five yards behind the Skinner home. Someone thought to ring the factory bell. One Skinnerville resident who heard it looked around to see what the trouble was, perhaps a fire or an accident at the mill. When he glanced upriver toward the village of Williamsburg, he spotted what looked like a huge cloud of thick smoke and remarked to his companion that "they are all burning out up there."

He had observed the torrent wrapped in spray and thought Williamsburg was in flames.

If Skinner had doubts about the validity of Graves's warning, the tolling of the factory bell chased them away. He dashed out of the house and glanced upstream in the direction of his factory, where he saw the wave encroaching on Skinnerville and his workers streaking out of the factory. Both he and the workers yelled, "To the hills! To the hills!" He hastened back into the house and ushered his family out the rear door and up the hill across the railroad tracks. With his back to the river, Skinner didn't see what happened next, but his workers and the other Skinnerville residents who had congregated on the tracks did.

They saw the deluge crowd past the train depot, leaving it untouched, then pound the village's only store. Storekeeper Salmon K. Wait and his family, who lived on the second floor, escaped. As the wave approached the silk mill it crushed a row of seven houses owned by Skinner—one was occupied by the depot master, others by families of silk workers, and two were boardinghouses. Those inside ran up the hill behind Skinner's house. Next was the home of the Hillmans. While Jerome Hillman was downriver in Haydenville collecting the mail, his wife Sarah heard the warning and left the house with their seven-year-old daughter Clara. But when Sarah decided to go back to retrieve something, the torrent broke down the house with her inside, making Sarah Hillman the first victim in Skinnerville.

The silk mill was next. The torrent reached for the storehouses, dye house, and wood house, consuming them all as it smothered the three-story factory and pulled the structure down. In one single swift moment, the mill workers saw their homes, their jobs, and all their possessions washed away. By the time Skinner turned around, no more than a minute or two after he left his house, the factory site was gone. He later told reporters that his factory was swept away so completely that it was hard to believe that it had been there at all.

Across the street, the flood swiped at Skinner's house, which stood just out of reach of its full fury. After knocking the front porch off its supports, it poured into the basement and the first floor to a height of three feet, where its weight collapsed the back parlor floor and whirled the bobbing furniture into the cellar, resting the piano on top. The large, substantially built house stayed put.

Below Skinner's, the torrent mowed down rows of shade trees and tossed about all the houses on the east side of the river for the next half mile. The devastated flat looked like a child's sandbox at the end of the day, with toys tipped, tossed, and randomly scattered, only it was real houses that were littered about. Some were upended, others canted on one end with the front door open to the sky. First overthrown was an unoccupied house owned by the silk mill. Next the wave hit the home of a brass finisher, his wife, and seven children, knocked off its rear addition, and slid it into a silk dyer's house, pulling away that house's back wall. Next door, it rocked the home of bookkeeper Nash Hubbard so violently while floating it downstream that when it came to rest, the two first-floor front rooms were neatly sliced out from under the upstairs bedrooms, leaving the interior configuration exposed as though it were a theatrical stage set.

The railroad engineer's house fell next, followed by that of farmer Thaddeus Bartlett, whose two sons and a daughter worked in the silk mill while another son labored at the brass works. The torrent picked up the house, dragged it past his neighbor's, pushed it back fifty yards, rotated it ninety degrees, tore off the rear addition, and collapsed the second floor. The mangled shell came to rest near Sarah Wrisley's house, which had been uprooted and carried downstream until it lodged against a pile of rocks with its rear section torn off. As the widow of a farmer, Sarah had supported herself by boarding silk-mill workers. Now, her home and livelihood were in ruins.

Below the Wrisley house, on a two-acre farm, lived Christina Hills with her husband, a daughter, and five sons, including Dick, Will Skinner's best friend. Just six weeks earlier, Will's parents had attended a surprise party there. As the flood approached, Christina ran uphill with one of her young sons but lost her footing and fell into the rising water. When the boy tried to pull her out, the wave was so close that she knew they both could not escape it, so she commanded him to run for his own life. He obeyed and survived. She drowned.

On the other side of the river, at the bottom of the village, lived Isabell and Joseph Lewis Hayden, their five-year-old son Joseph Jr., whom they called Robin or Robbie, and her father, seventy-seven-year-old Eli Bryant. A nephew of Joel Hayden Sr., Joseph was on the other side of the river on an errand. When Isabell heard the silk-mill factory bell ringing, she looked out and saw the wall of water, as high as a two-story house, charging down the valley toward her. Eli seized Robbie in his arms and carried him out and up a ladder that leaned against the side of a shed behind the house. Isabell yelled for her father to follow her as she sprinted up a hill beyond the shed. But it was too late: As Eli and Robbie descended the ladder, the water sucked them in and dragged them downstream, the grandfather holding the boy above the water for as long as he could. Isabell ran on the hill alongside her father and son until their bobbing heads disappeared into the current, which pulled them down to Haydenville.

On the morning of May 16, 1874, Joel Hayden Jr. awoke expecting to spend the afternoon dealing with financial matters related to his late father's estate. Several Boston businessmen acting as executors, his younger sister Isabella, her husband Acting Governor Thomas Talbot, and several members of the governor's executive council had already arrived in Northampton. They would all attend a memorial service for Hayden on Sunday in the Haydenville Church. Black banners hung between the tall columns that supported the Greek-styled triangular pediment, while inside huge floral arrangements sent from Boston adorned the sanctuary. The church's minister, James P. Kimball, had already written his tribute to Hayden in which he would describe Haydenville as his "most enduring monument."

By seven-thirty that morning, Haydenville was in full swing with the cacophony of manufacturing. Spinning frames clattered at the cotton mill, presses pounded at the tobacco mill, and hammers clanged against anvils at the foundry. In the brass works, leather belting whirred around drive shafts for the drills, grinders, and buffers that finished the brass fittings. Water-wheels and turbines groaned and vibrated; a steam engine hissed. Three hundred workers—pattern makers, molders, finishers, packers—labored full time after a winter of part-time employment because of a slack market and low water. Among them was twenty-year-old Francis Brodeur, a French Canadian immigrant who had joined his older brother in employment at the brass works. Francis removed his boots and slid into the slippers he probably kept at his workbench, as much to preserve the shoe leather as to be comfortable for the long day ahead.

Collins Graves covered the mile from Skinnerville to the Haydenville brass works in record time. He wheeled into the brass factory yard and dashed into the office, rain dripping from his coat onto the floor, to find superintendent Samuel Wentworth. Wentworth ridiculed Graves's warning that a flood was on its way. "It won't be down here for four days, and when it does come the water won't come to our first floor," Wentworth claimed.

Graves felt foolish. He hadn't seen the flood with his own eyes, but had taken Cheney's word that it would be there in minutes. Now he wondered if he'd alarmed the valley needlessly. He knew Wentworth was more knowledgeable about reservoirs and rivers than he and, in general, a man of greater judgment. Graves said to himself, "If what he said is true, the people will have the laugh on me all right." Graves decided not to risk public humiliation. He turned his wagon around and slowly headed back up the valley.

When he had covered a few hundred yards, Graves saw a man on horseback galloping toward him, waving one arm wildly and shouting, "Go back! A flood is coming!" When the man got closer, Graves saw that it was Jerome Hillman, who had ridden down to Haydenville on Skinner's horse to pick up the mail earlier that morning. As Hillman passed the brass works on his way back up to Skinnerville, Graves was inside talking to Wentworth so Hillman hadn't heard the warning. When he rounded the bend toward Skinnerville, he saw the wall of water churning over his village and knew instinctively what it was. He first thought of his wife and child, whom he had left that morning at their home next to the river, but he knew he could do nothing to save them or anyone else in Skinnerville. He turned around and headed full speed back down into Haydenville to warn the villagers there. The thunder of the flood was so menacing that the horse ran without urging. A reporter who interviewed him later wrote:

> Once he looked behind, and the air seemed to be full of flying timber. Great trees were turning end for end; now their enormous roots were in the air, and then he would see their trunks and branches whirling round. At the top of a perpendicular wall of water, advancing down the valley, 30 feet high, were seen houses and barns turning over.

Graves now saw the same scene looming behind Hillman. It was the first time he had seen the flood. With a burst of confidence and energy, he turned back to Haydenville. A moment earlier (or later—no one knows), Jimmy Ryan had ridden by on his way to warn his father at the brass works. When he arrived, he asked Benson Munyan, on duty at the shop gate, to summon his father and brother and warn the other workmen. In two or three minutes, his father and brother appeared and hopped into the wagon. As they drove to high ground across the street, they looked back and saw the factory gates thrown open and the workmen rushing out. Fifty years later Jimmy described what happened next:

> We had waited but a very few minutes when it became almost as dark as night to the north and a far-off roaring commenced, a sound the like of

which I have never heard before nor since. This roaring of the angry
waters increased in volume as the flood came nearer; at length we saw it
away up the valley, like a great wall about 40 feet high, some 20 feet
ahead of which was a froth of churning current as white as newly-combed
wool.

They watched and wondered if Mrs. Ryan and the two boys had made it to
ground high enough to escape the water that stretched clear across the valley from one side to the other.

Graves and Hillman entered Haydenville together, then quickly separated. Hillman first paused at the brass works where some men had come out
front, having heard Graves's warning to Wentworth and maybe Ryan's.
"Run for your lives!" Hillman cried. Hillman then raced down the street
past the Haydenville Church, calling to the sexton to ring the bell. When
Hillman flew back up the street, he saw no one in the church bell tower and
knew that the sexton had ignored him, probably because he didn't believe
him. Calling to him again, he asked where the bell rope was hung.
"Upstairs" came the reply. So Hillman climbed the bell tower but managed
only one or two peals before water surrounded the Haydenville Church.
Hillman waded up the hill behind the church to save himself. Three minutes had passed since he had reentered the village with Graves.

Meanwhile, Graves stopped at Hart's barbershop, where he warned a
group of men gathered in conversation. After pausing at a nearby store, he
made his final stop at the Haydenville House Hotel, where proprietor
Luther Loomis let his horses out of the livery stable to run for their lives.
With the wave nearly upon him, Graves wheeled up Church Street to the
high ground at the railroad tracks. With no more need to hurry, Graves
slowly proceeded up the tracks that ran parallel to the river behind a string
of large homes, including Lieutenant Governor Hayden's mansion, now
vacant. His widow had moved away a month earlier. He looked upriver
through the trees and between the houses, waiting for the flood to hit.

Above the village the broad, level land allowed the water to spread, but
near the village, hills on both sides of the river forced the water into a narrow
channel and down a short descent, from which it emerged slimmer but more
powerful. At this narrow outlet, on a sliver of flat land not one hundred feet
wide, stood the brass works' stone dam and factory. The hills receded immediately below the factory and the village sat on open land, rendering it
defenseless against high water rolling through the channel.

At quarter to eight, with a deafening roar, the torrent announced its arrival at Haydenville and the brass works. The employees there had been warned three times to flee the factory, by Collins Graves, by Jimmy Ryan, and finally by Jerome Hillman. By the time Hillman came by, the workers were standing out front looking up the river. He told them to flee. They didn't. Wentworth came out and asked why they were looking upriver. "The flood," they said. "Oh, it won't be here for three days," he replied. No sooner had he spoken, than they heard the roar and the torrent appeared. They dashed across the road and up the slope behind Joel Hayden's house, safe on the hill. Henry Brewster, the company's chief clerk, made it there, too. He had heard the alarm while eating breakfast at home and decided to go to the office to secure the books that he had been working on that morning in the vault. Never dreaming that there was any danger to the structures, he planned to stay in the building until the water passed, but once he saw the high water preceding the wave he ran back home and fled with his family to the railroad tracks.

Francis Brodeur, who had come out in his slippers, was safe on the hill when he decided to reenter the factory for his boots. Despite protests from coworkers, Brodeur went back in the building and retrieved them, but when he tried to get back up the hill, the water knocked him down. His coworkers watched helplessly as he regained his footing, only to be swept away when a section of a house cracked him in the head. He was the only brass worker to die.

As the blur of wood and water tumbled over the brass-works dam it slammed one of the houses it had carried from Skinnerville against the foundry building, creating a breach so large that the three-story structure collapsed in the center, the ends folding over the middle. The rush of water emptied all nine buildings of machinery, raw materials, patterns, molds, and finished goods, and then dissolved the buildings. One writer said that the brass works melted away "like a pyramid of sugar in hot water, sinking out of sight almost instantly." All that was left was the center section of the brick upper shop and a smokestack from the boiler. Minutes earlier the factory had been 600 feet long; now it was no more than 40 feet long. Boulders from the foundations, the immense safes of the brass works and the Haydenville Savings Bank, and the granite pillars from the office and bank building were strewn along a helter-skelter course that ended hundreds of feet downriver.

The impact exploded the steam engine boiler that the men had fired up that morning. At seventy pounds pressure per square inch, it blasted apart with a tremendous bang, throwing off pieces that were gobbled into the wave's general miscellany. The torrent picked up the other boiler, inoperative that morning, and carried the several-ton object one hundred yards across the street before depositing it on the lawn of Lieutenant Governor Hayden's home. It was five and a half feet in diameter and sixteen feet long, the length of Hayden's front hall.

Across the river from the brass works, Mary Thayer and her husband Edwin rented a modest home for their four small children. When Mary saw the flood coming, she grabbed two children in her arms and called upstairs to her two boys—George, age five, and Freddie, one year—who stood motionless on the landing, frightened by her hysterical cries to run down. With no time to get the little boys, she escaped out the backdoor with the two children in her arms, planning to go back inside for the other two. As she saw her house sucked into the current, she knew the boys upstairs would not survive. They didn't.

Below the brass works, the wave widened sufficiently to envelop almost every building on both sides of the river, toppling the structures one by one, like a row of dominos set in motion. It demolished about fifty structures on the west side of North Main Street and on the east side of South Main Street: one boardinghouse; twelve or more tenement houses; a dozen or more owner-occupied houses; several small businesses, among them the Hart barbershop, the Sharpe and Ames tinshop and stove store, Elam Graves's grocery, Chauncey Rice's boot and shoe shop, Pierce Larkin's grocery, Robert Cartier's blacksmith shop, Myron Ballou's shop, Luther Loomis's livery stable and barn, and at least eight factory buildings. It crumbled all four iron bridges. A few hundred inhabitants heard Graves's or Hillman's warnings and ran to the hills, where they shouted at those below to flee.

In the village, Edmond Mockler was standing in front of his house when he saw the flood. He tried to go inside for his wife and disabled son but was overpowered and swept away. Meanwhile, Mrs. Mockler had snatched the boy from his bed. The previous winter, he had fallen on the ice and sprained his ankle. Unable to move, his legs were frozen before he was discovered and he was left unable to walk. Mrs. Mockler and her son escaped the house but could not make it to dry land. For more than ten minutes she stood waist-deep in water, taking blows from floating rubbish. Despite being knocked down twice, she never let go of her boy until they were rescued after the water subsided.

At the bottom of the village, the tobacco-mill dam held back the wave for a second or two, long enough to push water and waste up into the neck of the millpond, where it backwashed over William Hayden's foundry and steam heater company, damaging the foundry building, its boiler house, and the blacksmith shop. It tipped over a worker's house next door and floated the foundry boardinghouse fifty yards before it came to rest next to the railroad tracks. When the stalled flood moved again, it collapsed twenty feet of the tobacco-mill dam and pulled down the mill.

Below the tobacco mill, the flood ignored the river's normal oxbow course. Instead, it charged forward in a straight path, bypassing the cotton mill, which it left undamaged, and breaking up the gas works, crunching the gasometer into a tangled mass. It uprooted six cotton-mill houses that stood within the curves of the oxbow. Inside one were the three children of Samuel and Mary Miller—ages ten, eight, and one—home alone while their father was at the barbershop and their mother at the cotton mill. Mary hurried out of the mill and attempted to cross the bridge to get home to her children. She was on the bridge when her coworkers called to her to come back because the bridge was about to be swept away. She obeyed and no sooner stepped back onto the riverbank when the wave jerked the bridge away. She survived but all her children drowned at home.

Stephen and Mary Kiely lived in another cotton-mill home with a daughter and son. They had emigrated from Ireland two years earlier to join three daughters who worked in the cotton mill. When the Kielys heard the warning, they accompanied the children to safety, but they dashed back into the house to retrieve some possessions and were killed when the house was carried away.

In less than eight minutes, Hayden's monument, which had taken him a lifetime to build, was a wasteland. Twenty-seven villagers were dead—the youngest was nine-day-old Joseph Bissonette, the oldest seventy-three-year-old John Kaplinger, a German-born shoemaker. Most of the dead were the Canadian women and children who lived in the vicinity of the tobacco and cotton mills and were at home together with no warning and no time to escape. This included baby Joseph Bissonette and his twenty-two-year-old mother Rosa, the Pouzee family—Theresa, forty-five, Isabelle, twenty-two, Ilocrain, fourteen, and Nayerene, eleven—and Margaret Wilson with her three little girls—Matilda, ten, Rosa, seven, and Margaret, five.

From the railroad tracks, Graves saw the torrent leave Haydenville headed into the long narrow river gorge that led to the village of Leeds. Graves's ride was over. He had outrun the flood through Williamsburg, Skinnerville, and Haydenville and had saved more than five hundred lives. The milk cans had rattled from his cart and his black mare was so lame that he would have no choice but to have her shot within the year. When Graves and the other survivors on the riverbank saw the wave move downriver they must have feared for the lives of the people in Leeds. They didn't know that someone from Haydenville was racing down to Leeds just ahead of it to warn them.

Sometime before seven that morning, twenty-two-year-old Fred Howard left his father's hillside farm for the button mill in the heart of the village of Leeds where he was a box maker. As soon as he stepped outside the house he heard the river roar. Passing a neighbor's farm, he headed a half mile down South Main Street where the road crossed and recrossed the S curve of the river. He went over the bridge at Cook's Dam, above the broad, noisy double waterfall (the water divided around a knoll) where the river plummeted thirty-three feet, the height of a three-story building. It was the greatest water drop on the river, such a good location for a mill that in 1681 the first in Leeds had been erected on this spot, but in 1874 the site was free for someone to build on. Turning left up Main Street, Fred crossed the river again, this time over a bridge supported by three large stone arches. He continued beyond the schoolhouse and the greening yards of three families he knew well, and made his way over one more bridge before entering the button factory gate. He walked past the brick building and into the smaller wooden one. The button company had been operated by George P. Warner since 1870, when an ailing Alfred Critchlow sold some interests to his son-in-law. With 250 employees, it was the largest button factory in the country.

The village of Leeds bordered both sides of the Mill River in the northern tip of the town of Northampton, a little more than midway down the river's course. Thirty-five of the village's seventy buildings lined the half-mile stretch of Main Street that ran parallel to the river, no more than fifty feet from the water. At the top of the village stood the Nonotuck Silk Company—the mill on the west side of the river and the boardinghouse on the east. Below the silk company's mill was the Emery Wheel Company, which made grinding wheels. On the east side of the river, at the top of Main Street, just below the silk company's boardinghouse, sat the fire engine house; the church stood in the middle; and the Mill River Button Company, where Fred worked, lay a little below that, just above the school. All the property along both sides of the river, with the exception of four homes, was owned by the emery wheel, silk, or button companies.

By eight o'clock, Fred Howard had settled into the box room on the second floor of the button factory's wooden mill building, where he fashioned shipping boxes for buttons that were made of vegetable ivory. His friend Charlie Brady was in the packing room, and the bookkeeper, thirty-one-year-old Ralph Isham, was in the office in the room below. Although Isham had been on the job only three months, he was well liked. He planned to return to New York the next month to meet his sister, who was returning from a several-month sojourn in Europe. Outside, butcher Mike Hannigan peddled meat along the main street. Two hundred men and women labored upstream at the Nonotuck Silk Mill, managed by Lucius Dimock. Three dozen worked at the Emery Wheel Company, whose owner, John Otis, a breveted brigadier general from Civil War service, was in New York returning from the reunion of the Army of the Potomac at Harrisburg.

Earlier that same morning, Myron Day—a farmer and an expressman whose job it was to deliver goods—had driven away from his Leeds farm in his light spring wagon to visit his sister, Laura Birmingham, who lived just above the woolen mill in Williamsburg. When he reached Haydenville, he saw a man across the river gesturing wildly and shouting, but he couldn't hear him and so continued upriver until he met Jerome Hillman near the brass works. Hillman told Day what was happening. When Day looked up the valley and saw the flood, his first thought was to notify people downstream in Leeds. He turned his horse and started down the valley "on a dead run," as he would later describe it. At the bottom of Haydenville he shouted "Fire!" as he passed the tobacco works, thinking it would get more attention than "Water!" It did and all escaped.

Day calculated that if he maintained his speed he could make it to Leeds before the torrent, but he would need to outrun the flood through a mile-long narrow gorge that offered no escape. If the flood caught up with him or if his horse stumbled, he and his horse would perish. With no more than an instant to weigh his options, he decided to risk it. He drove his wagon onto the road that topped the river wall, a route he had traveled a hundred times. With steep jagged hills at his right elbow and the rising rocky stream a few feet below to his left, he drove at breakneck speed and covered the two miles from the brass works to Leeds in ten minutes, he later estimated. When Day emerged from the gorge and saw the silk mill ahead, he knew he had beaten the floodwave.

Day rode over the river beside the silk mill, down Main Street, and directly to the button factory, bypassing the Emery Wheel factory and the Nonotuck Silk Company. He may have been intent on saving the button-mill workers because he had close associations with George Warner, the owner. Day and Warner were both town assessors and leaders of the Leeds Evangelical Religious Society. Day went into the button factory, where he warned bookkeeper Ralph Isham. Isham didn't know whether to believe Day or not, so he walked upstairs to the packing room to ask Charlie Brady what he should do. Charlie offered to go up the street to see what was going on. When Charlie stepped outside the factory, he discovered that the flood was there.

The flood struck Leeds a few minutes after eight o'clock. At the top of the village the torrent slammed directly into the west bank at the Nonotuck Silk Company's stone dam, crushing its west half. It yanked away a piece of the penstock, the pipe that conveyed water to the turbines, and tore off the stone embankment that housed the turbines as well as the shed built over them. On the east bank of the river, the wave jumped the bank and took out several hundred feet of railroad track, stranding some cars on the north side of the break. Freakishly, it left the village's only store, just below the destroyed tracks, unharmed except for water in the cellar. The storekeeper had pulled out his money drawers and run, leaving behind shelves stocked with shoes, clothing, hats, crockery, and wallpaper.

Correcting its course as it veered back to the west, the wave grazed the three-story Nonotuck Silk Mill, taking away piles of raw silk and the white board fence that enclosed the yard. Charles Stevens, who was writing in a ledger in the office of the Emery Wheel Company, saw it coming as he glanced out a window. He threw the ledgers in the safe, turned the combination lock, checked to see that the factory was evacuated, and fled across the canal to high ground. The torrent carried off a shop and storehouse and damaged machinery and stock. Below the Emery Wheel Company, it broadened to almost the entire width of the village, so that nothing and no one could escape its embrace.

The overseers of the silk factory gave the orders to leave quietly (no one knows for sure but they may have received the warning from a farmer named Field—perhaps Day called to him), and all three floors emptied quickly without panic. When Mary Harding, who worked on the second floor, and a group of other young women reached the yard and saw the wave spanning the valley, they didn't know where to go. Some workers shouted that they should run across the bridge to the higher ground on the east side of the river. As Mary and her roommate Mary Woodward started across, followed by a dozen others, rising water shook the bridge. From the east shore, their coworkers shouted "Go back! Go back!" The roommates ignored them and safely made it across. But seven at the rear hesitated, and before they could return to the mill, a mass of debris cracked apart the bridge, which fell into the water, killing them all.

Once on the east side of the river, Mary Woodward and Mary Harding ran into the silk company boardinghouse, which stood on the riverbank between the bridge and the store. Inside, the boardinghouse manager, T. F. Vaughan, was evacuating everyone. Mary Harding rushed out with other boardinghouse residents, but Mary Woodward remained inside for some reason. Vaughan went back in for her. As soon as he crossed the threshold, the boardinghouse was torn from its foundation, and water poured in the second-story windows. As the boardinghouse was carried hundreds of feet across the road, it picked up a wooden silk-mill office building and smashed into the fire engine house, pushing them fifty feet until all three shredded structures lodged against a sturdy maple tree and a small button company house. The shapeless mass was covered by the boardinghouse roof, mostly intact. Inside were beds, furniture, clothing, a fire pump, mud, wood, silk, and the bodies of Mary Woodward, age twenty, and Vaughan, age forty.

The three-building pile-up divided the current and protected three small button company houses, the only buildings on the main street left on their original foundations. Inside one house, six children huddled together behind a bed on the second floor as the water climbed up to their necks. They survived. The split current still had enough force to knock the other two button-mill houses off their foundations and hurl them against William Quigley's large farmhouse. Quigley and his son Will had heard the warning while working somewhere east of the river. Desperate to make it home to save the family but unable to get close, they watched the destruction from the railroad tracks twenty-five feet above the valley floor. Mrs. Quigley, daughters Nettie and Lizzie, and a visiting schoolteacher named Miss Marble had just finished breakfast and were sitting at the table talking when they heard the roar. They ran upstairs to a bedroom in the rear of the house above the kitchen. As the four stood motionless, the swell snatched away the large, front section of the house and bore it two hundred feet downstream, where it lodged in the mud. A second after the sections of the house separated, the women felt a crash as one of the button-mill houses plunged into the rear of the house. From the window, they spied Walter Humphrey, their neighbor, clinging to his roof. The women threw open the window to help him into their safe haven. As Humphrey crawled inside, the Quigley house was jolted ten feet off its foundation, but Humphrey made it and they all survived. Meanwhile, in Humphrey's house, his wife and mother each grabbed a child and stood on the beds to keep the children above water. They survived. From the railroad, William and Will Quigley watched the scene, not knowing the fate of their family. They saw their two barns go down, with a cow, bull, pigs, five vehicles, harvesting machinery, and farm tools inside.

Below Quigley's, at the button mill, seconds counted. Before Charlie Brady went outside to see whether Myron Day's warning was real, he, or maybe someone else, had alerted those in the box room in the wooden building where Fred Howard worked. In a letter to his brother, Fred wrote a firsthand account of the confusion that followed:

> [When] we first got the alarm . . . I rushed into the carding room. They tell me now that I ran back into the box room and told them to run, but I do not remember that. After the carders and looker-overs were all out, I ran down stairs and met Charlie who shouted to me to go over to the basement of the other [brick] mill and help get out stock. None of us real-ized what was coming.
>
> I ran to the steps that go into the brick mill when I thought of the school house and started back toward the gate (in the meantime all the hands had left both shops and Isham the bookkeeper, had unlocked the gate and advised the hands to remain in the shop. He evidently considered it a panic.) Most of [the workers] ran back through the yard by the dry house and up those stairs on the railroad. You will probably remember the stairs. They were directly back of the shop and were built for the hands who lived in the new tenements and the Fowl House. That was really the only way of escape and it's strange that so many should think of that way of get-ting out. Of course, some of them ran into the street and up the street to warn their friends and most of them were lost.
>
> Before I got to the gate, I thought that it was Saturday and no school. By this time, the hands were all out and gone and the water was pouring over the dike and into the yard. As I turned, Annie Chamberlain (a girl that worked in the carding room looking over buttons) ran down the steps from the wooden mill into the yard. I shouted to her to come with me and [bookkeeper] Isham stood in the door and shouted to [us to] come back. "I'll shut the door" [he said]. Little did the poor fellow realize what was coming. The girl turned toward the mill when I caught her by the arm and fairly dragged her from the yard, reaching the railroad not a second too soon, as the water was curling about us when we reached the stairs.
>
> Charlie came out close behind me and he was the last one out of the yard. I pushed Annie Chamberlain up the stairs and looking back saw Dave Duggan on top of the high fence that runs along the back of the

yard and the water almost up to him. [I] shouted to him to jump. I waded in and caught him by the collar and together we struggled to the railroad, and then came a scene that can never be described and I hope I may never see again.

A few feet from Fred, the wooden button mill where Fred had worked broke in the center and collapsed in a second like a house of cards. Five seconds later, the brick mill building next to it crumbled all at once, leaving only the three-story chimney. The five people who had remained inside with Ralph Isham were thrown out. Isham, Sarah Shaughnessey, and Arthur Sharpe died. Will Tunnicliff, the foreman's son, had jumped from the second-story door at the first sound of cracking timbers and floated on rafters until he was tossed ashore at the bottom of the village, battered but alive.

Charlie Brady and the meat peddler, Mike Hannigan, ended up near Will Tunnicliff. Charlie was trying to get others up onto the bank, but didn't reach the bank in time himself and was carried downstream over the three-story-tall dam at the bottom of the village. Somehow, along the way, Charlie plucked a child out of the water. Grabbing hold of a tree, he pulled them both to safety, bruised but alive. When Mike heard the warning, he drove around to the back of the button shop where he found Charlie, who tried to convince him to unhitch his horse so that Mike could escape with the horse up the stairs, but Mike wanted to stay with his horse and cart. Soon the water lifted the horse and cart, with Mike in it, fifteen feet up onto a pile of boards, which immediately collapsed. Mike grabbed the horse, still attached to the wagon, and floated downstream. Fred and his horror-stricken coworkers thought Mike would most certainly die, but Mike grabbed a timber and hung on until he slid into a tree and climbed away. The cart and horse were gone.

Watching such horror, Fred felt helpless on the riverbank. He explained to his brother:

> . . . all this time other houses were falling or sailing down the stream only to be dashed to pieces a short distance below. The whole valley was a wild torrent filled with men, women, and children, horses and cattle, trees and broken houses, the former waving their hands and crying for help till some timber struck them and either killed them outright or pushed them under and drowned them . . . We that had escaped this [were] running up and down the railroad—as helpless as infants and almost wild because we could do nothing to help them. I honestly believe that for a few min-

utes some of us on the railroad suffered as much as those in the stream. I can see the whole thing now . . .

You will remember Ed Hannum (Warner's gardener). He lost his wife and four children when we were on the railroad. He ran up and down wringing his hands and shouting at the top of his voice. I never saw a person act as Will [Quigley] did [when he saw his house destroyed and thought his mother and sisters were dead]. He threw himself on the ground and cried for his mother and sisters in such a way that any of us would have been glad to have risked our lives if we could have seen the slightest chance of reaching the house. There are many incidents of this kind that I cannot write of.

You must remember that all this occurred in a very short time, probably in one minute after I first saw the water . . . I was on the railroad [track] and in another minute both shops were gone and in less than ten minutes from the first warning the water had begun to recede.

As Myron Day drove back up Main Street, water started running over the riverbanks onto the road. Trapped on the narrow strip of flat land that was Leeds, he wheeled the wagon up the road to safety on the railroad tracks.

Three of thirty-five buildings on the main street were left on their foundations. Within the loop of the S, just below the button mill, the Fitzgerald, Fennessey, and Cogan houses were so thoroughly obliterated by the ruins of the button mill that later Fred couldn't tell where the foundations had been. The wave fell upon them like an avalanche from a height a dozen feet above the houses. At the home of widow Jane Fitzgerald, eight people spanning four generations died: herself, her mother, Ellen Dunlea, her four children, and two grandchildren, ages three and one. At the Fennessey house next door, Ellen Fennessey; her two daughters, Nellie and Kate, ages eleven and three; a son, John, age six; her sister-in-law Elizabeth, age thirty-six; and mother-in-law Ellen, age eighty, all perished. Elsewhere in the village, Ellen's husband Andrew also died. In the next house, forty-two-year-old widow Jane Cogan was home with two of her three daughters: Grace, a student at the Westfield Normal School, and her older sister, Annie, who taught at the West Farms School. Annie worked with Mary Birmingham, who had drowned in Williamsburg minutes earlier. A third daughter, Carrie, was not at home and survived.

Fred knew the Fitzgeralds, Fennesseys, and Cogans. In the first ten pages of his letter to his brother he had recounted so many horrible and terrifying incidents that he grew weary and numb to the destruction. By page eleven

Fred began to simply list the losses, starting at the top of Main Street and working his way down, building by building, until he had accounted for all the structures and their inhabitants:

> The red blacksmith shop of the Nonotuck [Silk] Co. went first, then what was left of the old woolen mill, then the large tenement house where Joe Shearn used to live occupied by Harley, a Nonotuck machinist. Jim and Sylvia and Dunning . . . all escaped but the old man Dunning who was found on the Florence Meadows the same day. Dunning himself was carried as far as Cook's Dam astride of the roof, but in some way got out of the stream there, how he done it I do not know and cannot imagine. The double white house where the Mongeons used to live was badly broken up and thrown against the maple trees in front of the house; I think that saved it from going down stream. The next house taken was the small tenement made from the barn that used to stand there and occupied by Davis, the mason who married Mrs. Sherwood. They were all saved but Eveline who ran up the street from the shop. She was found the same day on the flat stripped of everything but her shoes and stockings and her back broken. The next house occupied by Tom Bride and Jim Kennedy was not carried away but might as well have been for it [is] nothing but a wreck and was nearly thrown backward into the river. The next house taken [was] where Myrick lived before he left here. [It was] occupied by Walter Humphrey, Julia Hurley, and Mrs. Bonney. A lady visiting at Humphreys was lost as was Carrie Bonney [who] ran home from the [button] shop and would not leave the house which was turned completely around and thrown across the street some way. Sarah Jane and her child were lost from . . . [the] house farther down . . . Julia Hurley's mother was lost from the house [which] was swept from her grasp by the water. The next house standing near the chapel and occupied by [a] French family was carried away and several persons drowned, among [them] Mrs. Patrick who was sick abed. Quigley['s] old house where Mrs. Naramore has lived did not go, but the water went through the lower story. Mrs. N sent the children up on the hill but had no time to get out herself and sat at the [window] waving her hand to them expecting every minute to go down. The school house was damaged so that it will probably never be used again.

Jim Dunning, mentioned in Fred's letter, had been at work in the spool room at the Nonotuck Silk Mill when he heard the alarm. He went home and helped his wife and children escape but was caught upstairs with his father when the wave hit. Realizing that the house could not withstand the force of the water, Dunning opened a window to climb through. Just as he did, the floor gave way beneath their feet, and his father disappeared. Dunning clung to the window as the house tipped on its side. He grabbed for a fragment of the roof and sailed downstream in full view of his wife and children, who thought that at any moment he would submerge. When Dunning's makeshift raft broke apart, he grasped another and then a third when the second one splintered. Riding at a terrific speed, he didn't think about the button mill dam and Cook's dam which he was headed for. When he hit the button mill dam, he was thrown high into the air—what seemed to him like twenty feet. On his descent, he was plunged under the water, but managed to surface, grab another piece of timber and speed on. At this point, he realized that he could not survive the thirty-foot drop over Cook's dam and so tried to escape. Luckily, the section of the torrent on which he was riding surged toward the shore. He clambered across some broken roofs and leapt across water to solid ground. His cool head and experience as a raftsman on Canadian rivers had ensured his survival. His father, Amos Dunning, died.

From their house on the hill above the village, Fred's family could hear the torrent but not see it because a granite knoll stood between their farm and the village. If they walked down South Main Street they could have seen some of the destruction, but would have to wait to find out whether Fred was alive.

At the bottom of Leeds, a mile above the village of Florence, lay the meadows of a half dozen farms, hundreds of acres of the most productive land in the valley, made fertile by silt carried down the Mill River. For the last few weeks, farmers had been preparing "the garden of the neighborhood," as the *Hampshire Gazette* called the meadows, for spring planting. Moses Warner and Bela Gardner had spread manure on tobacco and crop fields, which were plowed and ready to plant. As the fields soaked up the rain, Austin Ross's farmhands were in the middle of the plain, near the river.

By half past eight, the torrent left Leeds. It had been rolling for forty-five minutes. Too fast, deep, and laden with debris to follow the river's sharp S curve at the south end of Main Street, it plowed straight south, dividing around both sides of a rocky knoll above Cook's dam. The split torrent tore away the abutments of the bridge over the dam and plunged into the gorge below where the current reunited. Then it fanned out over the wide, open Leeds and Florence meadows.

While the flood pounded Leeds, Edson Ross, the storekeeper, ran his horse down from Leeds to warn his father, Austin Ross, who lived at the bottom of the Florence meadows on the west side of the river. Ross raced out to warn his hired hands. As he pantomimed and shouted, they heard the thunderous fall of the torrent over Cook's dam. The workers sprang into the wagon and ran the horses at top speed to high land. One minute more and they couldn't have escaped. In Ross's residence, the water floated beds, bureaus, chairs, and tables on the first floor and left two feet of mud in the cellar.

Crossing the flat terrain of the Leeds and Florence meadows had the effect of putting brakes on the torrent, dispersing and shrinking it as it lost some of its momentum. As the water spread, the sediment and debris it carried snagged on the ground, slowing by friction the water filtering through. For almost a mile to the center of Florence, the flood spilled a layer of mud and gravel two to three feet deep, topped with a six-foot-thick carpet of debris. Scarcely an acre of meadow remained untouched, either doused with sediment and debris or scoured to hardpan. There was "not enough soil . . . left on the field to produce material for a decent breakfast," the *Hampshire Gazette* bemoaned. The grove that edged the banks captured hundreds of trees, thatching them into a fortress.

Its tidal-wave character gone, the flood hit Florence with less force than it had Williamsburg, Skinnerville, Haydenville, and Leeds. If the flood had maintained its original height and mass—with debris acting as a dam that mounded it higher and higher—the Florence brush shop, silk mill, cotton factory, and scores of homes would have suffered the same fate as those a mile up the river. Although destroyed itself, the topography of the Leeds and Florence meadows saved a half million dollars' worth of property in Florence and many lives.

At about this time, someone in Williamsburg telegraphed Florence and Northampton to tell them the torrent was on its way. Others raced down in person to alarm the village, so most Florence inhabitants had been warned by nine o'clock when it arrived. Led by a wall six to ten feet high, the flood was still powerful enough to snatch up all three bridges in Florence and carry them downstream. First went the upper bridge across Meadow Street—near Austin Ross's farm—which it hurled onto the Pine Street iron bridge two hundred yards below. The entangled bridges rocked and tumbled until they twisted themselves into a knot that plunged over the dam at the Nonotuck Silk Mill. A few hundred yards below, the surge took out the wooden structure that spanned Bridge Street. With all three bridges gone, the north and south sections of Florence were disconnected.

The wave reached four to five feet above the high-water mark and flooded adjacent meadows and scores of basements and first floors. The rise was so sudden that people hardly had time to see what was happening before escaping to upper floors. Peering out attic and bedroom windows, many expected the water to rise higher at any moment and drown them, but it didn't. Instead, it damaged their lower floors, swirling furniture and taking away larders stocked with butter, meat, eggs, and potatoes. Within an hour it was gone. It killed no one in Florence, but left a trail of damaged structures and piles of flood wood along the riverbanks and in the meadows, some as deep as twelve feet.

At the Florence Manufacturing Company, maker of hand mirrors and hairbrushes, the mill workers had been warned and all made it out safely. The wave seemed to loom up so suddenly that the factory was made an island in the current with uprooted trees crashing against the building. Two or three trees lodged in front of the coal house in front of the factory, protecting it from destruction. The water rolled containers of resin, shellac, and other stock around the basement. It submerged the first floor, the engine, and boiler, and sliced off part of the brick floor and one end of the washroom. At one end of the first floor, filthy water rose to the ceiling in the shop where O. C. Warner manufactured steel files. It destroyed his tools and finished stock.

The Nonotuck Silk Mill was next in line. The new stone dam, built within the previous year, withstood the pressure of the surge and the tangled bridges it carried, making it the only dam to remain on the river. Still, the massive ten-foot-long stone breakwater was flattened and the stones tossed into the wheelpit and raceway. The mill hands were no sooner out of the building than the water rose three feet on the floor, damaged the machinery and cloth set up on the looms, pared off the rear foundations, and sent some of the machinery downstream. Parts of the wooden mill and the dye house, as well as the blacksmith shop and iron storehouse, were destroyed, and more than fifty cords of wood were carried away. Next door the Greenville Manufacturing Company's cotton mills escaped major damage. The basement was flooded, the cotton supply soaked, and fences on the property were carried downstream. The pump house of the Florence Sewing Machine Company, not in use, was partially ruined, the wall crushed inward so that the side was open from roof to foundation.

In the village of Bay State, the torrent pounded the exterior of the International Screw Company, washing away fifty feet of the canal and filling the rest with sand. Below, in Paper Mill Village, the Vernon Paper Company lost part of its dam and embankment, while water swirled through the first floor of the factory and damaged some of the stock.

By the time the flood reached Northampton, the citizens were ready for it. Some stayed inside and rolled up carpets and moved furniture upstairs while others stood on the riverbanks and bridges in the cold rain. At least one spectator got caught in the flow. W. A. Clapp stood on the west side of the river checking the current when suddenly water lapped around him on all sides, leaving him stranded until it subsided. Residents reported that the water rose to their first-floor windowsills.

Below Paper Mill Village, the engorged river ran along the north side of the large grounds of the Northampton Lunatic Hospital, a state-sponsored asylum that cared for six hundred mentally ill patients. The river spilled onto the three-hundred-acre farm that was used to support the hospital, but the hospital buildings, high on a hill, were unharmed.

In Northampton, the only factory damaged was the Clement and Hawks and Company hoe factory. A one-hundred-foot chunk of the dam embankment was torn away and the forging shop took in six feet of water, which extinguished the blazing fires in the forges and sent off so much steam and smoke that it appeared as if the building were on fire. The floor was layered with six inches of mud and sand and all the tools wore a film of dirty, muddy water. Then the swollen river raised the iron bridge at West Street from its piers and floated it into the covered bridge of the New Haven and Northampton Railroad a few hundred yards below, pushing that bridge aside as it kept its downstream course. It continued through the meadow below, taking a thick apple tree with it. The West Street bridge finally came to rest when an iron projection caught hold of one of the South Street bridge's wooden underpinnings, so that the iron bridge dangled below the wooden one. As the railroad bridge was swept away, the engineer of an approaching locomotive realized that the track was gone, stopped the train, and backed up to the station. There were gaps in the track of ten, fifteen, or twenty feet and damage to the embankment.

For a distance of a mile the flood followed the river's twisted path as it skirted the town center of Northampton, running a block or two south of Main Street along the New Haven and Northampton Railroad through an area thickly built up with houses, small businesses, and schools, where it soaked some basements and first floors. The Northampton dike protected the houses within its limits. If it hadn't been there, much of the south side of town would have been submerged beneath three to six feet of water.

The same topography that gave the valley good waterpower made the flood extremely destructive. Rapid descents and narrow gorges like those in Williamsburg, Haydenville, and Leeds speeded and confined the water, greatly increasing its destructive force. It took the wide, flat expanse of Leeds's and Florence's farmland to dissipate the flood's energy. In Williamsburg, Skinnerville, Haydenville, and Leeds, the water passed any given point in twenty minutes. By comparison, it crept through Northampton, taking two and a half hours to pass the South Street bridge in the center of Northampton. There, the river began to rise at half past nine and reached its highest point at eleven o'clock. It fell rapidly. By noon, the river had settled into its natural channel again as the last of the flood-waters emptied into the Connecticut River. The Connecticut rose, turned muddy brown, and carried flood wood past Holyoke, Springfield, and Hartford. The flotsam that made it as far as Middletown, Connecticut, fifteen miles below Hartford, snagged on that town's riverbank where the river makes a sharp easterly turn.

In the space of four and a half hours—from seven-thirty when the dam burst until noon when the Mill River subsided—the contents of the Williamsburg reservoir, 600 million gallons of water, had rolled over and plundered an eleven-mile path down the Mill Valley. Those who survived were stunned at the wasteland they beheld.

That afternoon, two workers tending the Holyoke dam across the Connecticut, eight miles south of where the Mill River entered the Connecticut, watched debris slide over the dam. They saw a little girl floating on a bed, one hand clutching the headboard and the other grasping the mattress. The men grabbed at the bed with hooked poles, trying to pull it ashore, but as they jostled the mattress, the lifeless body slid into the river. The body was never found and the child was never identified.

CHAPTER 4

THE AFTERMATH

FOR an hour Elizabeth Cheney, the dam keeper's wife, sat on the cabin porch and watched the reservoir drain through the gap in the dam. The high wave thundered through first, followed by a swell that gradually shrank to the size of a small stream as it slowly slipped back into its natural channel. At the rim of the gap, the water pounded away the dirt, exposing the interior stone wall and chewing the wall's edge until the dam's mouth was wide and jagged. On the west side, a remnant of the wall spiked skyward looking like the skeleton of a tower in the ruins of some ancient castle. Through the gap, Elizabeth could see the wide, flat reservoir bed gently sloping toward her, like a bottle tipped on its side, emptying the last of its contents. Shallow pools filled low spots, and scattered tree stumps, a few here, a cluster there, stubbled the mud floor as a reminder of what had grown there before the dam was built.

When she last saw her husband, George, he was racing away from the barn on his horse to Spelman's house in Williamsburg village to tell his boss that the dam was about to break. Now she didn't know if he was alive or dead. He might have been swept away along the river road or swallowed when the flood hit the village. But George came back in an hour. He had reached Spelman's and tried to beat the flood down to Haydenville, but the first wave quickly passed him. Afraid for his family back at the dam, he rode home on the high road between farms. The river road he had ridden down on was washed out.

Once Cheney, his parents, wife, and children all saw that each other was safe, they each must have recounted what they had seen and heard. Elizabeth might have described how the dam burst open from the bottom; George must have told how the torrent washed over the village; George's father could have recalled the boom he heard as he ran to Hemenway's farm and how he saw a second large break west of the main breach upon his return; George's mother and children probably reported what they saw from the hill overlooking the dam and how they moved the furniture out of the house after the second break. Their family was lucky. Although the land around their house was scoured and rubble-strewn, their house stood and they were alive. Three miles above the devastated villages, the Cheneys were isolated from other survivors, but they wouldn't be alone for long. Within a few hours, newspaper reporters would find them.

George examined the dam. Water dripped from the gate pipe, still in place. A few stones were punched out from the low stone wall that the pipe rested on, but the top of the pipe casing was intact. He walked along the undisturbed western remnant of the dam toward the center. He faced a chasm, two hundred fifty feet wide and forty feet deep, where the center and east side of the dam should have been. All that remained of the east side was a small section, perhaps fifty feet long, clinging to High Ridge and a few stones resting at the bottom. From the top of the wall he could see the riverbed carved several feet below its original course and the valley sprinkled in some places, crammed in others, with boulders torn from the dam's interior wall. Trees that had once lined the river were missing, extracted by their roots or sheared off to stumps of varying heights. Others appeared ragged and worn, stripped of bark, branches, and leaves. Still others looked like gigantic brooms, their bark and branches pared off and white roots twisted into splints. The valley's smooth, spring-green hills had been cut by a jagged brown gash, a savage slash, which extended eleven miles from the reservoir to the Connecticut River. Along the Connecticut, heaps of demolished buildings and furniture piled on shore and snagged in the booms above the Holyoke dam. If Cheney didn't think to himself, *I told you so*, he had every right to. The east side was where he had seen the largest leak, the one he had described as the diameter of a man's arm when he reported it to Onslow Spelman and Lucius Dimock.

Down the valley, the overwhelming impression was of timber and rocks—large, small, strewn, sometimes piled, and always misplaced. New Englanders had always battled rocks, pulling them from the soil and using them to shape low walls along the edges of fields, to support buildings, line river banks, and buttress bridges and dams. Now those same rocks, combined with others the flood had unearthed, speckled the landscape. They would have to be picked up once again, along with more than a thousand loads of timber. By 1874, New Englanders had long since cleared most of the forest and sawed logs into lumber for fences and buildings, chopped it for firewood, and burned it for potash. For cash crops, they planted new trees like sugar maples, apples, and pears. Now trees of every variety and the things people had fashioned out of them lay helter-skelter like a valley-long game of pick-up-sticks. Property loss would be set at $1 million.

Miles downstream, survivors hoped for a happy reunion like the Cheney's. After the water rushed through, Isabell Hayden stood on the hillside overlooking her flooded Skinnerville farm. Her house was gone. Hundreds of people, most of whom she had known her whole life, were on the banks too, straining to catch sight of a husband, a child, a wife, a mother. She had seen the current whisk her son and father downstream when they tried to find safety on the roof of the shed behind the house, and now she had to find them in a place she didn't recognize. Her landmarks—streets, houses, sheds, fences, stepping-stones—had been replaced by heaps of timber and other tangled debris lodged against boulders stripped from factory foundations and mill dams. Her bright, colorful world had been transformed into a drab scene tinted with only the narrow range of shades in a brown-and-white photograph. Not a single blade of grass was visible on the valley floor. She must have thought about her husband, who had gone to the village that morning, and wondered if he was alive. There were no usable bridges between the reservoir and the Connecticut River to cross to find him.

Down in the valley, a few people wriggled free of the debris and crawled or walked away. Ten-year-old George Roberts floated from the breakfast table at his home in Williamsburg to Haydenville, two miles downstream. He untangled himself on the riverbank next to his neighbor's cow, which had also survived the journey. As George crawled up the bank, the cow followed. When George stopped to rest, the cow did the same. Four or five times up the riverbank, George and the cow crept, stopped, and rested, neither leaving the other's side. Jimmy Ryan, who observed the scene, wasn't sure whether the boy was caring for the animal, or if it was the other way around, but the two stayed together until they were both safe at the top of the hill. George didn't know that both of his parents and his two little sisters, ages three and one, had perished. One of twelve children orphaned by the disaster, George had worked for the past two summers with his father, a railroad engineer, as a water boy on the New Haven and Northampton line.

People on the riverbanks shouted names of loved ones across the trickling stream, some wet and chilled, and some still in their nightclothes; others, too dazed to move, simply stared for hours. In the rain, mothers and children huddled together, speculating about the fate of fathers who worked downstream in one of the mills. Fathers from the mills wondered if their wives and children had escaped their homes. Gradually, as if awakening from a long sleep, survivors began climbing over boulders and timbers. Immediately they began searching for bodies amid wreckage so dense and snarled that mattresses and quilts were knotted with belting and machinery, and hanks of raw silk were lodged with toys and potatoes. Everything was so mixed up that it was impossible to know where to begin or where anything belonged. It was as though the valley had been a life-size jigsaw puzzle of a pleasant and prosperous mill village scene that had been so suddenly and violently broken apart that the pieces depicting objects—natural and man-made—were rearranged in startling juxtapositions: ripped clothes dangling from trees, a cow tangled in a loom, a letter mixed with brass patterns, a blue silk dress wrapped around an old book, mangled machinery lying in a parlor, and a Masonic banner caught under a dam.

Within a few minutes of the flood, groups of men in each village, among them blacksmiths, storekeepers, and mill workers, gathered picks, axes, crow-bars, shovels—whatever tool they could find or make—to cull through the mounds along the riverbanks. Dozens of people had been swept away. If still alive, they needed to be rescued. If dead, they had to be buried. No one waited for orders from a town official or a mill owner. They simply set about the task in the customary way, the most practical and systematic way they knew—working in small teams—laboring together as if they were building a road, raising a barn, digging a pond, fighting a fire, cleaning up after a freshet, or any number of community activities that one man couldn't do by himself. It was as though all the work they had done together as citizens of a town and as neighbors had prepared them to respond to a disaster. In 1874, before the American Red Cross and the Federal Emergency Management Agency, res-cue, relief, and cleanup were local and voluntary.

Isabell Hayden and her husband, Joseph, found each other but they could not find their five-year-old son Robbie and Isabell's father, Eli Bryant. That morning someone had seen Bryant's dog Rover, a big St. Bernard, known to be so gentle that the village children wound ribbons around him and tied hats to his head. Rover was sitting on the riverbank, a half mile below their farm, watching over Robbie's lifeless body. Like fourteen other sets of parents, Isabell and Joseph lost at least one child in the flood. Some lost several.

Once Robbie Hayden's body was removed, Isabell didn't see Rover for three days. There was no sign of Eli. He was a hearty fellow and she may have thought he could have survived. Several years earlier on his farm in nearby Chesterfield he had been struck by lightning. He was on his way home when the bolt hit, burning his hair and beard, ripping his clothes, and knocking his boots off his feet. Paralyzed, he lay on the ground for what he thought was a minute or two until he was able to stand up and walk home. It was unlikely, but maybe he would survive this time too.

If Eli were dead, the place to look for his body was one of the five temporary morgues survivors set up by Saturday afternoon. From the Florence meadows, bodies were taken to Warner's carpenter shop on the hill east of the river; at Leeds, they were placed in the barn in the rear of the Ross store and at the schoolhouse; at Haydenville, corpses were laid in the basement of the church; and, in Williamsburg, they were moved into the town hall. Those in charge of these buildings may have opened their doors or it was just as likely that someone appropriated the space because it was needed. Since Eli was swept away a half mile above Haydenville, the logical place to look was the Haydenville Church, still cloaked in black banners for Sunday's memorial service for Joel Hayden Sr. Instead of celebrating Hayden's life, survivors brought his village's dead to the church.

Inside, women arranged the bruised, often naked, corpses in rows on crude wooden planks, covered each with a white sheet brought from home, and pinned on a slip of paper bearing the name of the deceased, if known. Before undertaking became a professional service, preparing the dead for burial was customarily women's work. The bodies were so badly battered that a shredded garment or a ring was often the only identification. All day long, silent, stone-faced men, women, and children gathered in front of the church, seeking a glimpse of the victims in hope of identifying a missing friend or relative. One observer wrote that "not a tear was shed by survivors. They seemed to be benumbed by grief, and their white faces and mechanical actions spoke volumes." Volunteers kept the doors closed and admitted only one or two persons at a time. If Isabell circled the room, she did not find Eli, but she would have recognized many other neighbors and friends among the dead and in the line of mourners outside. Those who found loved ones returned with wagons to pick up their dead.

In the morgues, the human toll of the disaster was collected and visible. Early estimates of the total number of victims ranged from 175 to 2,000, with most hovering between 200 and 250. By the end of the day, when officials started keeping a count, the number hovered around 157, higher than the final toll would be; some of the dead had been moved from one morgue to another and counted twice, and some missing persons had been counted among the dead. Most observers were shocked by how many children lay dead. One *Springfield Republican* reporter described the scene:

> In these "extemporized morgues" a horrible spectacle took place that made the stoutest heart quail, and the faintest nerve shudder and almost give way with sickening repulsion. There lay on the rude boards, often without a shred of clothing left, or, if clad, with every garment frayed to mere shreds, men and women in horrible invariableness of agony. . . . There lay children—many little children—their little, beloved faces beaten and bruised, and yet now and then one as sweet and placid as when its last good-night kiss was given. Many a veteran soldier, who had been hardened to death in battle, and cared little for the sight of dead men, found this spectacle of the innocent little ones more than he could bear, and many a strong man found his eye moistening with unwonted tears. No one was ashamed of tears . . . one would have been less than human to hold them back.

One third of the dead—a total of forty-three—were under the age of ten, killed at home with their mothers. Many elderly people who had been at home were also killed; the eldest was Electa Knight at age eighty. Twelve women became widows; nine men, widowers. Twelve more men would find that their wives and all their children had died. Five entire nuclear families—both parents and all the children—perished. The Birminghams and Johnsons in Williamsburg, and the Fitzgeralds, Patricks, and Fennesseys in Leeds all ceased to exist.

At the top of the disaster area, in the village of Williamsburg, almost three quarters of the victims had been born within thirty miles of town, while nearly a quarter were from Ireland, Canada, and England. In Haydenville and Leeds, where there were higher concentrations of riverside homes occupied by immigrant families, one half to three quarters of the victims were immigrants.

The Ryans were a Williamsburg Irish family that survived. When the flood was over, twelve-year-old Jimmy Ryan, his father Thomas, and his brother spent an hour driving through the mud to their Williamsburg home from Haydenville. When they arrived, they saw only the cellar hole with no house above it. Their two new barns, while standing, were swept clean of animals and fodder. A few minutes later, Jimmy's mother and younger brothers descended the hill to which they had fled, unharmed and wet. There was nothing for the family to eat all day. That night, they walked four miles down to Florence, where local volunteers fed them and gave them a change of clothes.

Downstream in Leeds, Fred Howard, the packer at the button mill who had yanked several coworkers up the railroad embankment to safety, couldn't get home to tell his family he was safe. Only six houses out of thirty-five remained amidst a sea of debris; all four bridges were gone. Sometime that morning Fred and his father, a farmer who had probably been on his own farm, found each other. They joined the search for bodies until the afternoon, when they finally piled together enough timber to cross the river, which rushed through, six to eight feet deep, its normal depth. Fred later wrote to his brother:

> We worked all day Saturday looking for bodies. Most were found on the meadows and flats from Cooks dam [tall dam at the bottom of the village] to [the] Ross place in Florence. Several were found near the stone bridge and back of the Cook house and other places in the village. The folks here could see the water, houses & timber going down the stream and that both [button] shops were gone but there was no crossing and they did not know that Father and I were safe till afternoon when we got some timbers across the stream near the silk mill. I can assure you that they felt relieved when we came home.

While Fred was home, survivors in the village continued to look for bodies. Someone searched the buildings that had piled into each other at the top of Main Street and found six cold and frightened children alive; they had huddled behind a bed on the second floor where the water had risen up to their necks. Soon, Leeds survivors learned that several dozen bodies from their village had been found two miles downstream in Florence; they had been brought to Warner's tiny carpenter shop there and placed on wooden tiers to save space. Empty coffins sent up from Northampton and Westfield were stacked outside or laid across carpenters' benches, to be filled with the forty-four bodies brought there that day. As in Haydenville, people waited quietly outside for their turn to enter.

Fred wasn't home for long before he too made his way to the Florence carpenter's shop. George Warner, owner of the Leeds button mill, had asked him to bring the bodies of Annie Cogan and Carrie Bonney to his house. While Warner was Fred's employer and a wealthy man, he was also a longtime resident who knew Fred well, and trusted him for this job. Fred had grown up with Annie, age twenty-three, and Carrie, age eighteen, who was probably one of the Cogan girls' friends. Annie had been a teacher in the West Farms section of Northampton; her sister Grace was twenty, a teacher-in-training at the Westfield Normal School.

Fred borrowed a hearse from Myron Day, the expressman who had raced from Haydenville to Leeds to warn the button-shop workers of the flood, and drove to the carpenter's shop. Fred was appalled by the sight of the cut, naked, mangled bodies, some of which he recognized, including that of Ralph Isham, the bookkeeper at the button mill who had refused to leave the building. Fred loaded Annie and Carrie's bodies into the hearse, and drove them to Warner's for the funeral the next day. There was no sign of Grace or her mother Jane Cogan. The nineteen bodies that remained at the carpenter's shop, all identified except for three women and a baby, were packed in ice for the night.

George Warner's house, untouched by the water, became an informal village headquarters for the Leeds relief effort. Warner didn't announce that he was in charge, but because of his economic and social position as a mill owner, he had an obligation to lead, and he fulfilled it. He dispatched people he trusted, such as Fred Howard, to do things on his behalf. He organized the burial for the Cogan family, a family of locally high social standing that his son was to marry into. Feeling responsible for his employees, he sent someone to Northampton to telegraph bookkeeper Ralph Isham's parents in Brooklyn, New York, that their son was missing. Someone brought three French Canadian children to Warner's house. All under age nine, the children told adults at the house that they could not find their three sisters, their brother, and their mother, but that their father was safe and helping find dead people. Many at Warner's knew that the brother and sisters were dead, yet no one had the heart to tell the children, and no one knew the fate of the mother. One of the silk factory overseers took the children home. Though several newspapers reported this family's sad story, none identified the immigrants by name.

Lucius Dimock, the reservoir company member and superintendent of the silk mill, lived in a big house on a hill next door to Warner. He had been a Leeds resident for twenty years, and it would have been unthinkable for him to have stayed home without assisting in any way. Outraged survivors would have made certain the newspapers reported it. But while he had the same obligation to lead as Warner had, there were no reports of his activities immediately after the flood.

Down in Northampton, when Joel Hayden Jr. heard of the disaster he hurried to Haydenville with his brother-in-law, Acting Governor Thomas

Talbot. Talbot, who had grown up in Leeds as the seventh of eight children of Irish immigrants—his widowed mother had moved there so her older children could find employment in the mills—spent time at the Hayden-ville Church boosting the spirits of the volunteers. The *Boston Evening Journal* called him "as electrifying as eloquent" as he spoke to those distrib-uting food and clothing and caring for the dead. A veteran of the Leeds woolen mills himself (at age thirteen, he began in the carding room), he took out all the money he had with him, $200, to start a relief fund.

Word of the disaster traveled fast. By nine o'clock that morning someone in Northampton had telegraphed Springfield, the closest large city. The *Springfield Republican* newspaper posted notices on bulletin boards, and word-of-mouth quickly spread the news through the city. Men left their shops and workrooms to gather in doorways out of the rain, wondering if the flood could be as bad as the first reports indicated. By noon, as the details grew more frightening and as hundreds of clerks were let out for lunch, eager readers surrounded bulletin boards and headed to the telegraph office to send messages to friends and family in the Mill Valley. Boston and New York picked up the news and telegraphed questions to Springfield, which relayed them to Northampton, the nearest available point, but still an hour by foot or horse-drawn vehicle from the devastation.

Businesses on Springfield's Main Street closed briefly while people stood on the banks of the Connecticut River and watched for an hour as the water rose, turned muddy, and floated wreckage downstream; they hoped to see in the debris some information on what had happened nineteen miles up-stream. The large volume of water lent credence to a rumor that the Holyoke dam had given way.

By the time the 12:15 train departed Springfield for Northampton, it was crammed with passengers, including six *Springfield Republican* news-paper reporters. One was William J. Denver, who set himself up at the Northampton telegraph office to act as special correspondent, tapping information back so quickly that by two o'clock the *Republican* issued a complete bulletin. By the end of the disaster coverage the Northampton telegraph line transmitted 75,000 words of description—enough to fill a two-hundred-page book. Disasters were a cultural preoccupation of the age, and the newspapers were not going to miss the opportunity to satisfy their readers' desires for tales of violent deaths of innocent people. In their first editions after the flood, newspapers compared the flood to other disasters.

The New York Times declared it was greater in loss of life than the Chicago fire in 1871 (they were mistaken; 300 died in Chicago as opposed to the 139 in the Mill River flood) and that the Avondale, Pennsylvania, mining disaster of 1869, in which 110 died, paled in comparison. Readers called to mind other notable recent disasters, such as the Peshtigo, Wisconsin, fire in 1871, which killed 1,500, and the Pemberton Mill collapse in 1860, in which a five-story cotton mill in Lawrence, Massachusetts, fell to the ground after a cast-iron column suddenly gave way. Seventy-six workers were crushed or burned to death as oil lamps ignited cotton fibers in the wreckage.

By early afternoon, the six *Springfield Republican* reporters were in the valley. Four spread out among the villages in search of knowledgeable citizens to show them around while one stayed in Northampton to transmit the story back to Springfield. The sixth reporter headed straight to the reservoir to examine the dam and interview gatekeeper Cheney, reaching him several hours after the dam's collapse. Cheney described his duties, the condition of the dam that morning, his opinions about its stability, the manner in which it slumped, and his discussion with Spelman about which side of the dam was breaking. Over the next few weeks, in the many times Cheney would describe the events leading to the flood, he would never change his story. That evening, a reporter, most likely the same one that had interviewed Cheney, called on Lewis Bodman, who had held shares in the reservoir company when he owned the Williamsburg woolen mill. With characteristic frankness, Bodman told the history of the dam, the mill owners' initial fear of the structure, and their growing satisfaction with it as the years progressed. Just the previous week, Bodman said, he had assured a local man that the dam posed no danger.

In the meantime, express teams leaving Springfield carried the news to towns east, west, and south of the city. In Pittsfield, thirty miles west of Northampton, bits of information filtered into town by the telegraph and passengers on the railroad. When the *Springfield Union* newspaper arrived late in the day in Pittsfield, people descended on the depot and the post office lobby to listen to repeated readings of the paper. It reminded some of the Civil War, when anxious people collected in public places to listen to newspaper accounts of battles.

All afternoon and evening, hundreds of people from around Massachusetts and Connecticut who had relatives in the stricken region flocked to Springfield. Some took trains up to the Mill Valley, but those who arrived after eight o'clock at night found the trains had stopped running and hired vehicles to take them there instead.

By midmorning the Northampton telegraph office was so overwhelmed by people anxious to send messages (the wires were down from Northampton to Williamsburg), that valley inhabitants crowded the Easthampton telegraph office, five miles away. Gaius Wood, the bookkeeper at the James woolen mill, sent someone there to telegraph Henry James, who was in New York expecting to sail for Europe at three o'clock that afternoon. This message reached James about nine in the morning:

> The Williamsburg Reservoir gave way this morning and washed away
> half the village. Our factory stands. Don't sail. Answer here. Spelman
> and Skinner's factory gone.
>
> Gaines [sic] O. Wood, Book-keeper

The word spread quickly through Easthampton. When Will Skinner, son of the silk-mill owner, left his Latin prose class at Williston Seminary on Easthampton's main street, he knew something was terribly wrong. "I noticed that the men were all standing around in groups on the street, and when 'Billy' Hill [a faculty member] saw me he called me up to him and said that the Williamsburg Reservoir had given away and had destroyed Williamsburg, Skinnerville & Haydenville & Leeds & also that 1200 lives were lost. I obtained a team and he drove me home." When they arrived, Will's house was one of the few standing. Dick Hills's mother, Christina Hills, and their grandfather, John Kaplinger of Haydenville, were dead. Will wrote:

> When I arrived at the house I found out that the family were all safe but
> in order to be so they ran to the hills. Our house is very nearly the only
> one standing & "Dick" Hills' mother was lost and has not been found so
> also was Mrs. Jerome Hillman. The men are now digging for bodies.

At eight o'clock that evening, Henry James, his wife, and brother arrived in Easthampton, where the train stopped; the track to Northampton was washed out. On the train they met Collins Gere, part-owner of the brass factory with Joel Hayden Jr.; Fred Warner, who worked in William Skinner's New York office; James Peck, an agent for Skinner's silk mill; E. W. Eaton, an agent of Nonotuck Silk Company; and brothers J. P. and E. L. Snow, New York businessmen who had grown up in Williamsburg. At every station the group received telegrams confirming the morning reports and giving new accounts of the terrible losses. The Snow brothers may have heard an early report that their mother and sister were dead, but a later dispatch to New York said they were alive. When the Snows arrived, they would find that their mother had perished and their sister had survived. At Easthampton, the men climbed into carriages that took them to their homes. The previous week, as Henry James prepared to leave for New York, he joked to Williamsburg friends that when he arrived in Europe he expected to be greeted with the news that his factory had gone up in flames or down in a flood. In the six years he had owned the mill, it had been damaged by fire and freshets so often that he predicted that his usual bad luck would strike again.

Before he boarded the train for Easthampton, J. P. Snow had told a *New York Tribune* reporter that he didn't know which of the reservoirs above Williamsburg had broken. The reports of the extensive damage made him think that both the Williamsburg and Goshen reservoirs must have broken away at the same time, but he acknowledged that would have been an amazing coincidence since they were four miles apart, at different elevations, and unconnected. Snow posited that perhaps there was a "set-back" where water from the Goshen reservoir ran down the West Branch of the Mill River until it reached the village of Williamsburg, where it was pushed back up the East Branch toward the Williamsburg dam, breaking it from the downstream side. The *Boston Evening Journal* reported that the Goshen reservoir had toppled due to heavy rain the night before. A *Journal* reporter called on Stephen M. Crosby of Boston, married to Joel Hayden Sr.'s daughter Anne Elizabeth. He described the setting of the reservoirs and the string of factories below, estimating that the capital investment along the river was $5 million and the immediate population affected was about 5,000 persons.

Within the valley, a few thought one or both of the Goshen dams had collapsed because the previous year the old Goshen dam had undergone extensive repair. But more attributed the flood to the Williamsburg dam because of their long-held suspicions about its weaknesses. Within hours, survivors buttonholed Lewis Bodman, a former reservoir company member, and insisted he do something to lower the level of the Goshen reservoirs. Acting on his own responsibility, Bodman sent someone with a note up to Goshen to instruct the dam keeper to hoist the gates and keep them up to relieve pressure on the dams until the present owners of the reservoir company told him differently. The dam keeper refused. The messenger threatened him with physical harm if he didn't comply. He finally opened the gates.

Panic about reservoir dams spread around the state. Fifty miles east in Worcester, citizens flocked to the North Pond dam, which held twice as much as the Williamsburg reservoir. Eight years earlier it had been pronounced unsafe by James B. Francis of Lowell, the eminent hydraulic engineer of his day. The Worcester County commissioners ordered the dam removed. But the city of Worcester, which owned the dam, did not comply and the commissioners finally agreed to let the dam stand if the water was kept below a fixed point partway up the embankment. But when citizens examined it on the day of the Mill River flood they found that the city had violated the order and the reservoir was full. Citizens demanded something be done, and within three days the city government ordered it rebuilt or repaired.

On Saturday night each of the flooded villages held a meeting of its citizens to organize recovery and relief efforts. In Williamsburg, Hiram Nash, a prosperous farmer who had served in the Massachusetts Legislature, presided at the Williamsburg village meeting. Because the town hall was filled with bodies, the meeting was held in the vestry of the Congregational Church. Prominent local men, including farmers, store owners, tradesmen, and the ministers of the Congregational and Methodist churches, attended. Storekeepers Lyman James and Lewis Porter, farmer and former wool manufacturer Lewis Bodman, and Albert Morton were assigned to a committee to attend to the search and burial of the dead. Farmer and deacon William A. Hawkes was placed in charge of collecting and distributing relief.

At a similar meeting in Haydenville, committees were appointed to clear away debris and bury the dead. Reverend James Kimball of the Haydenville Church and Dr. William Trow, the town's physician, were appointed to the relief committee. Dr. Trow urged an inquest to determine the cause of the disaster, and responsibility, asserting that they needed an explanation of why the dam should break at a time when no unusual pressure was placed on it.

Leeds held a meeting the following night in which they selected General John Otis, the Civil War hero who owned the Emery Wheel Company, as chairman of the aid committee. Otis was assisted by George H. Ray, an agent of the American Express Company, as secretary; storekeeper Edson Ross; and Mr. Whitcomb. Seven women, probably those who had already taken charge in the morgue, were also named to the committee: Mrs. I. B. Field, Mrs. George H. Ray, Mrs. Dora Van Slyke, Miss Lillie Field, Miss Emma Krager, Miss Nettie Quigley, and Miss Julia Marble. Button manufacturer George Warner was among those charged with the recovery and burial of the bodies, a task he'd already assumed. The purpose of the meetings was to codify the system already in place rather than to create a new one.

Local men employed their customary means of organizing and assigning work—they held a meeting and appointed committees. A few mill owners served along with the local men, most with long ties to the villages, who normally took care of the roads, schools, paupers, and other local matters. These storekeepers and farmers did not expect that in two days control would be taken away from them.

As the day of the flood wore on, the villagers slowly realized that they needed outside assistance. These were proud, industrious, self-sufficient people, and it was common for towns and cities at the time to understate the extent of damage, not wanting to appear weak or to destroy future business opportunities by giving the perception they were incapable of handling an emergency. But the Mill Valley's problems were too dire and too visible to underplay. In midafternoon, when Springfield's mayor John M. Stebbins telegraphed Northampton to offer police assistance, he received no response. Later that afternoon, the mayor again telegraphed Northampton to offer immediate assistance of any kind. The reply came, "We will telegraph if we need anything." It is not surprising that survivors wanted first to take care of themselves without outside interference; they needed time to assess their situation and get their bearings in their new world.

Certain that those in the flooded region didn't yet know what they needed, the Springfield city council appointed a committee to receive subscriptions for donations to the relief effort. The committee printed circulars to be sent to each of the churches in time for Sunday's morning service, but before the afternoon was over, pledges were coming in from people on Main Street: $100 to $500 from wealthy individuals and more than $100 collected by police officers on their beats.

Offers of aid also came from New Haven's mayor, H. G. Lewis. After telegraphing three offers of help and receiving no reply, he sent a midafternoon telegram instructing the selectmen of Northampton to draw upon him for $1,000 for the immediate necessities and more if needed. By nighttime, the Mill Valley residents were ready to ask for help:

Haydenville, May 16
To the Hon. H. G. Lewis, Mayor of New-Haven: Clothing and provisions are most needed, everything being swept away, which causes many poor

people, who are left without a mouthful to eat or clothes enough to cover themselves. A meeting of citizens is being held. Will telegraph again.

D. B. Carr

That afternoon a group of men in Williamsburg circulated petitions to the Massachusetts Senate and House of Representatives requesting a committee "be appointed to visit the localities above named and devise such measures of relief in the premises as the extraordinary circumstance of the case may suggest." Someone carried it up and down the valley for signatures of the most prominent men, who included merchants, farmers, and manufacturers. It was signed by Williamsburg and Northampton selectmen and eighty-six others and delivered to Boston on Monday morning. Among the signers were Williamsburg store owners Thomas M. Carter and Lyman D. James; Reverend Kimball of the Haydenville Church; farmers Thomas Nash, Otis G. Hill, and Lewis Bodman; manufacturers George Warner, Onslow Spelman, Henry James, and William Skinner; *Hampshire Gazette* editor Henry S. Gere; and Daniel W. Bond, the reservoir company's attorney.

The aid system had been set in motion. In the years before federal and state governments provided disaster relief, it was common for cities to offer one another financial assistance in the expectation that if a disaster struck, the cities they helped in the past would come to their aid. Federal and state assistance, an infrequent practice, was available only after legislation dealing with that particular disaster was passed, the necessary number of votes usually attained by promises of returning the favor if disaster ever struck a fellow legislator's community. But most aid in the nineteenth century was donated by generous Americans who opened their hearts and pocketbooks. Individuals, even those living far from the disaster scene, donated food, clothing, and money, often first as a pledge routed through a church or civic association.

Saturday night, few people slept. Some survivors searched the wreckage by lantern light, refusing to give up until they found loved ones. Some kept vigil in the morgues. Others with damaged homes stayed with friends who lived on high ground, or spent the night at the Williamsburg depot, worried that one of the Goshen reservoir dams on the West Branch of the Mill River might break and flood the valley again. Mary Hill, the twenty-six-year-old Williamsburg village housewife and mother whose backyard was bounded by the West Branch, remained in her home and wrote in her palm-sized diary:

Eventful day! Arose at seven—Got breakfast and was clearing away when we heard the roar of the coming reservoir. It was so sudden we stood like one stunned but terribly beyond description. The worst was past in 15 or 20 minutes, but the agony of those few minutes. Oh! We can never thank him [God] enough. I could do nothing the rest of the day. Of course, Mother came down at night and I went out for a short time. Called on Mrs. Hitchcock who had lost her dear husband. God bless and care for her. At home in the ev [evening]. Retired but not to sleep.

The flood had cut out the heart of Mary's world, destroyed much of the village she frequently walked, and severed ties to people she knew and loved.

Fred Howard's world had also turned upside down. The night of the flood, he went to bed late, exhausted. He and his father had carried five bodies into the Leeds schoolhouse sometime after ten o'clock. In closing his letter to his brother, he confided that "it's all over now and seems sometimes like a dream." If Fred slept that night he awoke to the same grim reality the next morning.

"All able-bodied men are summoned to the relief of the people of the Mill River Valley," read the notice posted in Northampton on Sunday morning, not yet twenty-four hours after the dam broke. Beginning at seven o'clock the bell of Northampton's oldest church tolled slowly and ceaselessly until men and boys old enough to wield picks and shovels filled Main Street. Men from Hatfield, north of Northampton, and from Hadley, across the Connecticut River, joined them. The volunteers boarded a special train that departed at seven-thirty for Florence, Leeds, and Haydenville, the tracks having been restored overnight. Acting Governor Thomas Talbot was at the depot to help local officials by offering encouragement. Those volunteers who found the train too crowded drove wagons of every type up the valley amid a swarm of men walking singly and in small groups carrying tools and lunch pails. Overhead, the sun shone brilliantly through a cloud-speckled sky. It was the kind of warm spring day that New Englanders had waited for through the long winter, but they had never expected to spend such a beautiful day—a Sabbath no less—in this way. Church services in the valley were canceled. The discordance between the delightful weather and the day's mournful activities struck one reporter as absurd. While he talked with a survivor about those she had lost, he was distracted by a bobolink that warbled loudly above her head.

Upstream in Haydenville, if survivors slept at all, they awoke to find announcements posted by Joel Hayden Jr., who had spent the previous evening in conference with his partners Collins Gere and Sereno Kingsley about the future of the brass works. The announcements read:

> Notice—Having decided to rebuild our works at once, we hereby give notice that we wish to employ a large force of workmen to clear away the debris, etc. Preference will be given to those previously in our employ. Applications may be made at once to S. C. Wentworth for particulars. All wages due our workmen will be paid just as soon as we can make up the accounts and anyone heretofore in our employ who is in want will receive aid by leaving name and wants with H. M. Brewster. We would ask as a favor that all Materials, Books, Papers, etc., that may be found by any person belonging to us be returned, or we be informed where they are, and we will defray all expenses. Offices for the present at house of H. M. Brewster.
>
> Hayden, Gere & Co.
> Haydenville, May 17, 1874

If brass-mill workers felt the irony of applying for cleanup jobs to Samuel Wentworth, the superintendent who had ignored Collins Graves's warning to vacate the factory, they kept it to themselves. Their future hinged on Hayden's decision to rebuild. They knew that the village had meant everything to Joel Hayden Sr. and now it seemed it was the same for his son. Overjoyed that the village would be reborn and they would have jobs at the brass works again, former employees went to work immediately.

The complete loss of a factory was not unusual or insurmountable to the businessman. Joel and Josiah Hayden had lost the button factory to fire in 1832. A fire had taken Lewis Bodman's dye house and the contents of the satinet factory in 1865. Henry James had lost a plane and moulding tool factory in 1869, and George Warner's button shop burned to the ground in 1871. All had been rebuilt. The difference this time was that so many factories and homes had been wiped out that many of the valley businessmen they might have relied on for financial backing to rebuild were also devastated. While a dozen of the victims had life insurance, flood insurance was not available in the 1870s.

When the Northampton volunteers arrived in the ruined villages, local committees directed them to dig in the largest concentrations of debris, where they assumed the torrent had dumped the most dead. One such place was Joe Wright's Brook just above the Williamsburg depot, where floodwaters had backed up into the little tributary. Over the next few days they would find seven bodies, including those of Williamsburg physician Elbridge Johnson and some of his family. Another was the wide Leeds and Florence meadow where the torrent spread out and dropped most of what it had gathered upstream. After several days excavating, the total retrieved there was more than sixty.

Most bodies were buried in sand beneath piles or hidden within layers of such compacted material that it was backbreaking work to budge the tangled articles to find them. Local farmers hitched their teams to huge beams and trees and ordered the animals to pull, releasing the largest pieces. Then men used saws, picks, axes, and crowbars to wrench apart the smaller items. They carefully probed the exposed earth with spades. Most often they found nothing, but when they uncovered a fragment of cloth they dug by hand until they found a body. The noisy crew turned silent and solemn. As one reporter described it:

Something that was once human is slowly, painfully, anxiously disencumbered of the flood's covering, and laid, bare and horrible, upon the sands. There is a mute moment when that happens—a sense of awe that stills the common voice, and sobers all.

Volunteers carried bodies to one of the morgues. This scene was repeated over and over on Sunday, as a reporter from the *Hampshire Gazette* wrote:

At almost every hour there could be seen a body of men carrying a corpse on a stretcher, or a team carrying one or more bodies, or a load of coffins. The scene was one of woe, woe, woe. Whichever way the eye was cast, and wherever a step was taken, it was one continuous scene of indescribable sorrow. People were often speechless, and hundreds took each other by the hand silently, or passed each other in the street, with simply a nod of recognition. Such a scene may have been witnessed somewhere before, but never here, nor in this region. And may God grant that it may never be witnessed here or elsewhere again.

The searchers' grim work was hampered by crowds of curious strangers—estimated at more than one thousand—who had come from miles around. Some wanted to help and others sought relatives, but most came simply to satisfy their curiosity. Residents lowered their heads as they walked through the swarm to protect themselves from strangers who gawked, joked, and jostled. One reporter described the scene:

> Into Williamsburg, the head of the disaster, came a steady throng all day
> long, mostly of idle sight-seers, though not a few came with offers of assistance, while others were newspaper men and those searching for friends
> and acquaintances. From Northampton to Williamsburg stretched a continuous line of conveyances, while the roads were lined with pedestrians.
> An unknowing person would have argued a cattle-show, circus, college
> commencement or other country-fete day, so miscellaneous and entirely
> un-Sunday-like was the procession.

It was the same in Leeds. Fred Howard observed that "extra trains were
run all day Sunday as fast as they dare go and every train brought fourteen
car loads crowded and the teams come in from every direction in an unbroken stream all day." On the hill above the village, people on foot, in vehicles,
and on horseback filled the road so that one man counted 470 vehicles passing his house in sixty minutes, while in the village center where the road
was washed out there were periods of gridlock that lasted for half or three
quarters of an hour. As drivers sought the smoothest surfaces, they wound
on and off the road, in and out of the streambed, and up and down riverbanks. Every day for two weeks, a deluge of curiosity seekers came from all
over western Massachusetts and as far down the Connecticut Valley as New
Haven, some from as far away as Boston and Baltimore to tramp through the
ruins. When Americans had the chance to see a spectacular disaster with
their own eyes, they did.

Most of the visitors headed for the reservoir, where they climbed down
into the chasm to walk along the gap at the base of the dam. Souvenir seekers snipped the tail and mane of Cheney's horse away inch by inch and
absconded with the Cheney children's puppies and kittens. With one kitten
left, ten-year-old Jane Cheney held tightly to it, but her eight-year-old brother Charles sold it for a dollar to a persistent buyer. Souvenir hunters probably also plucked chunks of stone from the dam wall or clods of earth from
the embankment, compromising evidence of the dam's construction before
engineers could examine the ruins.

Many sought family members. When Mrs. Orson Torrey of Chesterfield
heard of the disaster at five o'clock Sunday morning, she immediately set
out to locate her two daughters, Ida and Rose, who worked in the Leeds silk
mill. Mrs. Torrey walked up and down desolated streets, her heart pound-

ing until she found them, alive but with no possessions except the clothing they wore. Her son William Torrey of Haydenville also lost everything but survived.

Amid the throng were newspaper reporters, said to be "thick as berries in season." The Springfield, New York, and Boston newspapers had reporters and sketch artists in the valley by Sunday morning. Members of the New York press hired their own railroad car from Springfield. Milton Bradley went up from New York to sketch for *Frank Leslie's Illustrated Newspaper*, and other artists came from *Harper's Weekly* and the *New York Graphic*. Reporters sought out knowledgeable citizens to show them around, like Mary Hill's husband Henry, who spent Sunday morning with one. Most went up to the dam ruins. Americans' appetite for news was fed by the telegraph, which sped news around the country. Then, steam presses churned out so many papers so quickly that each cost only one or two cents. The Civil War had made the reporter a full-time professional, with deadlines and career ambitions. In the postwar years, news was a habit and Americans wanted on-the-spot telegraphic coverage of major events, like the Mill River disaster.

Through the Associated Press wire service, the Mill River disaster story appeared in newspapers all over the country at the same time it appeared locally. Sunday's edition of the *Daily Rocky Mountain News* from Denver and the *San Francisco Chronicle* headlined the story. The *Daily Picayune* from New Orleans on May 17 exclaimed "Floods in Massachusetts: Ghastly Spectacles, Whole Blocks of Houses Swept Away." *The Atlanta Constitution* led with the story on Sunday's front page: "Destructive Flood in Massachusetts: Over One hundred Lives Lost." On Monday *The Times* of London offered a dozen lines entitled "An American Disaster." On Tuesday, the *St. Louis Post-Dispatch* told locals where to send their cash or checks to relieve the sufferers.

While the press coverage attracted sightseers as well as an outpouring of charity, it also enticed pickpockets and scavengers who snatched souvenirs like a bobbin of silk, a brass water cock, a string of buttons, or a watch from a factory girl's trunk. When one woman who had lost everything spied her sewing machine among the ruins and was about to recover it, a man stepped out of a nearby carriage to take it. She stepped up to claim it and identified it by its number; he insisted that he didn't care whether it had been hers or not, now he should have it. He put it in his carriage and drove away. Looting became so pervasive that by Monday morning, special police were sent up from Springfield equipped with clubs and belts.

At three o'clock on Sunday afternoon, Mary Hill and other Williamsburg residents—some with no black to wear—crowded the Congregational Church yard for the first of a long string of funerals. She waited as men carried nine coffins out of the town hall, loaded them into hearses and wagons, and drove them up Main Street, across the West Branch to the church yard. Mary knew most, if not all, of the dead. Theodore Hitchcock, a miller, age thirty-four, was the husband of her dear friend whom she had comforted the previous night. William H. Adams, fifty-one, was Hitchcock's uncle and coworker at the mill. Emma Wood, twenty-one, was a friend who had visited Mary three days earlier with her baby Harold, age one, who had escaped the mothers' watch and climbed into the potato basket. Epaphro Hubbard, fifty-six, was Emma's father, a farmer whom Mary had known her whole life. Mrs. Electa Knight, age eighty, was an aunt of Mary's husband. Through church or town affairs, Mary probably knew the others—Mary Adams, thirty-six, and her son, William, age seven, who had lived near the woolen mill, and Eveline Sherwood, eighteen, who died in Leeds.

Three local ministers presided from the church steps. After prayers by Reverend Juchan of Goshen, who had been aiding survivors, and by Reverend Thorndike of the Williamsburg Methodist Church, Reverend John Gleason, the minister of the Congregational Church, spoke at length. He likened those present to the friends of Job who mourned with him after he lost his family, flocks, and riches. He reminded the mourners that the coffins present represented only a small part of the whole and warned them that now they were stunned, but that sorrow would grow as excitement wore off. He held up a Bible that contained the record of births and deaths of a family of which only the father was left.

A generation or two earlier, the ministers would have interpreted the flood as evidence of God's dissatisfaction with man's works. As late as 1860, after the Pemberton woolen mill in Lawrence, Massachusetts, collapsed, ministers saw God's hand in the deed and man's sinfulness as the provocation. But by 1874, Calvinistic Orthodoxy was waning and the ministers did not blame God but instead offered more practical and sympathetic messages to the sufferers. In sermons preached a week after the flood, many would condemn the mill owners.

Mary followed the cortege up Village Hill Road to the cemetery. In the coming week, mourners would climb Village Hill many more times. The next morning Reverend Gleason accompanied railroad conductor Edgar Chandler to Albany with the bodies of Chandler's wife, Caroline, and their

Views of the Flood in Mill River Valley.

Knowlton Brothers, Northampton, Mass.

View at Haydenville. (Descriptive List on the other side.)

View at Haydenville before the flood. Squeezed onto a narrow valley between two hills, the village's 100 buildings were clustered so closely along the Mill River that they blocked it in this picture. The Haydenville Church's steeple is at the left. A popular form of entertainment at the time, stereophotographs — two nearly identical images taken with a special camera — appeared three dimensional when viewed through a stereoscope. This "before" scene was one of more than 400 stereophotographs of the Mill River disaster that were marketed throughout America.

Joel Hayden Sr. (1798–1873). A brass manufacturer in Haydenville, he selected the location for the Williamsburg reservoir dam and later became president of the Williamsburg Reservoir Company. On rainy nights he often traveled up into the hills to the reservoir to make sure the dam was holding. He died six months before the flood.

Joel Hayden Jr. (1835–1918). At age twenty-two, he entered business with his father, Joel Hayden Sr., as one of the directors of the cotton sheeting factory in Haydenville. In 1861, his father took him into partnership in the brass works. After the flood, he repaired the cotton factory and rebuilt the brass works.

Isabell Hayden (1848–1917), left, and Joseph Lewis Hayden Jr. ("Robbie") (1869–1874), right. When Isabell Hayden, whose husband was a nephew of Joel Hayden Sr., heard Skinner's silk mill factory bell ring, she looked out and saw the flood wave charging toward her riverside home. While her father grabbed her five-year-old son, Robbie, in his arms and ran up a ladder leaning against a shed behind the house, Isabell sprinted up a hill behind the house. She called to her father to follow, but it was too late. She watched the water sweep them both downstream to their deaths.

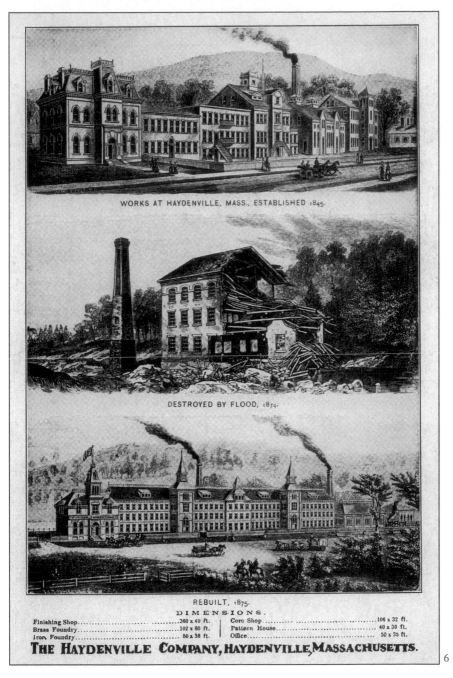

WORKS AT HAYDENVILLE, MASS., ESTABLISHED 1845.

DESTROYED BY FLOOD, 1874.

REBUILT, 1875.

DIMENSIONS.

Finishing Shop	360 x 40 ft.	Core Shop	106 x 32 ft.
Brass Foundry	102 x 80 ft.	Pattern House	40 x 30 ft.
Iron Foundry	50 x 38 ft.	Office	50 x 35 ft.

THE HAYDENVILLE COMPANY, HAYDENVILLE, MASSACHUSETTS.

6

Haydenville brass works advertisement. In the top image, the building at the far left is the Hayden, Gere & Co. office building, completed 1871, which contained the Haydenville Savings Bank and Masonic Hall. The river ran behind the row of buildings. The middle image shows all that was left after the flood: a forty-foot section of the brick upper shop, seen at the right of the top image. The bottom image is an artist's sketch of the new brass works; it was rebuilt without the turrets. The brass works were located directly across the street from Joel Hayden Sr.'s house.

William Skinner and Family, 1884. First row, seated from left to right, Ruth Isabel ("Belle"), Elizabeth ("Libby"), William Skinner, Katherine ("Kitty"), and Joseph ("Joe"). Second row, standing from left to right, Nancy ("Nina"), Mrs. William (Sarah Allen) Skinner, William Cobbett Skinner ("Will"), and Eleanor ("Nellie"). After the flood, Skinner abandoned Skinnerville and rebuilt his silk mill in Holyoke, Massachusetts, where it became the largest silk mill under one roof in the world. His sons William and Joseph joined the business.

View of the devastation at Skinnerville, looking southeast. William Skinner's house is at the center. Skinner's Unquomonk Silk Mills was located in front of his house between the river and the road. The white house to the right of Skinner's, tipped over by the flood, belonged to brass finisher John Coogan. Behind it are the partially wrecked houses of Thaddeus Bartlett and Sarah Wrisley.

Stockholders of the Nonotuck Silk Company in the late 1860s. Alfred T. Lilly, treasurer, and Samuel L. Hill, president, are first and second from the left in the front row. Lucius Dimock, superintendent of the Leeds mill, is on the far right in the back row. Lilly, Hill, and Dimock were members of the Williamsburg Reservoir Company, and Dimock was one of three members of the original dam building committee.

Men searching for bodies on Florence Meadows. On Leeds and Florence meadows, the flood wave fanned out and slowed, dropping a six-foot-high carpet of debris with dozens of bodies hidden inside. After the flood, a thousand or more volunteers culled through acres of flood debris to locate bodies of the victims.

11

Mill River Button Company before the flood. The first ivory nut button shop in the country, the Mill River Button Company turned out 216,000 buttons each day from the kernel of a palm nut. Fred Howard worked on the second floor of the wooden mill (the white building at far left) where workers sorted and packed the buttons. The flood killed several of the workers posing here in 1872.

12

Mill River Button Company after the flood. All that remains of the button mill is the smokestack from the boilers (not visible in the photo above) and the fly wheel from the steam engine, which supplemented the river's power. In the background at the right is a stairway leading half-way up the hill to the railroad track where Fred Howard and others pulled coworkers to safety and from where they watched the destruction of Leeds. This photograph was taken from nearly the same location as the photo above.

Collins Graves (1840–1910). The milkman who was lauded as a hero for racing down the river in his light wagon (milk cans in the front) to warn Skinnerville and Haydenville factory workers of the flood. He is shown near his home.

George Cheney (1844–1918). When he saw the first break in the dam, George Cheney raced his horse bareback, as he is shown here, three miles to Williamsburg village to alert Onslow Spelman, one of the shareholders in the Williamsburg Reservoir Company. Cheney had warned the reservoir company of leaks in the dam.

15

Ruined west wall of the Williamsburg dam with men standing in the riverbed. The masonry core wall that formed the center of the dam was supported by earthen embankments, most of which were washed away, exposing the stone wall. Gatekeeper George Cheney's cabin, which he shared with eight other family members, sat at the edge of the dam. From the back porch, visible here, Cheney's wife, Elizabeth, watched the east side of the embankment break and 600 million gallons of water pour through the gap, which enlarged to 250 feet. The wasteway ran past the cabin's front porch.

16

Gap in the Williamsburg dam. This photo, taken from the west side of the dam, overlooks the top of the ruins of the west wall (seen in the photo above) and across the gap to the east side of the dam where all that remained was a fifty-foot section of the core masonry wall. The man at the bottom of the gap stands on the stone wall that surrounded the gate pipe, which regulated the flow of water from the reservoir into the river and down to the mills. The dam, which was nearly 600 feet long and 43 feet high, spanned pasture-covered hills.

eight-year-old daughter Mary, who had died in their Williamsburg home. Gleason returned to a house full of needy people cared for by his wife. Nearly forty of the dead had regularly attended his church.

Meanwhile, Irish and French Canadian Catholics interred their dead in the Catholic cemetery in Northampton but no reporters covered their services or burials. Instead they reported on the services of the Birmingham and Johnson families and the young Mrs. Kingsley and her children, which took place in Protestant churches.

Down in Leeds, Fred Howard helped bury friends Carrie Bonney and Annie Cogan. He wrote to his brother:

> I went over [to Warner's] very early Sunday and worked till noon sorting out second hand clothing, identifying bodies & etc when I was bearer at the funerals of Annie [Cogan] & Carrie [Bonney]. We loaded them both into an express wagon, buried Carrie at Florence and went on to Northampton with Annie whom we placed in the tomb to remain till we found [her sister] Gracie & her Mother. I rode to Florence with Mr. Cobb and to No'hampton with Fred Warner (the one that was to marry Gracie) and Hannie Cogan. We heard in Florence that Gracie had been found and on the way out got a coffin for her but found it was a mistake. She was not found till Wednesday and I hear that Mrs. Cogan was found yesterday in Northampton.

Survivors maintained as many burial customs as they could, ensuring that each body was dressed, or shrouded, in what was called a winding cloth (to save clothing for the living), placed in a coffin, and buried with a short graveside service by a minister. Sometimes there were only one or two mourners because friends and neighbors were dead, busy, or had already grieved more than they could bear.

On Sunday night, as Mary Hill reviewed her day, she mourned the loss of her friend Caroline Roberts.

> Arose at seven or after—Done chores in morn—Henry [husband] went out with a Reporter in a.m. Mother came down about noon. Clarke Sampson called—I went over to the funeral services in p.m. Remarks made by Rev. Gleason there . . . Prayer by Mr. Juchan—sad, sad. Poor Mrs. Roberts—I loved her—but I hope she is in a better world than this— They buried nine of the bodies—I went up to the cemetery. Came home

and got supper. Had ham potatoes etc. I can eat but little. Called down
to Father Hills [father-in-law]—Retired as the day before—

Three days earlier, when Mary and Caroline Roberts saw each other at the
store, it had been a welcome surprise. Now Caroline, her husband Alexander, and their two daughters Nettie, age three, and Olivet, age one (the same
age as Mary's own daughter Myra), were dead. The Robertses' son George—
who had saved himself by climbing the riverbank escorted by a cow—was the
only member of his family alive. Caroline's body wouldn't be found until
Monday, and Alexander's and Nettie's bodies wouldn't be found until Tuesday. Mary's other friend, Mrs. Hitchcock, whose husband had been killed,
would leave in four days to return to her family in Rhode Island.

Earlier that day, local leaders began asking directly for money. A committee
of women sat outside a Williamsburg store to receive subscriptions from the
crowds of strangers, while Reverend Kimball stood outside the Haydenville
Church with a contribution box. Albert Smith, Northampton's town clerk,
telegraphed former Williamsburg resident George K. Snow of Watertown,
Massachusetts.

> May 17, 1874
> To George K. Snow:
> Matters grow worse. Anything gladly received, particularly money, blan-
> kets and children's clothing. Bodies being found all the time; probably
> 150 lives lost. Can we draw on you for money?
> > E. A. [sic] Smith, Town Clerk

Snow sent the sixty-dollar balance of Watertown's Chicago Fire Relief fund,
accumulated three years earlier to aid the victims of that disaster. The
Springfield Republican observed that "no disaster since the Chicago fire, at
least, has so reached people's hearts and opened people's pockets."
Snow's brother, a resident of New York, also begged for help:

> To the Editor of the Tribune:
> Sir: Please urge the people to open a subscription for the Williamsburg,
> Mass., sufferers. I am going up to-night to do what I can for them. It is my
> native town, and my mother and family are swept away. I shall stay to dis-
> tribute funds among the most needy. Collect and send me all you can.

Telegraph me what you can send, and how. Direct to me at Williamsburg, Mass., or at Northampton, care of W. F. Arnold. For God's sake, help the suffering. Hundreds are without food or house. Yours for humanity.

J. P. Snow

No. 648 Broadway, New York

By the end of Sunday, fifteen Springfield churches had pledged a total of $4,000. Some of the churches appointed committees to oversee the disbursement of their donations. Every town nearby—Springfield, Easthampton, Amherst, and Westfield among them—organized a relief committee, often separate from the committees established by churches, whose purpose was to gather local money and ensure that it was put to the best use by visiting the disaster site to determine that the need was real and that aid was distributed wisely.

Donations were sent to one of several temporary relief committees, one each for the districts of Williamsburg, Haydenville, Leeds, and Florence. Buoyed by a spirit of valley loyalty and optimism, the village committees had organized themselves to bury their dead and clean up, and they had worked together to petition for state aid. But after two days their hopefulness faded as the extent of the damage and suffering and the need for charity proved overwhelming. At some point on Sunday, as it became clear that they needed better inter-village organization and more funds, there was a cry to organize a permanent relief committee that could direct the effort for the entire valley. The Northampton Temporary Relief Committee called a meeting of the village committees to be held the following evening, on Monday, at the Northampton town hall.

On Monday, despite a cold drizzle and the mud it made, a crowd of spectators as large as the day before flocked to the valley, among them the students of Amherst College, whose president had granted them permission to come. The morning train from Springfield to Northampton departed with seats and aisles jammed with sad, impatient people, many of whom had come long distances. One woman, who had borrowed a newspaper from a gentleman standing nearby, agonized over each name she recognized. One man headed to see if his parents had survived learned from the paper that his mother, grandmother, and several brothers and sisters were among the missing or dead. Another young man carried a robe and had stored a casket for his sister, his only relative in this country, who had worked in the Leeds silk mill and was killed when the bridge went down as she was crossing to safety. According to the *Boston Morning Journal*, "The whole train of seventeen passenger cars bore the aspect of an immense funeral cortege, while the baggage and express cars contained caskets which could not be provided in Northampton."

When they arrived in the valley, they heard, from morning to night, the tolling of funeral bells, first at one church, then another, and another, and beginning again with the first church in a continuous round of mourning. To hear the bells was to feel part of each funeral.

In between the passing of funeral corteges, volunteers continued to search. On Monday, two hundred men from Northampton and Hadley were at the Northampton depot at seven o'clock. The first train from the north brought 253 volunteers from Greenfield, Deerfield, South Deerfield, Montague, and Colrain, in Franklin County. Every man carried a hoe, ax, crowbar, or saw. When they arrived at the Northampton station, each town's men organized in lines and boarded another train to take them to Florence. Next the train from the south arrived, bringing fifty men from Holyoke.

Monday's searchers concentrated on huge piles that were beginning to emit strong odors, from human and animal bodies. In the cove below the Williamsburg depot where Joe Wright's Brook entered the river, they found Mary Hill's friend Caroline Roberts and her daughter Nettie and the wife and three children of Dr. Elbridge Johnson. On Quigley's meadow in Leeds, volunteers found Mrs. Edward Hannum of Leeds. The supply of coffins used up, her body was laid in an express wagon side by side with another, concealed with a coverlet. Fair-haired Mary Woodward, age eighteen, the daughter of a former Springfield hotel keeper, was discovered in Leeds about two o'clock. Her name was embroidered on her untorn dress, which covered her unbruised body. On the Florence meadows below Leeds, searchers exhumed four dead. One was Mrs. Robert Fitzgerald, whose legs were severed; one leg had already been buried before anyone knew to whom it belonged.

In Haydenville, someone spotted Rover, the dog that had belonged to Isabell Hayden's father, Eli Bryant. It was sitting on the riverbank a half mile below their farm near where Robbie's body had come to rest. The dog had unearthed Eli's arm, his body still buried. After workers dug it out, they brought the body to the morgue in the Haydenville church. Isabell and her husband Joseph buried Eli and their son Robbie in the Haydenville cemetery.

By Sunday, Springfield had sent up guards as had Northampton because of reports of looting. Hayden claimed he had lost $20,000 because of pilfering in the riverbed just below his mill, which held the richest deposit of

brass goods. By Monday his factory was fully guarded and visitors were prevented from walking the riverbed below his factory and stepping behind
ropes where workers had collected the muddy brass goods.

On Monday afternoon rumors ran wild that the valley was about to be
overrun by hundreds, perhaps thousands, of "roughs"—thieves and drunk-
ards—coming from New York, Boston, and Baltimore. When the trains
arrived, the number of actual roughs dwindled to five, but in the meantime,
the Northampton selectmen appointed thirty special police who went on
duty under Sheriff Henry A. Longley. Fifteen state police from Boston, six
Springfield patrolmen, and members of the Peabody Guard of Springfield,
a division of the Massachusetts Volunteer Militia, arrived to restore public
confidence. At the end of the first week after the flood, Fred Howard wrote
to his brother:

> Telegrams were recd Monday from Baltimore and Boston that hundreds
> of roughs were on the way from both cities to plunder. The Peabody
> Guard of Springfield guarded Northampton Sunday night and we had
> Militia and state constables here nearly all week, but the excitement is
> less now and we begin to realize that the village is a ruin.

In the end, there was no great destruction or theft of property; instead there
was mostly what Colonel Parsons of the Peabody Guard called "relic hunting," people taking small brass castings and other souvenirs.

Survivors who looked through the ruins to recover their goods found
nothing. One man, whose family of seven had survived, laughingly told a
reporter that it didn't take long to collect his things after the flood took his
house. He couldn't find a single item that belonged to him; everything was
swept away. Holding his little boy's hand, "he said they had nothing in the
world except what they had on." The same paper quoted an unnamed
Irishman at Leeds who had lost everything but had been given dry clothing:
"Me body's me own, but me hat and coat, I don't know whose they be!"

Not waiting for additional police to protect their property, the mill owners tried to capture the bolts and skeins of wool and silk before thieves could
get to them. William Skinner's son and son-in-law spent two days seeking
silk. They found five bales and other company items. The Northampton
sheriff found Lyman James's wool and Skinner's silk stashed in several
homes and returned the booty to the mill owners. The industrialists repeatedly placed advertisements in the local newspapers claiming their goods
and requesting their return at the mill owner's expense.

Saturday and Sunday nights, survivors turned to family, friends, and neighbors who lived far from the river to take them in. Ten-year-old George Roberts stayed with Miss Nash, his Sunday school teacher. One homeowner put up a French Canadian family with ten children in a single spare room. William Skinner shared his large and relatively undamaged house with Jerome Hillman and Hillman's seven-year-old daughter, Clara; wife Sarah Hillman had been killed in the flood. Fifteen men had made Skinner's house habitable by shoveling four inches of mud out of the first floor on the afternoon of the first day. But after several days, accommodating neighbors began to "feel the added presence," as the *Springfield Republican* politely stated it, of their unanticipated guests, and there was a clamor to establish temporary housing.

But the stay was short, and not much temporary housing was used. Young women and men who lived in factory boardinghouses and who could return to their parents' farms or homes did so, and one by one, families moved back into their repaired homes or into other lodgings. Less than a week after the flood, volunteer workers had righted and cleaned damaged homes, readying them for at least temporary occupancy. Two days later, ten families in Williamsburg and five each in Haydenville and Leeds moved into dwellings with "sparse outfits" courtesy of the relief committees. The next day, a barn in Haydenville was converted into a six-tenement dwelling for brass workers. Acting Governor Talbot secured eighteen large tents through the federal arsenal to house twenty to fifty homeless persons. Erected about a week after the flood, the tents were used to accommodate searchers who stayed on for more than a day, as well as the men employed by the James woolen mill.

By Monday afternoon, two days after the flood, people in the valley had in their hands copies of that morning's *Springfield Republican*. Three full pages of the eight-page newspaper were devoted to the flood—the story of Cheney and the dam break; the damage caused as water cascaded over each village; the heroic rides of Cheney, Graves, and Day; miraculous escapes and tragic incidents; descriptions of the wayside morgues and funerals; and lists of the dead. Vivid prose painted the picture of desolation. Monday's edition sold 21,500 copies, about twice the usual number. Publishers estimated they could have sold seven thousand to ten thousand more copies if enough had been printed.

The *Republican* put the flood in context. In 1874 the Mill River flood was the most deadly dam failure on record in the United States. While there had been thousands of floods caused by rivers and creeks overflowing their banks in heavy rains, comparatively few had been caused by reservoir dam failure, and none as deadly or causing as much property damage as this. Survivors would have remembered at least four reservoir dam failures in the previous thirty-five years within one hundred miles. In 1871, in a great fall freshet, the reservoir between Conway and Ashfield, Massachusetts, broke, causing $15,000 worth of damage to the town in roads and bridges and more to individuals, but no one died. In the 1860s, in North Bennington, Vermont, a dam that carried a railroad across a ravine overtopped in the middle of the night when the small culvert used as a spillway overflowed, destroying a few houses and killing several people. In May 1850, in Ashburnham, Massachusetts, a 150-acre reservoir, swollen by a heavy rain, broke through the dam and ran down the valley, taking out the mill dam at the Naukeag cotton factory. Water rose five feet up the factory walls so suddenly that the women who worked inside had to be rescued by temporary bridges leaned against factory windows. A section of the Vermont and Massachusetts Railroad and every dam and bridge on the stream was swept away, for a loss of $200,000.

The Mill River flood was especially unsettling because, unlike other New England floods, where the dams had broken from the top during a heavy rain and then crumbled, the Williamsburg dam had burst open at the bottom. If it had concealed a fatal flaw that caused it to collapse under normal conditions, then all dams were suspect. If such a powerful flood could roll down the Mill Valley, then it could happen elsewhere.

While no floods the size of the Mill River disaster had ever occurred before in the United States, one had in Sheffield, England, ten years earlier. Built in 1854, the Dale Dyke dam, which formed a reservoir that supplied Sheffield with water, was 95 feet tall and 1,250 feet long with a core of puddled clay. At 11:30 P.M. on the evening of March 11, 1864, the dam broke, sending 200 million gallons of water roaring down the narrow valley, killing 250 people and destroying factories and homes. The investigation found that the dam's embankment, core wall, and gate pipe had been inadequately constructed. Newspapers were quick to highlight the parallels between the Sheffield disaster and the Mill River flood by reprinting pieces of Charles Reade's popular novel, *Put Yourself in His Place*, which was, in part, a fictional account of the Sheffield disaster.

The *Springfield Republican* took up the question of responsibility. It investigated the history of the Williamsburg dam and published four short articles at the end of its coverage, entitled "The Reservoir," "The History of the Reservoir," "Previous Opinions of the Reservoir," and "The Cause of the Catastrophe." The paper named the dam's builders and compared the written specifications for the structure with the measurements a reporter took at the dam ruins. Cheney told the paper about the leaks he had seen and feared, while Lewis Bodman was quoted as saying that in the matter of construction "the work as a whole was not satisfactory" and that the "proprietors were not satisfied with the reservoir when it was built and felt that it was not safe," although they became better, but not wholly, satisfied as the years progressed. One of the *Republican* reporters interviewed Albert Dwight Briggs, the Springfield civil engineer whose bid to construct the dam had been rejected by the reservoir company. He was a friend of Joel Hayden Sr. "Indeed the more intelligent people down the valley, Mr. Briggs says, have lived with the shadow of this disaster haunting them for years. Governor Hayden himself was particularly nervous about it, and any casual conversation concerning the reservoir was nearly always accompanied with some allusion of presentiment." Friends knew the dam was a matter of concern to Hayden.

Editor Samuel Bowles editorialized that it appeared that "serious doubts as to the safety of the reservoir have been entertained ever since it was built." He wrote that

> the responsibility probably rests upon a large circle of proprietors, engineers, builders, and county officials. But that there was sham work, there can be no doubt, — sham that was put into the dam either ignorantly or indifferently, and that was permitted to stay there because the inspectors didn't know sham when they saw it or didn't care to see it.

Of the mill owners he wrote, "They built the reservoir and they knew it was weak. . . . The manufacturers simply gambled with a fearful risk and lost." Without naming the mill owners or attacking them personally, Bowles spotlighted their negligence.

In 1874, the *Springfield Republican* had earned a national reputation as the nation's best daily newspaper published outside of a major metropolitan area. Its editor Samuel Bowles was considered second only to the *New York Tribune*'s Horace Greeley in political influence and notoriety. A champion of the free press and dedicated to exposing political corruption, Bowles was known for holding strong opinions and for printing them, no matter whose reputation he hurt. His opinions on the Mill River flood followed in this tradition.

The *Boston Daily Advertiser* offered a similar opinion: "It is said, with how much truth it is too early yet to judge, that the weakness of this reservoir was known, implying that to those who owned the structure and were responsible for its safety, the awful event that has occurred could not have been wholly unexpected . . . If these are not false charges, brought in the haste and excitement of the moment by those who desire to hold somebody to an account for the disaster, an awful responsibility rests upon those who were aware of the danger, and took no effectual means to avert it." The *Worcester Spy* was sharper: "There can be no doubt that this terrible catastrophe, the most fearful in the annals of Massachusetts, was caused or made possible by gross negligence."

The press didn't stop at condemning the dam owners and builders; they bored into the American character to find the true cause of the failure—the disease of sham—which linked the Mill River flood to such other man-made catastrophes as railway wrecks, boiler explosions, and bridge collapses. The flood was an example of just "one case out of hundreds of thousands" of the "rascality, carelessness, egotism and general dishonesty" that had been gradually ruining "political and civil order ever since the close of the great civil war," exhorted the *Springfield Republican*. The paper continued: "It is time there is a general revolt against costly and cruel shoddyism which is sapping the prosperity and eating out the morality of the land." The paper advised its readers that sham was not only morally wrong but was also the "poorest of all possible business investments." It concluded, "If this Mill river homicide sets the American public thinking on the subject, the dead will not have died in vain."

Like the *Springfield Republican*, the *New York Tribune* viewed the Mill River flood as an example of greed spun so far out of control that Americans readily took great risks for themselves and others. The *Tribune* moralized:

> We drive our railway trains over rotten rails and decayed bridges. We build houses that can only stand by leaning against one another. We go to sea in crazy ships. We sit over cracked boilers. We lack the patience to make life safe or properly secure. We are all in a hurry to get on, to win or to spend. Our feverish haste takes no thought of risk, or counts it only as the great stake that is played for a great gain.

On Monday evening, county men—who would have read or heard about the searing newspaper commentary—packed the Northampton town hall for a citizens' meeting called by Haynes K. Starkweather, head of the Temporary Relief Committee and chairman of the Northampton Board of Selectmen. Starkweather, well known to everyone in the room as an affable and courteous man and a druggist and grocer by profession, had been a selectman for fifteen years and had represented the district in the Massachusetts Legislature six years earlier. Before him sat shopkeepers, farmers, carriage makers, mechanics, lawyers, politicians, manufacturers, and bankers. People whose houses had been swept away shared the same room with proprietors of the reservoir company. Henry A. Longley, the county sheriff, presided. Reporters from the Springfield, New York, and Boston newspapers jotted notes and later described a contentious but orderly meeting.

Starkweather stated the valley's problem: as soon as the disaster occurred, telegrams poured in from various towns and cities offering monetary aid, but only $886 in relief money was in hand. Potential contributors had offered cash, goods, and labor, but insisted they would not follow through with their donation until they could be assured that it would be handled by properly organized committees of honorable men. Luther Bodman, Northampton banker and brother of former Williamsburg woolen mill owner Lewis Bodman, added that outsiders understood that it was not enough to feed and clothe people for a few days; they needed enough to rebuild homes, buy tools, and start again on a secure basis. To that end, the valley needed a permanent relief committee, a "committee of sufficient force and prestige to command public confidence and take the entire charge of the work," according to the *Springfield Republican*. Outsiders who wanted to give money needed the relief effort to speak with a single authoritative voice, not the individual voices of a handful of destroyed villages.

Once a valley-wide committee was mentioned, someone suggested Sheriff Longley appoint five men to serve as a nominating committee that would in turn name twelve men to a permanent relief committee. Village men immediately protested as long-held tensions between the villages and Northampton surfaced. From past experience, villagers knew that a committee chosen in this manner would be comprised of Northampton bankers and manufacturers who would promote their own interests at the expense of the villages'. There was a long discussion about the propriety of letting Northampton actively manage the funds and other aid to the sufferers in the villages. The *New York Times* reporter sensed "a jealous fear among the village representatives that Northampton should become too prominent. Williamsburg, Haydenville, and Leeds wanted to look after their own people." The reporter got it right. The villages wanted to serve their people independent of Northampton.

A villager named Ward made an alternate proposal: The general committee should be composed of one man from each village and one from Northampton. He was countered by Charles Delano, a lawyer and former U.S. congressman who would become the assistant coroner at the inquest into the flood. Delano thought there should be a committee composed of men of means, business, and leisure, large enough so that it could be divided into subcommittees on finance, labor, and supplies. Before the villages' disgruntlement could erupt into full-blown conflict, Delano's motion was voted on. It carried. The conflict was short-lived as villagers put up little fuss and quickly stepped aside, as they were accustomed to doing. The old power structure easily reemerged.

Sheriff Longley appointed a nominating committee of five men, who left the room. While they were gone, the villages reported on the plight of the people. General John Otis reported that 250 Leeds citizens were destitute, including thirty-six families, while contributions to their local relief fund totaled merely $300. Twenty of the fifty-one presumed dead from Leeds were missing. In Williamsburg and Skinnerville, sixteen of sixty-four presumed dead were not yet found. Aaron Morse of Haydenville stated that ten of their thirty-five lost were missing. He predicted that after the immediate crisis was over, the inhabitants of Haydenville would still need relief. Joel Hayden Jr. bristled at the idea of his villagers as paupers and announced that the immediate needs of all citizens would be relieved by Hayden, Gere & Co. whether or not they were his employees.

When the nominating committee returned, it was as the villagers had predicted. Almost exclusively, the committee had named Northampton manufacturers, bankers, and political figures to the permanent relief committee. Among the members were Haynes Starkweather, chairman of the Northampton Board of Selectmen; General John Otis of Emery Wheel Company and an investor in the Florence Sewing Machine Company; N. B. Hussey, manufacturer of furnaces and steam heaters and investor in Northampton Institute for Savings; J. C. Arms of Hampshire County National Bank; Oliver Edwards of Hampshire Savings Bank; and E. P. Copeland of the Florence Sewing Machine Company. Family members and business associates of the reservoir company were also among the twelve; these included Luther Bodman, president of Hampshire Savings Bank and brother of Lewis Bodman; S. W. Lee Jr., investor in Nonotuck Silk Mills and son-in-law of Lucius Dimock; and Daniel W. Bond, the reservoir company's attorney. Other members of the permanent relief committee included George H. Ray (a representative of the American Express Company), A. J. Lincoln, and Silas M. Smith. Albert E. Smith, Northampton's town clerk, was chosen secretary, and W. P. Abernathy was appointed to receive and take charge of supplies. A new supply headquarters was to be established at the Northampton town hall, where all donated provisions, clothing, and housewares would be sorted and stored. In the future, village committees would be required to make a request for specific goods. The general storehouse would fill their order, and ship it to the local committee, which would distribute it to the local needy. This was the kind of cumbersome bureaucracy that the villagers were trying to avoid.

Members of the reservoir company were reserved for the most powerful committee, finance. Joel Hayden Jr., William Skinner, and Lewis Bodman were placed in charge of the relief effort's finances. They were joined by John Otis, who assumed the chairmanship, and Luther Bodman, who served as the treasurer. This committee of five could exert its authority by refusing to pay bills for extravagant and unnecessary expenditures that the relief committee sent forward for payment; they thereby had the final word on the valley's relief effort.

Despite what the newspapers wrote about the mill owners' culpability, the citizens of Northampton and Williamsburg gave them a vote of confidence for their abilities to attract money and get things done, as well as their sense of civic duty. Their names and reputations were still good currency, and they were still linked with the promise of a bright future for the Mill Valley. Over the next few months, the Mill River manufacturers would use the finance committee to lay the groundwork for the revival and improvement of industry and the perpetuation of their own financial interests.

As the meeting concluded, Starkweather announced that he had collected six hundred dollars for the relief effort from those in attendance, and that he had received a telegram stating that the Massachusetts Legislature had responded to their petition for aid received that day by appointing a joint legislative committee of eight representatives and three senators. They were already on the train to Springfield, and would arrive in the valley first thing in the morning. The meeting adjourned. As residents of Leeds, Haydenville, and Williamsburg returned home, they found their villages patrolled by guards.

Onslow Spelman was likely not at the meeting and may have spent the night in hiding. It was rumored that a crowd of thirty Irishmen had hatched a plot to harm him and to damage his home, but that the plot had failed when someone tipped Spelman off, and he and his family hid for the evening. While the rumor of the planned attack was later retracted, the ill feeling against Spelman persisted. The next day's *Hampshire Gazette* reported that "the popular feeling against him grows very bitter, and people loudly condemn his not having heeded the repeated warnings of Cheney. Some go the length of charging him openly with being responsible for the loss of life."

If Mary Hill, who lived a few blocks from Spelman, heard the outcome of the Northampton meeting, she didn't record her reaction in her diary. Instead, she concluded Monday night's entry by describing her dreamlike state:

> Arose at seven or after. Done chores in morn. Mother came down in a.m. and washed and hung out part of clothes or most of them. Henry didn't come to dinner until two, tho Mother, Myra and I had eaten. Done up work. Don't feel as if I could do anything—Everything seems like a dream & I have no ambition to work.

CHAPTER 5

REBUILDING

A T nine o'clock on the morning of the fourth day, under fair skies, the Massachusetts Legislature's special committee—composed of three state senators and eight representatives—arrived at the Northampton depot for a tour of the disaster-stricken region. The lawmakers' purpose was to gather firsthand information on the causes and effects of the flood to determine the state's response to the sufferers' petition for aid. Senator Edson of Hampshire County, where the flood took place, chaired the legislative committee. He was joined by Senators Nye of the Island District and Wardell of Essex County, which encompassed the industrial city of Lawrence on the powerful Merrimack River. Five of the representatives were also from industrial areas: Sprague of Framingham; Robinson of Chicopee; Blunt of Haverhill; Bosworth of Taunton; and Howes of Reading. Three others were from small towns that mixed farming and manufacturing: Billings of Hatfield; Jenkins of Abington; and Jones of Spencer. The final representative was Henry Wilson of Boston, a well-respected engineer.

At the depot, the committee of lawmakers was greeted by Haynes Starkweather, chairman of the Northampton Board of Selectmen, and several other local officials, who led them to waiting carriages. Accompanying the group were Joel Bassett and Emory Wells, the contractors who had built the dam. Riding through Northampton's Main Street on their way to the village of Florence, the committee was immediately struck by the effects of the disaster. Northampton's center more closely resembled the "head-quarters of some non-descript army," as one *Springfield Republican* reporter labeled it, than the commercial center it was. Off-duty guards and police meandered around town, while clusters of men carrying picks and shovels paraded by on their way to the upper valley to join the search for the dead.

Wagons laden with food and supplies rumbled toward the town hall, the new central relief depot, where volunteers unloaded them and organized the goods, which they repacked for distribution to the villages. Inside, W. P. Abernathy, placed in charge of supplies the night before, set up his headquarters in the lower level. In one room, fifteen men and women fashioned a storehouse where they unpacked and organized shipments of clothing and food, including five horse-drawn wagons full of vegetables and cooked food from North Hadley, South Hadley, Amherst, and the South Hadley Female Seminary (later Mount Holyoke College). They took in forty bushels of potatoes from a Hadley farmer, twenty-five pounds of butter from four Deerfield families, and five hundred pounds of cooked ham from a Boston businessman. The committee's new procedure permitted messengers to visit each of the village relief headquarters daily and return with a written request for each village's needs. After women gathered the specified supplies, men transported them by train or wagon to the villages. For Leeds alone, they sent food for 250 people.

The carriages containing the committee and those who accompanied them rolled on to Florence, stopping above the village at the wide, flat Florence meadows, which spread out for several hundred acres on both sides of the river. A carpet of debris, waist- to shoulder-high, fanned out before them, so expansive that it looked almost purposeful, as though farmers had cultivated a bumper crop of flotsam instead of hay. One reporter estimated that if piled together, the rubbish would cover five acres at a depth of ten feet. Days earlier this stretch had been the most valuable farmland in the valley, costing $200 to $300 per acre; now skinned of its fertile topsoil and carpeted with timbers, boulders, and sand, the farmland was worthless. On the opposite side of the river, a one-acre grove of thick trees lay flat, either sheared off or bent over, all neatly arranged in the downstream direction, like hairs combed smoothly.

The Florence meadows were crawling with six hundred volunteers who had been searching for bodies since sunrise; among the volunteers were farmers, day laborers, mill hands, and a few businessmen from Holyoke and Greenfield as well as local men who had left their jobs for a day or more. Some worked for companies that had donated the labor of their men for a day, like the Belcher and Taylor Agricultural Tool Company and the Lamb Knitting Machine Company of Chicopee Falls. That morning they would find Mary Patrick of Leeds. As the committee watched, workers attacked the largest pile, which covered an acre of John Warner's farm and loomed ten feet high, several feet above the workers' heads. Within the last few days, twelve bodies had been found inside. This day's goal was to dislodge the entire mass systematically in hopes of finding most of the thirty-six bodies still missing. But with so much debris surrounding them, the problem for workers was where to place the material already inspected. Onlookers thought it a hopeless task, but the only choice was to forge ahead. In a week they would give up the search, satisfied that all the piles had been examined.

Nearby, cauldrons of coffee boiled over open fires, tended by neighborhood women who dumped in sacks of sugar and pails of milk. This was all some of the workers would have to eat all day. Bakeries in Northampton had been running night and day but were unable to keep up with the demands from sufferers, laborers, and visitors.

As the committee members' ears filled with the sound of workers' voices above the cracking and clattering of timber, they walked away, toward the edge of the meadow to the makeshift morgue at John Warner's carpenter shop. They arrived in time to see several men carting in two newly recovered bodies and trailed by a small downcast crowd looking for missing relatives. At first, several in the crowd identified one as Mary Hogan from Haydenville, but minutes later others determined correctly that it was Mrs. Spencer Bartlett of Williamsburg. No one could identify the other body.

The committee hiked over the washed-out roads to Leeds because their carriages couldn't pass. Before the day was out, they would walk most of the nine miles to the dam, their destination. Everywhere they went, a moving fringe of spectators circled the destruction, peeking, pointing, and commenting. Locals said the crowd was more orderly and slightly smaller than it had been on previous days. From the railroad track at the bottom of the village, the committee looked out at Leeds which, despite three days of work, appeared the same as when the flood first retreated. Only four habitable houses stood on the main street. The towering accumulation of debris lodged against the stone bridge was, at three stories high, the tallest pile along the course of the river; it was still untouched. Searchers supposed there were bodies trapped inside, but they couldn't untangle the mass until they cleared enough debris to set up tackling gear to extract the trees stretched across the top. The pile would have to wait. When they did finally excavate the pile ten days later, they found mattresses and household furnishings soaked with mud at a depth of twenty-five feet.

Along Main Street in Leeds, the committee wandered for more than an hour. On the site of Warner's button mill, they saw only rubble, a section of a steam engine, and a smoke stack. They saw militia posted around the depot like a picket fence. They listened sympathetically to survivors' stories and their concerns whether they would still have jobs and saw some Leeds industries getting back to work. At the Nonotuck Silk Mill, mechanics repaired machinery and installed steam engines to use until the mill dams were in operation again. At the Emery Wheel Company in Northampton, John Otis's workers had started to dam the Roberts Meadow Brook, a tributary of the Mill River, which ran behind the factory, to power the mill. No one had given up on the Mill River; they used steam or a small brook until they could harness the river again.

Residents of Leeds were anxious about whether George Warner would rebuild his button factory. For several weeks before the flood, he had paid his workers half their wages, promising the rest after he took orders at the spring trade shows he planned to attend in New York. Now there were no wages, Warner hadn't announced whether he would rebuild, and he couldn't take orders without a factory. Warner had lost $59,800 on his brick and wooden factory buildings, machinery, raw and finished stock, and tenement houses. He needed $75,000 to rebuild. But there was hope. The previous day's *Springfield Republican* had reported that Horatio Knight, a wealthy Easthampton button manufacturer and Samuel Williston's partner, had offered Warner $25,000 toward rebuilding. Years earlier, Knight had found Warner a New York market for his ivory buttons. The village waited to hear whether Warner would be able to find the other $50,000.

The committee pressed on to the riverbank at Haydenville, where they observed Joel Hayden Jr. uncharacteristically wearing a dress shirt and no coat, personally directing his employees as they salvaged goods along the dry streambed that ran the length of the village. The day before, workers had plowed a new course for the river so they could mine in the flood's track. On this day, one hundred men, in rolled-up sleeves and brimmed hats, trained their eyes on the ground as they carefully wielded picks and shovels to uncover, but not damage, the treasure hidden in the mud. Women and children followed to extract buried brass goods, much of them still in the original boxes, and the patterns used in manufacturing, which were more valuable than the finished products. They found a cache of plated brass goods, which were to have been shipped on the afternoon of the day of the flood to the Boston Post Office. Over the next few days, they would recover $50,000 in brass goods and $60,000 worth of manufacturing patterns. A cordon of police stationed on the riverbank guarded the excavation site and the booty. Behind them milled a crowd of onlookers. Other workers set up a derrick, which they would use later that day to hoist out of the river two company safes in which they would find the papers soaked but legible. In the vault that had held the safes, the Haydens and two or three other families had stashed silver forks and a prized Paisley shawl; there was little hope of their recovery.

Meanwhile, Hayden's partner, Collins Gere, was in their temporary office in Brewster's home dictating notices to trade publications and letters to customers stating that the firm still had enough goods on hand to fill orders. Business would not be interrupted.

Joel Hayden Jr. was the biggest loser of the flood, with $288,000 washed away from the brass works and an additional $29,500 lost from the cotton, tobacco, and gas factories of the Haydenville Manufacturing Company, of which he was the principal investor. At the time of the flood, Joel Jr. was one of the wealthiest men in western Massachusetts. The 1870 census showed that he possessed real estate worth $140,000 and a personal estate of $50,000. He was also a principal owner of the Stebbins Manufacturing Company of Springfield and the Travelers Brass Company of Chicopee. He had become president of the Haydenville Savings Bank after his father's death.

Hayden and Williamsburg manufacturers Henry James and farmers Hiram and Thomas Nash joined the committee before they proceeded to Skinnerville, where there was little activity. The torrent had rolled over the village so fast that it had deposited little flotsam and no bodies. All that stood in the village were a few twisted houses and Skinner's massive home. One man valiantly wrestled with his upturned house, trying to figure out how to return it to its original site, but he couldn't find its old location. Like many older structures constructed of stocky upright posts pegged to thick horizontal beams, the heavy wood-framed houses had stayed intact. Newer buildings with lighter, nailed wooden frames, like the tenement buildings, and brick structures, like Hayden's and Skinner's factories, had dissolved instantly under the water's force.

Locals knew that it was doubtful that Skinner would rebuild. The channel that had carried water to the mill was washed down to bedrock, making it impossible to reconstruct. All that remained of his factory was a large turbine for waterpower and a bucket someone had dug out of the sand. His tenement houses, worth $45,000, were demolished or beyond repair. In all, Skinner had lost $192,000, making him second to Hayden in the amount of his loss. His factory buildings had been worth $40,000, but at $60,000, his silk stock was worth more. Skinner had sent his son Will and his son-in-law Fred Warner to hunt for bales of raw silk down the valley. Whether he moved or not, he could make use of the raw material.

Skinner joined the group as they pushed on to Williamsburg, where they were met by Lewis Bodman; wool manufacturer Henry James; his brother, storekeeper Lyman James; farmer and former legislator Hiram Nash; and others. Henry James told them that he had asked his employees to remain in the village because he expected work to begin in a few days in his largely undamaged factory. Machinery on upper floors was untouched, and wound bobbins were still in place. James's problem was his power source; the river's course had shifted from the north to the south side of the mill. He planned to install a steam engine until the river's course could be corrected. His losses totaled nearly $50,000, most of it from his waterpower system and the loss of a dozen workers' houses.

The search for the dead continued along the river in Williamsburg; twenty bodies still had not been found. Searchers, who had already worked for four days and nights, foresaw no immediate end. The legislative committee bypassed the morgues where inside toiled many women who were related to the men accompanying the legislators: Mrs. Onslow Spelman, Minnie Bodman, Nellie Nash, Mrs. D. H. Alvord, Jennie White, Ada Evans, Susie Nash, and Mrs. George Smith—all prominent in the community.

As the legislative committee neared the center of Williamsburg village, they relied on their tour guides to tell them what had been there before the flood. Two days earlier, a correspondent for the *New York Tribune* with the pen name of John Paul had stood on the same spot and remarked to a bystander "what a fortunate thing it was that no one had built there." He was told that he was "standing near the junction of two streets," on land once covered by twenty-six houses. John Paul then pointed to "some twisted leaden pipes . . . which at odd intervals protruded from the ground and spouted water into the air in an apparently aimless way" and was informed that these were the remnants of the gravity plumbing system that brought spring water into the kitchens that had stood above them. The committee saw signposts—sticks with boards nailed to them supported by stones— placed around the village by Reverend Gleason. One sign read: "Mill Street, 17 lives [lost], one mill, 5 houses, iron bridge." Another read: "Main Street, 32 persons, 17 houses, lost from this point [south] to James mill." The *Springfield Union* reporter thought the signs looked like crosses erected in some Catholic countries where a murder has been committed, and the pile of stones increased as each passerby cast one. As the committee left the village, members saw the scoured site of Onslow Spelman's small button factory, a loss of $6,000. He would not be able to rebuild in this location because the dam and canal were washed away, and the site was stripped to bedrock, leaving no soil into which a trench or building foundation could be dug.

The committee's ride up to the dam was filled with compassionate talk about the plight of the victims and sympathy for the manufacturers' losses. At about two o'clock when they reached the dam, they quickly descended to the base and stood in the gap. As they gazed at the empty reservoir through the hole, a solemnity fell over the group as though they had entered a tomb, or a cathedral. After a few minutes, they began to walk around, stepping along the base to inspect the wall and embankment. They were shocked by how carelessly the dam had been constructed. Each layer of stones was grouted or mortared less and less securely until the top row seemed more like a row of ill-fitting cobblestones than the flush top of a stone wall. The irregularly shaped boulders at the foundation appeared to have been rolled into place from nearby fields. At least one was significantly smaller than the boulders it supported. The material between the stones crumbled in their hands. Someone mumbled that the dam was "child's play;" another said it was no more than "a boy's dam." Sympathy changed to indignation. The New York Times reporter recorded what happened next.

Little was said until Joel Bassett, the contractor who built the dam, took out a copy of the specifications he had used, and began to read them aloud, pausing now and again to call attention to what he termed "the evidence of their fulfillment," which he felt would lead to the exoneration of himself and those who worked for him. Bassett commented that he had exceeded expectations and that the fault should be placed with the reservoir company's engineer who designed the dam and with the county commissioners who accepted it.

Bassett had nearly finished his impromptu presentation when Henry Wilson, the Boston legislator and civil engineer, interrupted, "This dam was not built according to the specifications of that paper in your hand."

"But, Sir, they are—"

"Excuse me, Sir," replied Wilson, "you are talking now to a man who fully understands this kind of thing, and can see just how it is. Mr. Bassett, we are standing on your own witness, and its testimony condemns you."

Wilson stepped up to the astonished contractor and took the specifications from Bassett's hands. Wilson was a well-known civil engineer who had constructed the Hartford reservoir twenty years earlier. The day before, Wilson had introduced into the Legislature an order to provide for a supervisor of reservoirs, stating that three cases—the papers didn't say what they were—had arisen within a year that demonstrated the need for such a measure. The order was adopted, but later dropped.

Tall, square-shouldered, with a massive head of curly black hair and a heavy moustache and goatee that nearly hid his mouth, Wilson took center stage and compared the dam ruins to the specifications, point by point, speaking decisively and clearly. Wilson showed the committee that the embankment was forty feet narrower than the contract specified. From the banks, which were supposed to have been made of "clean" dirt, free from any organic matter, Wilson pulled at half-rotten tree stumps and decomposing roots; these had left spaces into which water had seeped, saturating and weakening the banks, and causing abundant leaks. Wilson scooped up a handful of earth and showed the group that the high gravel content caused the soil not to clump together, but instead to slip apart like dry sand. He told them that the gravel-laden soil had caused chunks of the bank to slide off. In the stone wall, which was to have been thoroughly grouted, Wilson's hands found cavities where there was none. In other spots, he plucked grout so sandy it crumbled between his fingers.

Then Wilson turned to the foundation of the wall. He pointed out that the specifications required Bassett to lay the wall in a trench at least three feet deep on a base of bedrock or hardpan. The group examined the ground where the boulders, which now dotted the valley, had been. They could see that the wall had not been laid in a trench, but on level ground, sometimes on hardpan, sometimes on gravel. In several places, springs had dug fine channels through gravel under the wall, undermining the dam's foundation. Wilson hypothesized that water moving through such openings broke the dam and wondered aloud why it hadn't happened sooner. Senator Edson, the chairman of the legislative committee, remarked that it looked like the dam had "slid off as though the ground was greased." Wilson asserted that while the specifications were faulty, if they had been carried out the dam would have stood. The constant leaking should have told the reservoir company to take strong remedial measures.

The *New York Times* reporter quoted Wilson's conclusion: "In short, the specifications have been entirely disregarded and the accident which has desolated this once fair valley, was inevitable. The only wonder is that it did not occur before. The terrible neglect and gross ignorance displayed in the construction of the dam was criminal, and its recent evil consequences, murder."

When Wilson was finished, silk manufacturer William Skinner walked up and said to Bassett and his partner Emory Wells, "Look here, if you want to know what I think of you two, I'll tell you that you ought to have a rope around your neck, and something ought to be done with the rope, too." Afterward, Skinner told the *Boston Globe* correspondent: "Mr. Reporter, you may say that William Skinner said just that thing, and that he sticks to it." It was probably one of the few times Skinner had visited the dam in the eight years he had been a member of the reservoir company.

Onslow Spelman was glad Skinner had threatened the contractors for their poor work. The popular perception that Spelman was responsible for deaths in the valley had persisted. At some time during the day, Spelman addressed the legislative committee and swore that he did not detain Cheney. Spelman's friends told reporters that they hoped that Wilson's charges against Bassett and Wells would remove bad feelings about Spelman and stick them on the contractors.

The legislative committee's tour was over. Reporters buttonholed engineer Wilson and the mill owners to capture their reaction to the day's events. Wilson told the *New York Times* reporter that "he could not regard [the flood] as an accident because the dam could not hold any body of water in, as the earth at the bottom under the wall, was slowly but surely being washed away daily." After another examination on his own the next day, he said that "such work is homicide; the dam was a perfect abortion." For the *New York Tribune* correspondent, Lewis Bodman repeated frankly and earnestly his long-held doubts of the dam's strength, confirming the villagers' rumors that from the beginning the dam was not trusted.

Henry S. Gere, editor of the *Hampshire Gazette*, sought out Joel Hayden Jr., whom he knew well. Gere's brother, Collins, had been Joel Hayden Sr.'s and now Joel Hayden Jr.'s partner in the brass works; his other brother, Edward, was in charge of Hayden's New York office. After seeing the ruins, Young Joel told Gere what was on his mind: that his "father was always in fear of this reservoir dam. He believed it to be weak and dangerous, and 'a thousand times,' . . . have I heard him express such fears. It worried him, and when there was a heavy rain he could not sleep at night, so great was his apprehension that the dam would break away. Several times I have known him to get up in the night and drive up to the reservoir to examine it, so as to personally satisfy himself that it was all right." Gere published Hayden's story in the *Hampshire Gazette*. At the coroner's inquest, the examiner would repeat Hayden's own words and ask him to explain why his father was afraid of the dam. Hayden would then try to take the words back.

The committee returned to Williamsburg at four o'clock to dine at the Hampshire House Hotel. After dinner, they retreated to an upstairs room to discuss what the Legislature could do to help the stricken region. Sympathy, outrage, and heart-wrenching sights of devastation turned to tallies of financial losses, projections for rebuilding, and strategies for securing money. Lewis Bodman stated his desire that the Legislature appropriate money to cover the town's losses on public roads and bridges, and presented an itemized list:

Ashfield Road	$20,000
Bullard's Bridge	3,000
Grist Mill Bridge	8,000
Mill Street and Mill Street Bridge	11,000
From Mill Street to railway station, including two bridges	30,000
From Carr's [house] to Haydenville, three bridges	15,000
Road	2,500
Three bridges at Haydenville, each	6,000
Road to Northampton line	7,000
Total	$114,500

Williamsburg's assessor, Hiram Nash, declared that the town had lost $500,000 in taxable property and that if the mills were not rebuilt the loss would be greater. Haynes Starkweather said that Northampton could not yet present a detailed budget because its citizens had been so busy caring for the victims that they hadn't done the necessary calculations, but his best estimate of their losses was $60,000. Chairman Edson adjourned the committee until Thursday morning at nine at the State House in Boston, where Starkweather and other citizens of Williamsburg and Northampton could make statements about their losses, both public and private.

On the way to their carriages, committee members freely discussed with the press the need for a board of state engineers to review plans and contracts for dams and other structures, one that would operate like the boards of building commissioners in large cities. There was talk of introducing a bill to establish a board that might have oversight of dams, canals, reservoirs, natural basins, and streams to prepare for and prevent the spring freshets, which periodically devastated some of the state's narrow valleys. Someone proposed a board of inspectors to thoroughly examine all dams and reservoirs in the state every year and the creation of strict rules for materials and construction of all works in the future. They lamented that the order Wilson had introduced on reservoir inspections the day before hadn't gone forward. They mentioned that other Massachusetts reservoirs similar to the one that broke free—the Richmond reservoir near Pittsfield, the Berkshire reservoir near Berkshire Village, the Ashmere and Plunket Woolen Companies' reservoir near Hinsdale, and the Goshen reservoirs in Goshen—would be inspected. All were positioned high above manufacturing villages that could suffer the same destruction and loss of life that the Mill Valley had. The *Springfield Republican* concluded their report of the day's events with this sentiment: "Nobody can call to mind the miles upon miles of heavy canals in this commonwealth . . . without apprehensions of their security." The legislative committee's visit to the valley was a call to action.

Before nightfall on Tuesday, as the legislative committee rode back down the valley to Northampton, the searchers on Florence meadows were stopping work. They had found eighteen bodies that day; fifteen to twenty more were still missing. A half dozen others lay unrecognized in morgues. Organizers estimated that not one tenth of the flood's deposits had been examined. Hoping to have one thousand men at work the next day, the relief committee had already telegraphed Springfield to request four hundred workers, Chicopee and Chicopee Falls to request three hundred volunteers, Holyoke to ask for two hundred, Easthampton and Westfield to request one hundred each, and Greenfield and Deerfield for as many men as they could spare. The relief committee stipulated that, in addition to their own tools, volunteers should bring full dinner pails. The governor had promised tents that they could sleep in if they could spare another day's labor.

As the legislative committee boarded the seven o'clock train, engineer Henry Wilson stayed behind. The legislative committee's chairman had asked him to remain in the valley to inspect the Goshen reservoirs so that he could enlighten the committee about reservoir construction in Massachusetts in general. One manufacturer, Frank Hinsdale, who owned the Ashmere and Plunket Woolen Companies' dam in Berkshire County, was worried. He had examined the Williamsburg dam and, noting its similarities to his own, vowed to drain his reservoir by nightfall. Meanwhile, Easthampton residents voiced their fear of the Loudville and Manhan River dam in the Westhampton hills, which had never been inspected by county commissioners.

On Thursday, two days after the Massachusetts Legislative Committee toured the flood district, Senator Edson opened the hearing at the Boston State House to consider the petition for aid by the selectmen of Williamsburg and Northampton. Haynes Starkweather, chairman of the selectmen of Northampton, was the first man to report. Northampton had lost ten bridges, and the one remaining bridge was in poor condition; although it was still in use, it was considered not structurally sound. The cost to replace and repair all the Northampton bridges and the stretches of road between them totaled $80,750. The loss of taxable property was $200,000, which included damage to the meadows and to the factory buildings in Leeds. When Starkweather finished, a committee member asked if the town couldn't get along with fewer than ten bridges. Starkweather replied no.

Benjamin Johnson, a Williamsburg selectman and cashier of the Haydenville Savings Bank, reported that the town lost half its $1.5 million valuation. The town debt was about $15,000. Lewis Bodman stated that the figures for rebuilding bridges and roads, presented earlier in the week when the committee was in Williamsburg, stood at $114,500.

Elisha H. Brewster of the Governor's Council, who had been chairman of the county commissioners in 1867 and 1868 when the dam was inspected, underscored the importance of rebuilding all Williamsburg roads. Hiram Nash and Elnathan Graves, father of Collins Graves, advocated returning the river to its original course. While costly, it would help the town revive by recovering land that had formerly been available for building but was now washed over and susceptible to repeated flooding. To the question of whether he could do without a few of the town's bridges, Nash replied no.

Lewis Bodman of Williamsburg suggested that the town be relieved partly of its taxes for several years. If their roads and bridges could be restored and waterpower replaced, they could do the rest themselves. He added that although his property wasn't damaged, he would be glad to sell it now for two thirds of its valuation, implying that the flood had so devalued Williamsburg's land that he would be happy to sell his at a 33 percent loss.

Attorney Henry H. Bond of Northampton, the counsel for Williamsburg and the brother of the reservoir company's attorney, concluded the hearing with a plea to establish precedent. He urged the committee to relieve the towns from taxation and to rebuild the roads and bridges. In addition, he thought it would be "perfectly constitutional" to give relief to the one hundred families who had lost everything. He reasoned that the Legislature had the same right to relieve these people—made temporarily poor by the flood—that it had to delegate to the towns the obligation to provide for their poor. These families were really in the position of paupers, and the Legislature ought to appropriate money for their aid. He admitted to practical difficulties in administering the money, but was confident they could be overcome. He believed there had been some precedent for this relief by the state in the previous few years, but wasn't specific.

No one took up Bond's proposal, not the town he represented or the legislative committee. Brewster countered that the people expected to provide relief through donations of money and goods and the most practical thing was to make an appropriation for roads and bridges. Lewis Bodman and others from Williamsburg sided with Brewster. They didn't expect a charitable handout from the state to relieve the suffering of their townspeople; that was a local responsibility they planned to meet. When disaster struck, no matter what the cause, people took care of their own and gratefully accepted charity. The Mill Valley didn't expect or desire state aid for its population.

Mr. Robinson of Chicopee suggested assessing taxes on the real valuation and providing for an abatement to the sufferers in the fall. The reaction was favorable. The committee adjourned.

Committee members grappled with new questions about relief for survivors of a man-made disaster, but ultimately sided with tradition. In a May 28 report to the Legislature, they said they knew of no "precedent in this state for the grant by the legislature of direct pecuniary aid to towns that have lost public property by flood, fire or other uncontrollable causes." They decided that it wouldn't be "prudent and safe for the legislature to enter upon the distribution of charity to relieve cases of personal hardship and distress." But they noted they had to do something, since the disaster wasn't an act of nature but had been caused by a "creature of the state," the reservoir company, which had legally interfered with the flow of the Mill River. Deeply impressed by the seriousness of the issue, they asked for recommendations and suggestions and "searching criticism" from their fellow legislators.

On June 11, the Massachusetts Legislature voted $100,000 for Williamsburg and just $20,000 for Northampton to repair roads and bridges. Northampton was angered by the small sum; it appealed and lost. Some thought that Northampton received so little because legislators assumed that Leeds was a village in the town of Williamsburg rather than Northampton. The aid came in the form of a grant to rebuild and repair roads and bridges and a tax abatement for citizens whose property had been destroyed. Following the committee's recommendations, the Legislature did not consider the request for direct aid to individuals; however, since the reservoir company was chartered by the state to build the dam, legislators agreed that the state shared some responsibility for the disaster and agreed to contribute to the repair of public property. The towns started to work on repairs with the state's money immediately.

While the Massachusetts Legislature considered relief for the Mill Valley, the U.S. Congress in Washington debated aid for the sufferers of a Mississippi River flood that occurred one week prior to the Mill River disaster. A bill passed, which authorized President Ulysses Grant to distribute rations to the sufferers in Arkansas, Louisiana, and Mississippi. A few days later Congressman Charles W. Willard of Vermont tried to include the Mill River sufferers, but Congressman Charles Hays of Alabama, who had originally introduced the Southern flood bill, refused, and no further action was taken. Disaster relief on a national level was a political issue. If influential lawmakers or a sympathetic legislature supported "pork barrel" relief legislation, usually because there was precedent set by a previous disaster, then the disaster-stricken region was likely to be granted aid.

The sixth day, two days after the legislative committee's visit, began with a cold drizzle. As it became a heavy rain, the valley's general anxiety about the Goshen dams turned to fear that the reservoirs might become so filled that the dams would topple by the next morning. Villagers worried that the upper dam, thought to be the weaker of the two, might fail. This would send the reservoir contents cascading into the lower reservoir until they spilled over the lower dam, forming a combined torrent twice as large as the one that had destroyed the valley six days earlier. The previous day, Henry Wilson had inspected both Goshen dams and offered an ambiguous assessment of their safety. Wilson told several local men that the dams were essentially safe but deserved "constant watchfulness" and should be strengthened as a precautionary measure. The reservoirs had been full the day the Williamsburg dam broke and the water level had fallen a foot per day since the gates were hoisted after the flood, but rain was raising the level again.

Downstream from the reservoirs, the river roared and rose steadily, snatching away a temporary footbridge in Leeds. As night fell, a downpour swelled the river higher. Somehow the river was more frightening after dark—when one could hear but not see it—and a nighttime panic swept up and down the valley amid rumors that the Goshen reservoirs were nearly overflowing. From eight to ten o'clock, people along the river carried their property to high ground. One man was seen walking uphill with two children on his back. A woman struggled to a knoll with a trunk on her shoulder. Lyman James removed some goods from his Williamsburg store while other villagers headed for the railroad depot or for homes of neighbors who lived on higher ground. In Leeds, those in the few remaining riverside houses abandoned them for the depot, where they stayed until morning. Those who remained in the villages burned lights all night, ready to run if alerted by someone from the self-appointed Goshen reservoir warning committee—a committee formed that evening.

As a precaution, Williamsburg farmers with their swiftest horses stationed themselves along the potential flood route, ready to carry the alarm down the valley at the first sign of a break. Lewis T. Black and Edward Hyde watched the reservoirs while Charles Tileston waited two miles below. One mile downriver from Tileston, at Searsville, three other men waited with their horses, while in the vestry of the Williamsburg Congregational Church thirty men stood ready to fan out across the village if alerted by one of the Searsville men.

But nothing happened. The morning ushered in a fine warm day and the water subsided as quickly as it had risen the day before. Sunshine dried the land, absorbing the immediate fear but leaving a new underlying sense of vulnerability and dread. A year earlier, the villagers would have welcomed the rain that filled the river, millponds, and reservoirs; the water made the industries hum and the Mill Valley economy prosper. But after the flood, residents were skittish about a heavy rain and uncomfortable with the Goshen dams above their heads. Some weren't taking any chances. Leeds farmer and selectman William Quigley relocated his riverside house to a hillside lot above the railroad tracks a short distance below manufacturer George Warner's. For his new structures, Quigley used the one thousand dollars given to him by friends to show their sympathy and esteem.

Henry Gere of the *Hampshire Gazette* understood the depth of anxiety about the Goshen dams and warned the manufacturers directly to listen to the people or they'd have a riot on their hands. He threatened:

> It took considerable red tape to get the gates opened after the Williamsburg disaster, and the gate-keeper had to be told in earnest that it would be *good for his health* to move in the matter before anything could be effected. And it may be as well for the manufacturers or reservoir owners to understand, that the people in general in these valleys will have something to say hereafter about death-traps being built over them, and that if they are not willing to put more money into a reservoir dam than they can make in a few weeks, there will be more than one dozen men to say whether the reservoirs shall be filled or not.

As a young man, Gere had learned well from the elder Joel Hayden and the antislavery movement about confronting a moral wrong by writing eloquently against it. Now Gere was using his own strong arguments against Hayden's son and the other members of the reservoir company.

By the time the Goshen scare subsided, the survivors were weary. For six days they had sustained sleeplessness, shock, and grief as they met heightened activity with increased energy. But when they realized the extent of the death and damage and that they still lived beneath two potentially dangerous reservoir dams, a kind of depression took hold. A *Boston Globe* reporter who noticed wrote: "The excitement of the week before had settled into a mournful and exhausted silence." Fred Howard described it to his brother:

> It grows worse every day as the excitement grows less . . . We had militia and state constables here nearly all week, but the excitement is less now and we begin to realize that the village is a ruin . . . You must not expect to see Leeds as you left it. Probably it will never look at all as it did.

For hundreds like Fred, the misery of the moment was compounded by the uncertainty of the future. Fred didn't know whether he would have his old job back because button manufacturer George Warner hadn't yet found financing to rebuild. Fred continued:

> Warner of course lost the most [in Leeds]. I have been working since Wednesday noon. We have found some of the machinery, most of it on the flats back of [farmer] John Warners and have been cleaning it up at his barn. The safe was found yesterday in the river directly back of Fennessey's place. It was under water and the books soaked but drying will make them all right. [Bookkeeper] Isham put them into the safe and locked it before he left the wooden mill or else he had not opened it that morning. I think the former was the case. Charlie told me today confidentially that they would hire room & power at the Florence Sewing Mach[ine] Shop and commence work at once and build as soon as possible at the Cooks Dam. I think this is a pretty sure thing. Of course there will be a new company formed as Geo Warner has lost everything but Williston Knight [Horatio Knight's son] will back him again as they did after the fire [three years earlier].

While Fred waited, he worked on his father's farm and for Warner cleaning up the button mill lot. Fred prepared himself for the worst, confiding in his brother: "If Warner don't start here, I don't know what I shall probably go away from here."

Skilled workers like John Coogan who owned their own homes were also concerned. If the factories that employed them didn't reopen, they wouldn't be able to resell their homes, even if they could afford to repair them, and move to another job. At age thirty-seven, Coogan, who had been recruited from Ireland by Joel Hayden Sr. to work at the brass mill, had made enough to buy his family a house in Skinnerville. His house may have been heavily damaged in the flood, and he now stood to lose his job. If the brass mill did not reopen, he would have to abandon any plans he might have made to send his children, who ranged in age from five to fourteen, to school, and instead move the family to a place where most of the family could work.

Coogan's neighbor, widow Sarah Wrisley, needed the factories to rebuild too. At fifty-four, she rented part of her home to a female silk-mill worker, who gave Wrisley an income and companionship. Wrisley also rented out her fields to local farmers. But if the silk mill were gone, she would have no boarders, and without a factory population, local farmers might not need her fields to grow food for factory workers.

Some survivors who couldn't wait for the mills to rebuild moved near friends or relatives who were able to provide support. Others considered newspaper ads that beckoned them to relocate out west where they could "buy a farm wholly on credit" in Nebraska. But in the immediate aftermath of the flood, most villagers felt that waiting for the mills to rebuild was the best option.

Deciding to remain in the valley was an emotional issue as well as an economic one. Like other New Englanders, Mill Valley villagers were sentimental about their home villages, drawn to civic, social, and church activities, good neighbors, a small scale that lent security and familiarity, and a heritage of self-sufficiency. It was no coincidence that many of the biggest donors to the Mill River Relief Fund were local men, like the Snow brothers, who had moved to Boston or New York but maintained strong family ties to the valley. Banker Luther Bodman of Northampton still retained the "old paternal acres" at Williamsburg that had been in his family for over a century. If survivors had to start over someplace to rebuild their lives, it might as well be in a place they knew and were known in. In the 1870s, when the nation was expanding in overwhelming ways—bigger cities, more people, larger mills, and more immigrants—it was a comfort to think one could hold on to a small, familiar place.

Hayden's plans for rebuilding, announced the day after the flood, set the tone for the valley. The next day, he had contracted Emory C. Davis, a Northampton civil engineer, to survey the site to determine the size and location of the new buildings. By the sixth day, Davis's site plan called for a large new complex of 20,000 square feet, one-fifth larger than the old factory. The largest building would run 700 feet parallel to the river, with a foundry and coal house perpendicular to it. Hayden knew the cost would approach $300,000 and he didn't think he could afford to rebuild his father's elegant marbled office and bank building, so he omitted it from his plan. More important to Hayden was a branch railroad track—a spur—connecting the Northampton and New Haven Railroad across Main Street directly into the factory yard to provide cheaper and more convenient transportation of raw materials and finished products. Hayden no longer wanted his brass workers hauling freight by wagon to the Haydenville depot. The new branch would cost $5,000, and he proposed that the railroad pay for it since his company was a good customer.

As the railroad company considered underwriting the branch track, Hayden took steps toward reestablishing Haydenville. After paying his brass employees their past month's wages, he outfitted a damaged Hayden Foundry Company building at the south end of the village with salvaged machinery in hopes of turning out some goods by the end of the week. By May 26, six lathes operated and they expected to begin casting a week later. Some workers moved into a six-tenement dwelling made from a converted barn. Boston and Northampton architect Clarence Luce drafted plans for the new factory: a long two-story brick structure with towers rising from each end and bright attic rooms filled with sunlight passing through dormer windows. As Luce designed, several firms competed for the construction contract, which Hayden planned to let as early as June 1. At Hayden's cotton factory, ninety factory hands began work on machines powered by a newly installed steam engine.

On May 26, just eleven days after the flood, the railroad announced that it would not pay for Hayden's branch track, arguing that their profits from the $4,000 monthly fee the brass works paid were insufficient to justify the expense. Hayden sent a shockwave through the valley when he responded to the railroad's decision by declaring that he had changed his mind. He was no longer sure he would rebuild in Haydenville.

At thirty-nine, Young Joel didn't plan to recreate his father's world. While he faced a huge financial setback, he saw the destruction of his factory as an opportunity to start over with his father's former business partners, Collins Gere and Sereno Kingsley. He envisioned a grander factory than the old one—larger, more efficient, with better access to rail transportation—and he assumed others would help pay for the improvements. Hayden insisted that he could not afford the track himself. Besides, he had other opportunities. Someone, perhaps Hayden himself, told the *Springfield Republican* that he had received inducements from other cities with large waterpower supplies to rebuild there. If he couldn't get his branch track, he would move.

Holyoke, Hartford, Chicopee Falls, Miller's Falls, Turner's Falls, and Springfield, Massachusetts, along the Connecticut River, as well as Norwich, Connecticut, on the Thames River, all made offers for the brass works. In addition. Bridgeport, Brooklyn, Jersey City, Providence, Worcester, Northampton, and Greenpoint, Long Island, all invited Hayden to consider relocating to their towns. When Hayden arrived in Norwich to tour the town, a brass band and a Norwich citizens' committee met him at the train and enticed him with the gift of a $50,000 brick factory if he would move there. But Hayden took Holyoke's offer the most seriously.

In the 1870s, Holyoke was undergoing an economic expansion (its population jumped from 11,000 to 14,000 between 1870 and 1873), as local paper and textile industries grew and were joined by outside firms. The city fathers hoped to reap the benefits of the Mill River disaster by luring both Hayden and William Skinner away, for they saw the profit in adding two industries with complementary workforces; husbands and fathers would labor in the brass mill while wives and daughters worked at the silk factory, as they had in Williamsburg.

The terms of the offer were not disclosed, but the Holyoke Water Power Company had abundant waterpower to sell and it was anxious to sign up large, well-financed businesses such as the brass works. Holyoke's power came from the Connecticut River, which had been harnessed by a dam and a series of locks and canals that brought the power to mill sites. Interested in promoting the most effective use of its water supply, the company had induced James Emerson to move his testing flume from Lowell to Holyoke, where it became a national center for testing the efficiency and performance of hydraulic turbines; thus, mill owners had an objective evaluation of turbines on the market.

For Hayden to remove Haydenville's largest mill would have meant financial ruin for the village. In addition to his industries, Hayden owned thirty-one single-family houses, two double houses, a seventeen-unit tenement, and one boardinghouse. If he left, real estate prices would plummet as houses glutted the market, and the bank would fail as customers demanded their deposits. Methodist and Congregational churches would lack for members and financial support, and small businesses would collapse, particularly those that had already started reconstruction based on Hayden's early pledge to rebuild. Robert Cartier had erected a temporary blacksmith shop and was making plans to locate his carriage shop nearby. Pierce Larkin had reopened his grocery store in another building in Haydenville. Ezbon Sharpe and George Ames had started up their tin shop and stove store in a vacant spot near the old location. Nearby, hotel owner and livery keeper Luther Loomis had begun repairing and rebuilding, while shoe dealer Chauncey Rice patched his damaged shop. If Hayden left, not only would these small businesses likely fail, but the town coffers would be significantly poorer. Hayden, Gere & Co. was the town's top taxpayer with a tax bill of nearly $2,000 for 1873, while the tax bills of most other factories hovered around $400.

If Hayden's intention in exploring the proposals from other cities was to shock Mill Valley citizens into offering him inducements of their own, then he succeeded. On June 3, Haydenville's nervous residents held a large public meeting to determine their response to Hayden's sudden indecision. If the financing of the railroad was the impediment, they would provide the money themselves, and they raised it on the spot. Afraid that the brass works' departure would hurt Northampton's economy as well as Williamsburg's, forty of Northampton's businessmen pulled together an attractive package. Fifteen Northampton men agreed to lend Hayden, Gere, & Co. $100,000 (almost one third of the total Hayden needed) to assist in reconstruction, while the Hampshire County commissioners (two of the three commissioners had approved the failed dam in 1868) and the railroad assented to cover land damages and to purchase and lay rails and ties for the branch track.

But still Young Joel remained decided, so the Hampshire Gazette's Gere had a fatherly talk with Hayden via the newspaper. He referred to the brass works as "the most complete establishment of its kind in the world" whose goods were "beyond competition" and which his father surely would have rebuilt because "with him it was largely a matter of pride" to maintain the community that was "in great part his own creation." By contrast, Gere continued, the younger Hayden saw the question of rebuilding as one of "mere dollars." Gere reminded Young Joel that "the business grew up at Haydenville," and that much is still due to the place from its creators. He continued:

It is not a light undertaking to remove a large business from its birth place and the place of its mature years, to a new locality. In Haydenville, the people employed in the works were a community in themselves. The company there has complete control—it can make and unmake its own laws. In larger places it must do more as others dictate . . . we speak the voice of the people for miles around, where we express the earnest hope that the company will not leave the spot where it has flourished so well.

As Hayden's indecision dragged on, the newspapers flip-flopped. One day the paper reported Hayden would rebuild, the next day the opposite. The *Springfield Republican* on June 4 said Hayden and Gere had "virtually decided to stay." Two days later it proclaimed that their future was uncertain. Everyone grew impatient, including young Will Skinner, who told his diary on June 21, "Hayden, Gear [sic] and Company have not yet decided or at least [that] Young Joel will let out." Six weeks after the flood, Haydenville's future was unsettled.

As Hayden weighed his options, he spent much of his time in the swarm of activity at the relief committee headquarters in Northampton's town hall, where he attended continual rounds of meetings for the finance committee headed by banker Luther Bodman. On May 21, while others telegraphed Springfield, Easthampton, and Boston for supplies, Bodman, a savvy older gentleman with muttonchop whiskers that framed his prominent cleft chin, sent a dispatch to the Associated Press.

To the Associated Press: The impression has gone abroad that we have funds enough. Such is not the fact. Our actual receipts are $6391. Our necessities will require over $100,000.

L Bodman. Treasurer of the Relief Committee.

Individuals dropped by headquarters to donate, and the fund grew steadily. Early one morning two businessmen from Maine left two hundred dollars each as they started their trip up the valley to see the ruins. W. F. Prindle of Northampton came by to contribute four stoves. Benefits and concerts raised as much money as spirits. The Florence Musical Association presented a grand vocal concert in Cosmian Hall on Wednesday, June 3, while the Florence Dramatic Club planned an entertainment at the same location on another night.

Most of the money was contributed by subscription, in which people signed papers pledging to contribute specified amounts. Police, city councilors, businessmen, ministers, bankers, and other prominent citizens handled subscriptions in their respective communities. Unfortunately, people were often more enthusiastic in pledging than they were in paying. Nearly one week after the flood, the *Springfield Republican* chastised its readers because less than $500 of the $1,000 in pledges made at some local churches had actually been counted.

In addition to money, services of all kinds were contributed. The Connecticut River Railway and the American Express Company both offered free delivery of money and packages to the victims. Arms and Bardwell, a Northampton manufacturer, cleaned one hundred carpets for free, and a local watchmaker agreed to repair water-soaked timepieces at no charge. A writer to the *Western Hampden Times* proposed that Westfield mechanics give a week's free labor toward the construction of a house for a homeless family. Amherst offered to give one family a tenement, set them up in housekeeping, and "take care of them until they are independent." The Springfield orphanage was willing to take up to twelve children, but all the parentless children found homes among friends or relatives. A Northampton woman, who clipped hair from the heads of thirty girls who had died, offered to twist and braid it into hair jewelry (a broach or a ring made of girl's hair) as a keepsake for their bereaved family members. In the nineteenth century, when death was an ever-present reality for young and old alike, hair jewelry reminded the wearer of a dead loved one and served as a memento mori, a forewarning of the wearer's own death.

Goods of all kinds, particularly bedding and clothing, were also donated. The Boston Young Men's Christian Association sent one hundred mattresses, which were matched by two bales of blankets and a bale of comforters from Sargent Brothers of Boston. Two Springfield women sent six barrels of used clothes they had collected, while a Greenfield group delivered eight more. A Boston sewing circle contributed 321 new garments, the only new ones to be donated. Survivors who smoked were particularly thankful for twenty pounds of tobacco and a box of pipes courtesy of a Northampton firm.

While there was a great outpouring of charity, some people who might have been expected to give did not. Reservoir company members whose mills were only slightly affected by the flood—including Lucius Dimock, Samuel Hill, and Alfred Lilly—neither appeared on the rosters of contributors nor took a public role in the relief effort or rebuilding. Samuel Williston of Easthampton, western Massachusetts's wealthiest citizen, who had recommended the contractors who built the dam, contributed two hundred dollars; his employees easily topped that with five hundred. Instead, the manufacturers focused on rebuilding industry and made charitable gestures that maintained their social position, and they continued to perform cere-monial functions. Skinner, for instance, maintained a supply depot at his home for a short time and personally presented his former mill hands with checks from the relief committee.

Many people, perhaps distrustful of the committee's ability to distribute relief fairly, gave their donations directly. The students of the Westfield Normal School for teacher training made up a "purse" for classmate Carrie Cogan, the younger and surviving sister of Annie and Grace Cogan of Leeds. Within the first week, the Silk Association presented $2,150 to Skinner to distribute to silk-mill workers. The town of Sunderland gave part of its $230 contribution directly to the destitute and put the balance into the hands of Haydenville doctor William Trow, "to be dealt out as he thinks best." Their skepticism may have been fueled by the stories of attempts to defraud the committee. One woman from out of town caught the sympa-thetic ear of several Northampton residents by claiming she had worked for Skinner but had received no relief money. When Skinner heard the tale he confronted her: He did not know her, she had never worked in his mills, and her name was not on the rolls. She left town. Another woman with a young daughter convinced a kind Northampton woman that she was in need and the committee had given her nothing. When the committee reviewed her case they found she had already received $100 and the girl $54. The *Northampton Free Press* reassured its readers: "send what you wish to give, to those who have the best means of knowing the needs of sufferers, and trust to the committee, charged with the duty of applying relief."

A week after the flood, the general relief committee turned their atten-tion to providing for the long-term support of the survivors. Chairman Haynes Starkweather requested that each village provide a total of the num-ber of destitute and the amount of their losses, including houses, furniture, and other personal property, for a meeting on Saturday, May 23. The vil-lagers complied. Williamsburg counted 195 destitute persons, Skinnerville 122, Haydenville 173, and Leeds 250, for a total of 740 destitute persons in the valley representing 146 families. Their property loss neared $250,000.

As the relief committee considered these numbers, they kept in mind their business goal—to retain a strong, skilled workforce to rebuild the local economy. To this end, the committee established a two-tiered compensa-tion system. On the higher rung was a package for families, who tended to be headed by skilled workers, all male. Families were to receive a "fresh start," determined to be up to $300 in cash and goods for setting up house-keeping, distributed at the local district's discretion. The second package was for single individuals, who were mostly unskilled workers, both male and female, who could easily be replaced when the factories reopened and who the committee did not want to remain on the relief rolls until their jobs were reestablished. The committee allocated each single, destitute man a maximum of $50, while every single, destitute woman was to be presented with $100 and a trunk filled with clothing. Surely the trunk was useful, but it was also symbolic. These people were mobile; they carried their possessions with them and moved on whenever a mill fire, low water, or a freshet-caused factory washout put them out of work. With this allowance, the committee "considered themselves relieved from all further responsibility for such persons." After they were granted their allotment, they were stricken from the books and expected to leave town. Several of William Skinner's mill girls found employment at a silk factory in Warehouse Point, Connecticut. But when the factory burned down in December, they telegrammed Skinner to ask him to employ them again, and he did. They took their trunks where the jobs were. Mill hands didn't protest; continued employment wasn't guaranteed.

For some workers, the allowance was a great deal of money, but for others it did not even approach compensation. For the women who worked in the James woolen mill, $100 represented about one hundred fifteen days of labor, or about nineteen weeks, but, for men employed at the same place, their $50 represented less than thirty-five days' labor, or slightly less than six weeks. Homeowners fared the worst. Joseph Page, whose son was a friend of Will Skinner, had made brass patterns for many years and purchased a house and property in Haydenville worth $4,000. He lost it all and recouped only $300 cash from the relief committee. At middle age, Joseph Page was starting over. Payment according to need, rather than loss, made the flood a leveler of fortunes, but all were not leveled equally. While manufacturers had eager business investors and a hearty supply of cash and the unskilled operatives were given a financial cushion to relocate, skilled middle-class homeowners were hurt the most. They would recoup some losses as long as they could repair their homes and get their old jobs back, but that was not assured.

Names were removed from the relief roster almost immediately. On Monday, May 25, the tenth day, the papers reported that three single women from Williamsburg accepted their $100 and left town; three families from Haydenville departed the following day with their due; and four families and five single women from Leeds did the same on Wednesday. For the most part, those who left scattered across New England, often returning to their previous homes. Theodore Hitchcock's widow rejoined her family in Rhode Island. One silk-mill worker, his wife, and four children returned to their native England; their passage was partially paid by the steamer company. Some Haydenville families returned to Canada. With the nation still feeling the aftershocks of the depression and financial panic of 1873, most people found it hard to envision big changes.

Aware of the intense public scrutiny under which they operated, on May 28 the general relief committee required the district committees to visit the applicants to determine their exact needs and ascertain their worthiness to receive aid. That day a group of Haydenville women visited all the village's destitute to compile a list of articles needed. As a consequence of the new plan, the supply depots were soon closed and aid brought directly to people's homes. A Connecticut Legislature committee came to review the relief procedures, as did one composed of Boston citizens, which reported that the relief committee "seems to us to perfectly understand what is required of them, and received our entire confidence." The record books of the relief committee were left open in Northampton for the public to review.

In the end, a total of 566 persons and firms gave sums ranging from five cents to $10,000, with donations sent by rich and poor individuals, schools and clubs, churches of all denominations, and state governments and corporations. The citizens of Boston and New York each provided about $20,000, the state of Connecticut donated $10,000 from its treasury (the largest single gift), and the city of New Haven offered more than $1,000. The Shakers gave $125, and a Greenfield manufacturer of children's carriages sent $50 from himself and his employees; each donated a day's wages. A Connecticut brass manufacturing company sent $100. One of the smallest amounts came from an eight-year-old Springfield girl who sent the fifty cents she had earned selling flowers. The final donation arrived in November from a Chesterfield native, working as a missionary in India, who sent fifteen rupees, which amounted to about eight dollars. The final accounting showed that the relief donations reached $93,000: $75,683 in cash receipts and an estimated $18,000 paid directly to the sufferers or to other organizations, such as local churches who agreed to distribute aid at their own discretion. A total of 8,400 days of labor had been donated by men searching for the dead.

While Hayden publicly equivocated about whether to rebuild in Haydenville, William Skinner deliberated so privately that the only record of his considerations appears in son Will Skinner's diary. While Will was concerned with the possibility of his parents moving his childhood home and with losing lifelong friends who shared an ebullient social life, he was also studying his father as he made a difficult business decision. For as much as Will chafed at the confines of school and social customs, he was headed for a career like his father's, and his father was his role model.

Will's initial shock and sadness over the flood soon turned to high adventure. He was only too happy to write that he "did not go back to school" for several days. Five days after the flood, he "was all ready to go back to school but missed the train." The next day he wrote, "Since I missed the train yesterday little has been said about going back to school so [future brother-in-law] Fred and I went after silk. We found three bales . . ." Instead of preparing for his exams, which would be held in three weeks, he and Fred Warner spent their days retrieving some of the $60,000 worth of bales and spools of silk his father had lost. One day he took a trip to the reservoir and on another he and Fred directed one hundred laborers from the Boston and Albany Railroad to clean out the cellar. When he finally returned to school after a week's absence, he basked in his newfound notoriety:

> Did not know I was so popular as I now find I am. Always surprised as pretty [well] all the fellows come up to shake hands and are sympathetic with me.

Adventure aside, the world was changing around him. The Hibbards, a Skinnerville family, left for Europe, and the family of Edward Van Vechten, a railroad engineer whose house had been destroyed, moved into part of the Skinner house. Ed Bartlett, a silk dyer, went to work in Connecticut. Will's carefree social life had been consumed by the flood. His pal Dick Hills was no longer much fun. Dick and his father were out of jobs at the brass works, his mother was dead, and he had four brothers and a sister. If there were any hard feelings toward Will or his father about the flood, they went unsaid or Will didn't notice. After a month's silence, the friends picked up where they left off as best they could. "Went to church in the forenoon and in the evening went down and saw Dick Hills. Nothing of any account happened since the flood for it is all devastation."

Will worried with his father about the future. "Father does not intend to build here again," wrote Will on the fourth day after the disaster. The next day, he reported: "Found the safe and Father feels better." Workers had unearthed it a half mile downstream filled with mud and water. The company books, railroad bonds, and life insurance policies were still legible.

Two weeks later, Will met his father on the train as the latter returned from New York after settling with creditors. Will described his father's mood: "Everyone had sympathy and consolation for him. He went to Brooklyn and looked at some mills there but was awfully disgusted with them." The next day Will reported, "Father went to Holyoke and looked at a mill there and was very well satisfied with them and now has Holyoke on the braine [sic]." The following week he wrote, "Father and Mother went to Holyoke to look at the place and see how they would like to live there. They do not think much of it. Father hasn't yet made up his mind where he will go." The next day, Dick Hills's father and Onslow Spelman visited Skinner, probably asking him to rebuild Skinnerville. According to Will, "Father has not yet decided what to do. He has a great many very good offers to go, but the people all beseech him to stay."

If the disaster disturbed young Will Skinner, it deeply troubled Fred Howard, who was six years older. Their extreme reactions highlight class differences in the Mill Valley, as well as two different personalities' reaction to the same event. Fred had escaped the torrent, pulled people to safety, witnessed death and physical destruction, searched for bodies, and helped bury the dead. He lost many friends right before his eyes. He unflinchingly fulfilled his responsibilities to his neighbors, employer, and village. The event so depressed him that he took a vacation after two weeks of flood-related activity. He walked up into the hills, west to Worthington, Massachusetts, and then northwest on to Windsor, covering twenty-five miles. He pushed on another ten miles to Dalton and Pittsfield, in the heart of the Berkshires, visiting old friends and fishing in mountain streams. By the time he walked home again, a week had passed and his future was still uncertain.

Will Skinner had arrived home after the flood and helped out by finding silk and supervising workers, but he never did the gruesome work Fred did. For a respite, Will rode the train back to school where he accepted his classmates' sympathy, concentrated on exams, ball playing, and staying out of trouble. His mother watched him graduate on June 17. Will's father had the means to ensure that he would attend school again and that enter a professional position. Fred might also have his father's encouragement, but Fred would have to find his own job even if it meant leaving Leeds.

Saturday, May 30, two weeks after the disaster, was Decoration Day; today called Memorial Day. Before the flood, Williamsburg had allocated $100 to honor its fallen soldiers with speeches, a musical program, and a procession to the cemetery. Williamsburg had sent 250 men to the Civil War. Twenty-seven died at such faraway places as Baton Rouge, Winchester, Spotsylvania, and Andersonville. Many villagers were veterans of the war, among them George Cheney, Jerome Hillman, Joseph Hayden, Andrew Breckenridge, Reverend Gleason, Charles Tileston, and Lewis T. Black. (Among the 655 sent from Northampton were Alfred Lilly, Henry Gere, and John Otis.) But with so many new dead—eighty-eight Williamsburg citizens had been killed in the flood—and with so many other needs the town decided to use the $100 to rebuild roads instead. On Decoration Sunday, May 31, the day the program would have been held, Mary Hill and her husband hiked up to the Williamsburg cemetery to see how relatives and friends had decorated the graves of men they had all known. Then they walked down below Williamsburg village to view the flood destruction. "Oh! it is dreadful," Mary wrote that night. For survivors like Mary and Henry, the war and the flood were burdens that would weigh on their minds and hearts for the rest of their lives.

CHAPTER 6

THE INQUEST

AT nine o'clock on Wednesday morning, May 20, 1874, the fifth day after the flood, Ansel Wright, the Hampshire County coroner, arrived at the temporary morgue in the Williamsburg town hall to begin the coroner's inquest. Under Massachusetts law, a coroner's inquest was the legal method for investigating the cause of death of persons who may have died as a result of a violent act, such as by murder, suicide, assault, or accident. The push for an inquest came on the evening of the day of the flood, at the emergency relief meeting in Haydenville, when William Trow, a town selectman and the village physician for the past twenty years, urged his fellow selectmen to petition the Northampton district attorney to appoint a special coroner to investigate the cause of the disaster. The district attorney then authorized Ansel Wright, the county's deputy sheriff, to conduct the investigation. Wright determined that it would be impractical to investigate all the deaths and so decided that one victim would serve as a representative of all. He chose John Atkinson, whose body lay in the morgue at the Williamsburg town hall.

At the town hall, Wright met the six men who had been handpicked by the constable to be jurors and subpoenaed to appear before the coroner at this day and time. It would be their task to return an inquisition; in other words, to write a report that would "find and certify, when, how, and by what means, the deceased person came to his death" and the circumstances that caused it.

Wright knew all of the jurors, either personally or by reputation. The six were highly respected, financially successful men, so well esteemed for working in the public interest that the *Springfield Republican* called them "some of the most intelligent citizens of Hampshire county," and the *Boston Globe* praised their "excellent reputations for intelligence and fairness."

They were William Trow, forty-seven, the Haydenville physician and Williamsburg town selectman who initiated the inquest; Enos Parsons, about fifty, a Northampton attorney; John Mayher, nearly forty, an Irish-born Easthampton pump manufacturer, practical mechanic, and bank director; Silas Hubbard, a fifty-year-old Hatfield farmer, tobacco dealer, and bank director; Hiram Nash, sixty-five, a Williamsburg farmer, bank director, and former state representative; and George Hubbard, about sixty, the president of the board of trustees of a large local charitable fund for the poor called Smith Charities, a trustee of Smith Female College at Northampton, and a former state representative.

Wright and the jurors entered the town hall through the large front door. It was a white, wooden churchlike building with one high-ceilinged room, topped with a cupola. Bodies rested on boards stretched across the benches where citizens sat for town meetings. Their first order of business was to agree on the scope of the investigation. They decided to explore beyond the obvious fact that Atkinson was killed when the Williamsburg dam failed and determine how the dam was constructed, maintained, and managed. In other words, they planned to investigate who was responsible for the disaster. They named Northampton attorney Enos Parsons foreman.

Procedures in place, the inquest began. Wright and the jury viewed the body of John Atkinson. He had been dead five days; his body had been recovered only the day before and packed in ice. Standing over the body, Wright swore in the jurors: "Do you solemnly swear, that you will diligently inquire and true presentment make, on behalf of this commonwealth, when, how, and by what means, the person whose body lies here dead came to his death; and you shall return a true inquest thereof, according to your knowledge and such evidence as shall be laid before you; so help you, God?"

The jurors affirmed that they would. Three witnesses had been named who would testify. Abner Miller identified the body as that of his brother-in-law John Atkinson, age forty-eight, a native of England. Thomas Brazel recounted that as the flood approached the Henry James woolen mill in Williamsburg, he saw Atkinson leave his post as foreman of the weaving room to run home to warn his wife and daughter; he watched as Atkinson was swept away by the water, unaware that his family had already fled safely. Henry Cragin described how he had recovered Atkinson's remains in Leeds. Wright ordered the body removed and buried.

A group of reporters followed Wright and the jurors out of the town hall where a small crowd had gathered. A friend called to Wright, asking who would be on trial at the inquest. "It's the dam we are trying," Wright shot back, loud enough for a reporter to hear. The next day's *Boston Morning Journal* published his remark, which set the framework for a thorough investigation of the dam, its owners, builders, and engineers. The paper called it "one of the most important inquests held in New England for a century." In all, the jurors would hear testimony from forty-two witnesses over five days.

But first, Wright and the jurors wanted to examine the dam by themselves. Upon leaving the town hall, they climbed into waiting carriages and rode to the reservoir, where they fanned out over the dam. Attired in black coats and top hats, they poked, prodded, and measured the ruins just as legislators, reporters, and the public had during the past five days. One juror inserted a crowbar into the wall to see if he could loosen stones; he could, easily, perhaps because the stones hadn't been cleaned of dirt before they were placed on the wall and the grout hadn't adhered to them. Another measured the stone wall at various points along the base and determined that on average it was five feet three inches thick, not five feet nine inches as called for in the specifications. He guessed the width of the top of the wall to be less than the two feet it was supposed to be; when he saw the high ragged-edged wall of loose stones he would have to scale to take an exact measurement, he decided that an estimate was good enough. Another juror jammed a stick under the base of the wall to probe for hardpan. When he found none, he moved down the wall to try it again and again until he was satisfied that the wall had not been built on hardpan. Other jurors yanked out grout specimens that crumbled in their hands, then added drops of water and watched the material dissolve into sand. As they prepared to leave, jurors questioned Elias Cheney, the gatekeeper's father, about his opinion of the structure. He admitted his misgivings about it and proudly explained that his son had always said it would break on the east side where it did. If the jurors sought out the gatekeeper, he might not have been home; he had taken a job digging graves at the cemetery.

None of the jurors had ever closely inspected the dam before, but they had certainly heard about it, perhaps from the members of the reservoir company, with whom they had overlapping business, political, and social interests. John Mayher was the treasurer of the Valley Machine Company in Easthampton, which manufactured bucket, plunger, and steam pumps, and the president of the Easthampton Savings Bank. Silas G. Hubbard was a director of the First National Bank of Northampton, of which Joel Hayden Sr. had been president from 1862 to 1873. For juror Hiram Nash, the dam was such a close neighbor—on the other side of High Ridge from his northern Williamsburg farm—that its break must have rattled his windows. Nash's sister Emily was married to Lewis Bodman, a member of the original reservoir company board of directors; Nash himself used to raise sheep whose wool supplied Bodman's woolen mill. Nash had also served as a selectman with Joel Hayden Sr. and followed him as the town's representative to the Massachusetts Legislature. He had been an officer of the Greeley-Brown Club with William Skinner in 1872. As these connections became known outside the valley, some papers noted the interrelationships of the jury and the mill owners and voiced skepticism of the ability of these men, or any local men, to be unbiased. The *New York Tribune* described the valley as a place where "capitalists and manufacturers are so thoroughly mingled and distributed among all classes of people that it is not easy to obtain a competent and impartial opinion."

On May 25, five days after the viewing of Atkinson's body at the Williamsburg town hall, Wright and the jury reconvened at the Hampshire County courthouse on Northampton's Main Street to begin hearing testimony. Wright would preside. They were in the heart of downtown, next to the *Hampshire Gazette*'s offices, and diagonally across from the First National Bank, where several jurors and reservoir company members held directorships. The courthouse was a long, white, clapboarded building, columned in front and topped with a cupola and bell. It was no accident that the courthouse, like the older factories, resembled the Congregational churches of the Connecticut Valley; the town fathers had styled the courthouse to evoke parallels between the law of man and the law of God.

At eleven o'clock, Coroner Ansel Wright opened the inquest. Nearby sat Charles Delano, fifty-four, a Northampton attorney whom Wright had appointed assistant coroner. Delano, a former two-term congressman in the U.S. House of Representatives and another director of the First National Bank of Northampton, was skilled at conducting lengthy and detailed examinations. He had a broad face, deepset eyes, and a pointed nose. He was known for trying his cases with energy and perseverance. Near Delano sat John H. Slade, an expert court stenographer brought up from Boston to record what Wright expected to be voluminous testimony. By the end of the inquest, Slade's transcript would fill over one thousand sheets. District Attorney Hopkins observed the proceedings.

In the courtroom sat two dozen members of the public, a small crowd, and a cluster of reporters who listened attentively, ready to scribble frantically to summarize testimony and record the tenor of the proceedings. Representatives from the *Springfield Union*, the *Springfield Republican*, *The*

Boston Globe, the *Boston Daily Advertiser,* and the *New York Tribune* were all present. When it came time to write up the testimony, some relied on the *Springfield Union,* which published every afternoon, while others printed the Associated Press reports spiced with a few of their own observations.

The first three witnesses called were Abner Miller, Thomas Brazel, and Henry Cragin, who gave their testimony about the circumstances of John Atkinson's death. George Cheney was next. He recounted the early-morning inspection, the slumping of the bank, his ride to Spelman's, and his effort to race down the valley before the floodwaters blocked his route. In the two and a half years he had been gatekeeper he had noticed leaks the length of the dam, "running year in and out," mostly at the bottom, but drying up when the water fell below their level. The largest one, which had already been there when he took the job, was a stream "as big as a man's arm" running a rod or two east of the gate, a little below the level of the pipe. The previous summer, he had spoken to Lucius Dimock about it; Dimock had said he thought the large stream was nothing more than a spring bubbling up from under the dam. Dimock never visited the dam again. Cheney had often spoken to Onslow Spelman, the secretary-treasurer of the reservoir company to whom Cheney reported, about the large leaks, but Spelman had never asked him to repair them. A year earlier, a chunk of saturated earth—about two wagon loads—slid off the west side near the gate, and Spelman had never asked him to patch the gap. He had no instructions other than to report to Spelman.

Captain Parsons, foreman of the jury, asked, "Have you said, within a month, that if the dam broke away it would break where it did?"

"Yes," Cheney replied without hesitation.

Cheney's father, Elias, followed. The *Springfield Republican* couldn't resist poking fun at his "genuine Yankee dialect" as he described seeing the first slide of the bank while "sorter throwin' his eye out the winder" after breakfast. When he referred to the "stun wall" as a "pretty slimsy thing," Elias wasn't trying to provide local color; he was doing his best to convey the poor quality of the dam and his son's warnings of its failing condition. He recounted the visit of Lucius Dimock and Isaac Stone, the clerk of the Williamsburg and Mill River Reservoir Company and agent of the Northampton Cutlery Company, the previous summer. Elias had called their attention to the large leak on the east side; they dug in the bank but discovered no cavity as evidence that the dam was wearing away. Elias had heard his son predict that if the dam ever broke, it would break on the east side, as it did.

The gatekeeper's wife, Elizabeth, and his mother, Jane Ann, testified next. On the morning of the flood, Jane Ann had turned her back to the dam because the prospect of seeing it collapse made her sick, but Elizabeth had watched it intently, the only person to see it break. Her testimony confirmed that the dam had exploded upward, bursting open from the base; it did not slump or overtop—important information in determining what caused the failure. Years later, Elizabeth would recall that she had once told Dimock about leaks, and he had admonished her, "Don't be a damn fool."

The Cheney family testimony ended the morning session. If there were possible repercussions for the family testifying against their breadwinner's employer, they ignored them and described the dam, leaks and all. Members of the reservoir company had listened from a table near the front of the courtroom, close enough for eye contact with the Cheneys and other witnesses. Their attorney, Daniel Bond, was at their side but within easy reach of Delano so that he could slip written questions to Delano to be asked on the mill owners' behalf, which he did occasionally. Counsel was not permitted to participate in any other way. While the mill owners were not on trial, they made a strong presence. The examiner was an arm's length away and witnesses were never beyond their gaze.

When the jurors returned from dinner break, the morning's thin audience had swelled with people anxious to see local celebrities, Collins Graves and Myron Day. "An electrical stir and thrill [moved] through the court room," as Graves walked to the stand in what the *Springfield Republican* labeled the moment of greatest public interest in the inquest. The *Republican* described "a young man, probably under 30, with a well-knit figure of medium height, a quiet, strong, honest face, with thick brown mustache and hair negligently overlying square, firm brows and a well-balanced head; and a demeanor that was even shy." Graves retold his much-repeated story: He was driving in the village when he saw Cheney enter Belcher's stable yard looking scared and nervous. When he heard Cheney's news that the dam was breaking, Graves raced down the valley, shouting as he went, and warning the factories in Williamsburg, Skinnerville, and Haydenville.

Myron Day, who outraced the flood from Haydenville to Leeds, generated as much excitement as Graves. Day was an older, more serious-looking man than Graves, bereaved by the loss of his sister, Mrs. Birmingham, whom he had been driving to visit when he spied the flood. Her husband and three daughters had also died. He recited the tale of how he saw the water as he approached Haydenville, turned his team around, and raced through the gorge to warn factory workers in Leeds. Considered as honorable as Graves, Day prompted the *Republican* to write that he wore "an air of business-like resolution and a keen sense of duty and principle."

The chronology of the morning of the flood established, the inquest turned to the dam. First, Eugene Gardner, who had a role in overseeing the construction, was called to show some diagrams of the structure and explain them to the jury. Some he had prepared from memory, others from the specifications. He described the wall, foundation, and the embankment.

Next, Delano sought to establish who had been in charge of constructing the dam. He examined several mill owners, including Spelman, the secretary-treasurer of the reservoir company, and William Clement and Lucius Dimock, the two surviving members of the original three-member building committee. William Clark Jr. had died in 1868 of pneumonia at age forty-four.

Onslow Spelman, the first mill owner called, had been secretary-treasurer of the reservoir company since its beginning. Of all the mill owners, Spelman lived closest to the dam and his factory was powered exclusively by the East Branch of the Mill River while all the other reservoir company members benefited from both the East and West Branches. Before the dam had been built, Spelman often had no water in the summer. His investment in the company was $1,000 or ten shares.

Delano began slowly, in a quiet tone. "You are a mill owner in Williamsburg."

"I *was* a mill owner in Williamsburg," Spelman snapped back. He was pale and fidgety, so agitated that he couldn't keep his thin angular body still. His black hair and patchy gray beard stood up in tufts, as though they were nervous too. He had reason to be anxious. Yesterday's *Springfield Republican* had printed a sermon delivered by Reverend Meredith at Springfield's State Street Methodist Church the previous day in which he pronounced Spelman "guilty" because he knew the poor condition of the dam. A week before, the newspapers had reported, then retracted, a story about a gang of Irishmen from Haydenville who had planned to storm Spelman's house and harm him, angry that he had detained Cheney so long that Cheney had missed his opportunity to warn the villages. Even though the threat to Spelman wasn't real, he knew people were talking about him, trying to make him the scapegoat for the loss of life.

Delano tried to set the record straight by asking Spelman how long he talked to Cheney. Spelman asserted that he spent only a moment or two with Cheney before telling him to ride to Leeds. Delano probed further:

Did he tell Cheney to give the alarm as he went? Spelman didn't remember doing so. "One can't think of everything in one half-minute," he retorted.

Delano brought out the Williamsburg Reservoir Company's record book, a hardcovered book of lined pages. In his own neat handwriting, Spelman had recorded the act of incorporation, the constitution and bylaws, the stockholders' assessments, and the minutes of the meetings of stockholders from 1865 to 1872. Delano handed Spelman the book and instructed him to locate the names of the building committee and those in charge of the dam. There was a long, uncomfortable silence as Spelman flipped the pages nervously. "Out of mercy for Mr. Spelman's evident inability to do it," the *Springfield Republican* reported sharply, Delano took the book back and skimmed it himself without finding the appointment of a building committee, only a reference to Hayden being added to the committee on March 10, 1866. Delano read:

Moved that one be added to the building committee—Honorable Joel Hayden was nominated and chosen.

That was the entire written record concerning who was responsible for building the dam. Spelman had gone to the trouble of recording meeting attendance, assessments, and election of officers, but so effectively avoided anything of substance that the record book held no information about the construction and operation of the reservoir. He wrote up no summaries of discussion about designs for the dam, the selection of contractors, the construction, or its condition. No reports were appended or referenced. Examining the book today one finds that following the minutes of the meeting for May 27, 1872, the next ten pages had been clipped out with scissors. There is no indication when they were clipped, by whom, what they contained, or whether they had anything to do with the reservoir company. At the back of the book were coupons for shares in the company, the receipts remaining.

The Williamsburg Reservoir Company wasn't unusual in having insubstantial minutes; indeed, it was unusual in having recorded anything. In neighboring Berkshire County, Massachusetts, several reservoir companies had no records at all. They relied instead on verbal understandings and handshakes. That didn't change Delano's line of questioning, though.

Delano put the book aside and asked Spelman to name the members of the building committee. Spelman replied that he didn't know who they were and, furthermore, knew of no records on the subject. Delano tried another tack, asking Spelman if he knew who *acted* as the building committee. Reluctantly, Spelman acknowledged that Lucius Dimock, William Clark, and William Clement had served in that capacity. The newspapers, of course, had already named these men. Now Spelman opened up a little. He admitted that he had bought the reservoir land in his own name and that he was at the construction site often—not as frequently as three or four times per week, but approaching that number. Later, he was always there when repairs were made. Still, he insisted he had nothing to do with contractors Joel Bassett and Emory Wells, whom he saw each time he visited the site. He never saw their contract, never held it in his hand. He believed they began early in the summer of 1865 and finished in January or February of 1866, but couldn't remember for certain.

Spelman squirmed as he let small details about the dam slip out, then tried to deny them. The *Springfield Republican* observed that he was "restless in every limb, hurrying, yet hesitating and uncertain in speech, and apologetic in all he said,—he was an object for profound pity, even to those whom his oddities irresistibly amused."

Spelman admitted even less about the construction of the dam than he had about those responsible for building it. He knew of no complaints by members of the reservoir company about defective or insufficient workmanship. He had no idea of the width of the wall, either at the top or the bottom, had never measured it nor questioned its strength. He was, however, certain that the bed of the stream was hardpan as hard as stone, and he thought the builders had struck hardpan along the length of the dam, but couldn't recollect with certainty. He knew definitely that they hadn't dug into the hardpan when they laid the wall. He had no opinion whether the wall was thick enough or not; he had nothing to do with it. His excuse was that he acquiesced to those more powerful; as one reporter summarized, "he owned a share in the company but so small a one, he didn't want to press anything and he gave way."

Delano asked Spelman to explain the origins of the large leak Cheney had described streaming from the east bank. Spelman dodged the question by speculating about a different leak, a spring boiling up from the ground downstream from the bank, offering a long-winded theory of its origin. His off-the-point response was so rambling that Delano gave up trying to pin him down and moved to a final topic, for which he picked up the record book again.

Delano instructed Spelman to read a specific section, the meeting notes for May 14, 1867, when Joel Hayden Sr., president of the reservoir company, entertained a motion about liability from John Payson Williston. This time Spelman complied:

. . . it was moved that A. T. Lilly be a committee to consult with D. W. Bond, Esq. concerning the personal liability of stockholders in case of damage or loss by the breaking away of the reservoir and to take such measures as are necessary to relieve them from the same.

A month before Spelman had entered those words in the reservoir company record book, a mass of earth about eight feet thick, forty feet long, and two thirds the height of the slope had slid off the west side. Emergency maintenance spurred renewed anxiety in the villages, particularly in Williamsburg where citizens openly lobbied stockholder Lewis Bodman to remove the dam if it was not safe.

Then, at the reservoir company meeting in May 1867, John Payson Williston articulated what was on the minds of the other mill owners when he broached the subject of their liability if the dam broke. Alfred Lilly consulted with their attorney, Daniel Bond, and reported back with a strategy to reduce, if not eliminate, liability. An 1854 Massachusetts statute allowed anyone "owning [a] mill or other property liable to destruction or damage by the breaking of a mill or reservoir dam" to apply to the county commissioners to "view and thoroughly examine" the dam. If the commissioners judged the dam as "not sufficiently strong and substantial to resist the action of the water" under reasonable circumstances, then the owners were required to repair the structure. If the required alterations were not made, the commissioners were authorized to remove a part or the whole dam, as they deemed "necessary for the safety of property, roads, or bridges on the stream below."

But this law was far from complete; it said nothing about liability if a dam approved by county commissioners broke, neither affirming liability nor immunity from liability. Under common law, however, directors or stockholders of a reservoir corporation might still be criminally liable if a dam broke and caused damages, providing it could be determined which members should be held accountable, a difficult prospect since each member would likely argue that another was more responsible. But if members were charged, then having had the dam inspected by the county commissioners, as provided in the 1854 statute, would have demonstrated that the company stockholders had taken all reasonable steps allowed by the state to ensure the dam's and the public's safety. An inspection would have shown they had carried out their civic responsibility and that any break that occurred was out of their control, a freak occurrence that they might label "an Act of God." Practically speaking, then, inspection would be a preventive measure. It would be an easy step for the Williamsburg Reservoir Company to take, and Attorney Bond surely recommended it.

While the 1854 statute appeared to protect citizens like those of the Mill Valley, it actually had the opposite effect. One provision called for the examination costs to be paid by the party making the application for inspection if the dam was judged to be safe. Thus, it could be financially prohibitive for citizens to call for the inspection of dams. County commissioners, who were elected officials, were usually peers of mill owners (Joel Hayden Sr. had been a commissioner for six years) and dependent for information about dams on the mill owners themselves, and so were more inclined to judge dams safe than not. Engineer Henry Wilson from Boston had already spoken out about the uselessness of county commissioners inspecting dams. With the *Worcester Spy* as his mouthpiece, he declared that county commissioners are "ill adapted" to render a fair judgment because they had no engineering expertise, they couldn't see the inside of the dam once it was finished (he compared it to inspecting the lumber in a house by looking at the exterior paint), and they tended to give the benefit of the doubt to completed dams rather than require that the structure be removed at great expense. After all, they needed the good influence of the mill owners to be reelected.

Delano inquired of Spelman if there was any talk at the May 1867 meeting about the danger of the dam. He denied that there had been any such talk—and there was no written record to prove otherwise—but he understood that, as a result, the county commissioners had inspected the dam. Lilly made no written report of his consultation with Daniel Bond. At the same meeting, the reservoir company voted to assess themselves an additional 15 percent of the company stock they owned to pay for repairs to the dam that they expected would be required by the county commissioners. Later in the meeting, they voted to build a house for the gatekeeper to live in, so that he could keep a constant watchful eye over the dam. Spelman's testimony had taken up most of the afternoon. The inquest adjourned until the following morning.

The mill owners must have watched Spelman anxiously, anticipating their turns. Spelman had made a fool of himself, but he had also set up the story that other mill owners would follow: that they were uninvolved and had trusted others to do the work. Some mill owners were better at hiding behind the corporation, and their success at bluffing often had much to do with how well they played the role of honorable businessmen who wouldn't knowingly build a poor-quality dam. Spelman wasn't convincing, but others—such as Isaac Stone and William Clement, who would take the stand the following morning—were.

When the inquest resumed at ten o'clock the next morning, the courtroom held fewer members of the public than the day before. With no more heroes expected to testify, popular interest waned. While the human story of the disaster became a public spectacle, the investigation into its cause did not. The public who had read the results of the newspapers' investigations expected no new revelations at the inquest. Perhaps, too, some stayed away because they did not want to be seen delighting in the manufacturers' embarrassment. Others simply may have had too much to do, restoring the valley and caring for family and neighbors. The public's absence left the courtroom almost exclusively occupied by representatives of the manufacturing interests in the valley, most of whom had a personal stake in the outcome of the inquest. Among the gentlemen mill owners and their attorneys were two rough-looking men—Joel Bassett and Emory Wells, the contractors who built the dam—who listened intently to what the witnesses said about them. Their attorney, Samuel T. Spaulding, sat with them.

Isaac Stone was the first witness called on the second day of testimony. A stockholder of the Northampton Cutlery Company of Bay State Village, Stone was clerk of the Mill River and Williamsburg Reservoir Company, a consolidation of the Williamsburg Reservoir Company and the Mill River Reservoir Company formed in 1872. The company owned the failed Williamsburg dam, the two Goshen reservoir dams, and a dam in Searsville on the West Branch. Stone's restrained manner and elegant appearance contrasted with Spelman. According to the *Springfield Republican*, Stone was "tall, erect, formal, somewhat over middle aged . . . [whose] careful, even punctilious manner, bespeak the man of business, with every faculty under discipline and every utterance under control." Stone's politics and gentlemanly bearing had earned him an appointment by President Abraham Lincoln as a consul in Singapore and easy treatment by Delano.

Delano asked Stone who had charge of the Williamsburg dam. Stone replied that because there had never been any indication that anything was wrong with the Williamsburg dam, no one had responsibility except the reservoir company directors, who were William Clement, Lucius Dimock, and Joel Hayden Sr., the president, who was deceased and not replaced. He didn't mention that Spelman informally oversaw the dam. Stone recalled that in 1869 and 1870, when he and the other mill owners discussed the reservoirs and ways to improve waterpower on the Mill River, the question of the strength of the Williamsburg dam never came up. Since the reservoir companies had been consolidated two years earlier, no one held direct responsibility for the Williamsburg dam and no money had been appropriated for repairs. He repeated that he had no idea that there was anything wrong with the Williamsburg dam. Neither Delano nor the jurors probed Stone's moral obligation to be vigilant about maintenance. Nor did Delano bring up the dam keeper's father's assertion that within the past year he had called Stone's attention to a large leak on the east side, which Stone and Dimock had probed with a shovel. Perhaps Stone's polished confidence intimidated him, or perhaps Delano didn't want to tarnish the reputation of a fellow Republican.

William Clement was the next mill owner called. A member of the building committee and the first president of the reservoir company, he was a major stockholder of Clement and Hawks Manufacturing Company, Northampton, a cutlery factory. Clement owned twenty-five shares of the reservoir company, a total of $2,500. On the stand, Clement distanced himself from the other mill owners by professing to have been a conservative among the directors, one who had wanted a stronger dam than was finally constructed. He portrayed himself as an observer of the building process, no more knowledgeable than the others. He testified that he hadn't known about the county commissioners' inspection and he hadn't attended the 1867 meeting at which Lilly was charged with consulting their attorney about liability. But if the jurors had closely examined the record book, they would have found that he knew plenty about the dam. He was president of the reservoir company during the years when fundamental decisions about the dam were made. He presided over five meetings: two in May 1865, one each in September and November 1865, and a final one in March 1866 at which the main topic of discussion must have been the development of the specifications, selection of the contractors, the appointment of a superintendent, and a review of the construction progress. Clement admitted only that he had reviewed the plans of Smith and Raymond, Stewart Chase, and Lucius Fenn.

When Delano asked how often he was at the dam site during construction, Clement maintained that he was only occasionally there in the winter months of 1865–66 when the work was being done. (Bassett would claim Clement was there two to three times per week.) Clement recalled complaints made about the contractors, but could remember only one specifically. Spelman had called his attention to the fact that the contractors were not reaching the hardpan in digging the trench for the west side of the wall. They offered to take down the wall and rebuild it on hardpan, which would cost $150, but Clement and Clark thought that the builders were right and told them to continue building. The wall was created in steps, some places nearer the hardpan than others, but always on firm mountain gravel. That wall—the west one—was still standing. On the east side, the soil was wet and mucky, but he thought the hardpan was touched all along. Clement's greatest concern was the use of cement in cold weather, but the contractors assured him that covering the partially built wall with brush and earth kept out the frost.

Delano asked Clement if what he saw of the ruins matched his expectations. Clement responded with indignation: "It looks as if the main earth had never been taken away for the dam," meaning that it appeared as though the site had never been cleared. In addition, the cement had a bad appearance. A juror asked if he would have approved such a foundation if he had seen it. "Not for a moment," he huffed. He insisted he had seen only small sections of the work.

Days later when Clement was recalled, he stuck to his moral high ground. He denied the statements of the contractors that they had warned him that laying the stone on gravel would cause the west side to leak. Had these men, "whom he trusted to do honest work," consulted him and told him the dam would leak, he would never have violated their advice just to save $150. He "had confidence in the contractors," he repeated. He would not have accepted their work if he had seen it.

Delano asked him about Lieutenant Governor Hayden's opinion of the dam. Clement said Hayden thought the work was not done thoroughly and wanted Eugene Gardner on site more, to oversee the construction as project supervisor, but Clement demurred on what the specific complaint was. Clement repeated: If he had known something was wrong, then he could have done something about it. Delano inquired about the history of the dam's condition. From the time the dam was first filled, Clement said, water oozed out of the lower part of the dam at two points, one near the wasteway and one large stream on the east side that came, in part, from a leak in the embankment and, in part, from springs under the embankment that were not diverted. When the reservoir was full, the underground rills flowed downstream as the weight of the water in the reservoir squeezed them out.

These leaks hadn't signaled any special danger to Clement. But if Clement didn't know that leaks were a problem, there were more than a dozen professional engineers living within a hundred-mile radius who could have told him that water running through a dam will slowly destroy it. He could have called on Albert Dwight Briggs, John R. Smith, George Raymond, or Phineas Ball of Springfield. He could have contacted James B. Francis of Lowell or Henry Wilson of Boston, who would have told him that even a watertight dam can't choke off underground streams, which can harm the inside of a dam. Engineer Henry Wilson would later testify that leaks through a dam didn't necessarily have to run thick and discolored to be a problem, explaining that it was unpardonable to allow water to continue running from the base of such a structure on the supposition that it was simply a diminutive spring.

Today's engineers know that while every earthen dam will seep water, minor seepage is not necessarily dangerous, but leaks that show actual water flow are, so it is important to identify the source for even a small amount of water on the downstream side of a structure. This flow of water, which carries mineral materials (some microscopic) through the dam, is called piping, a process that was not well understood until the 1940s. When piping occurs, water moves through the embankments via tiny gaps left by shifting minerals or decaying organic material, such as roots and leaves, through interstices in grout or masonry, or under the dam's foundation. As it moves, the water collects tiny particles of soil and carries them out of the structure hollowing out the soil so that seepage increases. A chain reaction is created: The water erodes the soil in its path, and the erosion allows the water to increase in velocity and create a greater flow. Uncontrolled, it can erode material from the downstream slope or foundation, backward toward the upstream slope. Soon, a channel running through the dam may further erode the interior by creating a larger channel. A channel, or "pipe," may collapse over time, but eventually the flowing interior water will find another exit and enlarge to such an extent that the dam will fail. Blocking up leaks can increase the already tremendous water pressure and create another pipe elsewhere.

Clement's turn was over. Dimock was next.

Later that afternoon, Lucius Dimock, agent of the Nonotuck Silk Company in Leeds and the only living member of the building committee beside Clement, was called to the stand. The *Springfield Republican* had reported that he was the "boss engineer" and the "moving spirit" of the project, the leader of the building committee, who understood gate pipes and reservoirs. The jury expected him to tell what had gone wrong with the dam. Since Spelman, Stone, and Clement had contributed little information, they hoped Dimock would be more forthcoming.

Delano started by posing simple questions. What designs were presented for the dam? Dimock could not recall. What were the costs of the plans? Dimock didn't remember. What were the specifications for the dam that was finally built? Dimock didn't know. Was there a contract? Dimock had no distinct memory. Who was present when the specifications were accepted? What circumstances led to their approval? When did it occur? Dimock professed that it was all too loose in his memory. He had no recollection of hiring the contractors to do it, nor did he remember having any objections to the contractors' work, and he knew of no repairs made after their job was complete. Exasperated, Delano asked if as a director, stockholder, mill owner, or person having memory, he had any idea as to when the reservoir dam was approved. It was too vague in his mind. He could not remember whose plan was accepted and couldn't recall when the contractors built it. Did he know for a fact that a dam had been built? Dimock was forced to answer yes. Delano's persistence angered Dimock, which amused the *Springfield Republican*. He was described as a "spare, nervous, active gentleman, with keen features, piercing eyes, and an excitable temperament that animates every hair on his head, and gives character to his very beard and mustache." He looked shifty and on edge, yet had the mannerisms of a buffoon.

Delano asked about laying the wall. Dimock could not remember anything about the wall except that he believed it was laid on hardpan at all points except the sections high up on both ends where it attached to hillsides. Any evidence of a trench had probably all been washed away. Delano probed the reasons the reservoir company called the county commissioners. Dimock insisted that calling them wasn't caused by any fear of the dam, but was the result of caution, "the same that leads a man to insure his house." Dimock knew of no commissioners' objections to the dam and knew of no repairs taken as a result of the commissioners' exam.

Delano asked if he had ever considered the possibility that the dam might break. Dimock had never doubted its safety enough to call together the directors to discuss it, although he had known about the streams that ran from the dam during certain seasons of the year. He implied that if anything was wrong with the dam, it was hidden by the builders, whom the directors had trusted to do honest work. He insisted he was no more responsible than any other director.

Angered by his stonewalling, foreman Enos Parsons demanded to know whether he considered himself competent to be a director building such a dam. Dimock mumbled that "the *Springfield Republican* could tell," then stepped down.

In the next day's edition, the *Springfield Republican* editorialized:

The [reservoir] corporation . . . either by design or by accident, carried
out the policy of irresponsibility to the full. The books of the corporation
scarcely show that a reservoir was built at all, names no building committee, or responsible superintendent, and are as pertinent as the Talmud
to the questions now raised . . . How can we dogmatize about Troy and
Stonehenge when we search through the Connecticut valley in vain to
find the responsible builders of a dam not ten years old? . . . There was
no record evidence of work done, no building committee appointed or
instructed, no plans formally adopted, no engineer made responsible, no
contract signed, and almost no trade made with the supposed contractors.
The next most logical conclusion was that no dam was built, and so, alas,
it proved.

If Spelman and Dimock had answered the questions put to them with
directness and clarity, and if they had looked and acted with the presence
and confidence of someone like Isaac Stone or William Clement, they
wouldn't have been portrayed as fools by the newspapers. In the 1870s, the
physical appearance and demeanor of a businessman were important. The
right clothes, manners, and posture bespoke a trustworthy, rational, prudent, and levelheaded man. Spelman's and Dimock's odd looks and quirky
behavior marked them as bumbling small-town men, and the press was
keen to exploit them for comic relief.

When Lewis Bodman of Williamsburg was called, he appeared far too
dignified and direct to be ridiculed. Delano asked, "Had there not been
considerable discussion and anxiety among the mill owners as to the security of the dam?"

Bodman responded, "Why, we *knew* it wasn't safe at first. We thought the
weakness was all on the west side, not the east which broke." However, he
added, the feeling of insecurity about it the first year wasn't shared by the
stockholders further downstream in Northampton. But after the first year or
two, after the repairs and the acceptance by the county commissioners,
there was no special fear. For the past five years the reservoir had been considered to enhance property values in the valley.

Delano asked why the reservoir company called the county commissioners. "We aimed to escape a personal liability," Bodman answered,
adding that the community was nervous and talking about calling the commissioners themselves if the reservoir company didn't. Some of the mill

owners thought that if the dam gave way the water would spread out and do little damage, but he and Governor Hayden, as many people called him, thought that the result would be as devastating as it was.

William Skinner was equally blunt. When Delano asked if he had anticipated a break, he said yes, but thought that it might destroy only a few bridges. He recalled that during construction there was ill feeling between the contractors and Governor Hayden and Lucius Dimock. He explained: "Dimock would cuss and swear and damn 'em all, and Governor Hayden, well, he didn't exactly swear, but he acquiesced in it, anyhow." His early fears of the dam had been erased by Governor Hayden's assurances within the last year that it was all right.

Lucius Fenn was called next. Delano asked him if he had prepared the specifications for the dam. In spring 1865, Fenn had been supervising the construction of the Williamsburg link to the Northampton and New Haven Railroad when his close personal friend William Clark Jr. asked him if it was possible to build a dam at Williamsburg that consisted of a two-foot-thick stone wall covered by earthen banks that sloped at an angle of 45 degrees, a base-to-height ratio of 1:1.

"I shouldn't build such a dam," Fenn had replied. Such steep banks couldn't have withstood the pressure of the water in the reservoir. The more gentle the gradient of the bank, the more area to absorb water pressure. Fenn advised a ratio of two feet in horizontal distance for every one foot in vertical height; a 2:1 ratio would have a gradient of 27 degrees. Fearing the cost of the dirt and labor for a gently rising embankment, the directors inquired if a dam with a slope of 1½:1 would "fill." Fenn said he thought it would fill. "We can fix it afterward," one mill owner had offered, meaning they could add more earth if it looked like the slope wouldn't hold after the reservoir had stood full for some time. As Fenn and the company talked further about the dam, Clark showed him a design by engineers John R. Smith and George Raymond—a tall stone dam sheathed in chestnut planks and covered with gravel, costing almost $100,000. Clark explained that they "couldn't think of the expense of a stone dam" and had asked Fenn to propose several designs and estimates of his own. He did and included at least one stone design, which he testified he always thought best. But the reservoir company was only interested in the earthen designs and asked him to write up specifications for one.

By May 28, 1865, when Fenn had completed a first draft of the specifications, the committee had already chosen the contractors, Joel Bassett and Emory Wells. A month later, an oral agreement was made between the building committee—Clement, Clark, and Dimock—and the contractors, using the not-yet-final version of Fenn's specifications. The parties trusted one another, so the contractors began work without signing a written agreement. On August 1, Fenn staked the trench for the wall; it would be the last time he would visit the dam. Nine days later, six weeks after the contractors had first started work, Fenn delivered the final specifications to Clement. Fenn knew the contractors weren't happy with the change in the plans from an eighteen-inch pipe to a sixteen-inch pipe because the smaller capacity wouldn't be adequate to divert the river's flow as they built the dam. He recalled that at one time he had discussed a stone sluice twenty-four-inches in diameter, but had no idea why the pipe capacity shrank as the plans became final.

Delano asked Fenn if he had superintended the dam. No, he said. After he completed the specifications, Clark asked him to visit the dam site periodically, pointing out that Eugene Gardner would be there some, but that he wanted Fenn there too. Fenn recalled that he was happy to say he could not. His work on the local railroad was finished and he was going "out west." He didn't know Gardner or his reputation; the first time he saw him was in the courtroom. Before he left for the west, Fenn told Clark that superintendence by a competent engineer was necessary. Fenn had no further connection with the dam, admitting to the jury that he didn't want the responsibility. He did not hear about the dam again until he was called to testify.

Delano asked Fenn if it was his opinion that a competent engineer was needed, because in his judgment the dam would involve danger to life and property. Fenn protested: He wasn't responsible for the specifications; he had made calculations for a thicker dam of $1^3/4{:}1$ because he knew a slope of $2{:}1$ would not be accepted. He told Clark not to trust the work to any contractors even if they were his most intimate friends. Finally, Fenn admitted "yes," danger to life and property were in his mind when he advised Clark to have the work looked over carefully.

Jury foreman Enos Parsons questioned Fenn about the quality of the specifications. Fenn answered that he did not consider the specifications definite or definitive; they were vague and depended on proper superintendence and he had put in such a proviso in the specifications. The *Springfield Republican* summarized the exchange that followed:

He [Fenn] was asked if his sense of duty did not demand of him better service than that, and he thought it would have if he had had any power to enforce a single idea, but as his opinions were all disregarded, he felt that his specifications were equally at the option of the committee, who, he understood would take intimate charge of the matter . . . Left to his own option, he never would have built such a structure . . . He had thought it possible that the dam might break away, and expected it might go at the pipe.

After the jury posed a few follow-up questions about the specifications, Fenn stepped down.

Fenn could hardly defend himself. Earlier that afternoon, the jury had listened to George Raymond, one of the team of engineers who had submitted a bid for the stone dam, give a two-and-a-half-hour tutorial on dam building. Raymond had built two reservoir dams in Leominster, Massachusetts, on the same general plan as the Williamsburg dam. After discussing the deficiencies of the design and execution of the Williamsburg dam, Raymond addressed the cause of the break. When one is building a dam, he explained, one must consider opposing forces. There is one law that governs the pressure of all fluids: The pressure is always at right angles to the surface it presses against. To take the specifications for the dam as an example, with a ratio of $1\frac{1}{2}$ feet horizontal to 1 foot vertical, the pressure of the water on the inside slope was divided between a vertical pressure, which tended to press the earth down into the ground, and a horizontal pressure, which pushed at the earth in the downstream direction. He went on to explain that when water reached under the dam's wall, creating an opening, then those two pressures combined. The vertical pressure pushed upwards and the horizontal pushed out, together with a force of $1\frac{1}{4}$ tons to the square foot at a depth of 40 feet. That was why, he explained, Elizabeth Cheney saw the dam burst upwards from the bottom. Raymond stated that builders of grouted work often failed to take horizontal pressure into consideration since they never encountered it elsewhere, such as in a building or a freestanding wall, and don't know how to provide for it. The *Springfield Union* summarized one of Raymond's concluding statements: "No such work should be constructed without the supervision of a competent engineer, who understands and can provide against these special forces."

Eugene Gardner was called and questioned to find out if he had been the dam's superintendent. Gardner, too, maintained that he had not. Although he visited the dam twice a week, spending two or three hours each time, his purpose was not to oversee the manner of the work; he was only there to take measurements of additional work, which was to be paid for by the cubic yard. He did not act as a superintendent, nor did he think it was expected of him. Gardner claimed he never found any fault with their work and, as far as he knew, the directors didn't either because all the work was done according to the specifications. Delano suggested that he must have known about the clause in Bassett and Wells's contract, which stated that all work was "to be done in a thorough and workmanlike manner, and in all respects in strict conformity with the directions, plans and specifications, and to the acceptance of the said committee, or the superintendent employed by the said committee to take charge of the work." Gardner was acquainted with the clause, but he insisted that he was not the superintendent, with so many directors on hand who knew more about building dams than he did.

Gardner explained that he visited the site regularly in July and the first part of August, but was then absent until October on account of illness and absent again in November because of sickness and death in his family. No one had complained that he spent too little time at the dam. He recalled on several occasions having examined foundation stones with Clement, Clark, Hayden, and Dimock. Consulting notes he had made during the project, he testified that an additional wall was built in the eastern portion of the embankment to stabilize the moist patches that came from underground springs. (It was customary for engineers and contractors to make day-by-day or weekly notes during a construction project.) Wells had made notes too, but neither the coroner nor the jury examined them. At this point in his examination, Gardner complained of faintness, perhaps to buy time to collect his thoughts before more questioning. Coroner Wright excused him and adjourned the inquest until after dinner.

Parsons queried Gardner about his qualifications. Gardner stated that he was no engineer, but an architect and a surveyor, unqualified to oversee the work. This was his first and last effort in dam building. Parsons asked if the contractors had ever passed him money. They had not, he replied.

In colonial America, when building and manufacturing were on a small scale, engineering didn't exist as a distinct occupation; those functions were assumed by artisans and mechanics. Civil engineering emerged in the early years of the nineteenth century in response to the nation's need to improve the transportation network as a stimulant to trade. But with Americans fearful of a strong central government (the result of years of English rule), it was left to state governments and private enterprise to hire engineers to build roads, canals, water systems, and railroads. The engineer worked as an individual, with no governmental oversight of his work, and no one to enforce his sound technical judgment against a sponsor's eagerness to save money. Engineers came to the profession in one of three ways: on-the-job practical training through apprenticeship or work; education at one of the national military academies; and education in a civilian academic engineering program. In 1864, when the reservoir company began soliciting dam designs, only 30 percent of engineers were educated in an institute or college of engineering.

Many nonacademically trained engineers were extremely knowledgeable, wrote treatises on engineering topics, and exhibited a high standard of ethics. But in a growing nation eager to build bridges, railroads, and dams, there was plenty of room for a man like Fenn, who had little practical knowledge of dams, to design one, and for a man like Gardner to be given the job to superintend one.

West Point began training engineers in 1802 (but contributed few in numbers to civilian service), and the Rensselaer School (later Rensselaer Polytechnic Institute) granted its first degree in 1835. As the nineteenth century wore on, on-the-job training declined while the proportion of academically trained engineers rose until higher education became the primary source of engineers. By 1900, there were 100 formal engineering training programs. Academic training triumphed, in part, because a large number of engineering accidents, such as the Mill River flood, showed the necessity of competent engineers.

The creation of professional associations, which were key to promoting and diffusing new engineering knowledge and to standardizing and improving practice, had a slow beginning. Only a few local technical societies, like the Boston Society of Civil Engineers (incorporated in 1851) existed before 1860. After it reorganized in 1867, the American Society of Civil Engineers became the first national society of engineers. The emergence of such societies illustrated the shift from a conservative, craft tradition of engineering to a more dynamic, science-based approach. It also helped engineers gain social recognition for their profession and gave them a way to express their sense of social responsibility. The importance of regulating engineering practice for the public interest was exposed by the Mill River flood.

Wright called Joel Bassett three times. His first time on the stand, Bassett was relaxed. He removed his coat and leaned back in his chair as he spoke calmly and slowly. Delano first pursued the topic of superintendence. Bassett replied that Lucius Fenn first acted as superintendent, then Eugene

Gardner, and finally the committee consisting of William Clark, William Clement, and Lucius Dimock. Clement visited the site two to three times a week, Dimock less often. Fenn gave him and Wells instructions; Gardner did not but was on hand. Bassett never heard anything said against the way they were doing their work. He and Wells never signed a contract. They seriously thought about quitting the job when they received the revised specifications from Fenn, calling for a reduced-sized gate pipe, which they thought would endanger their work. But they had already spent $8,000 on the job and so opted to continue.

The *Springfield Republican* took note of Bassett's straightforward, frank manner as he described the things that rankled him about the project:

> Mr. Bassett's testimony was blunt and direct, as one would expect to look at the man. A figure sturdy, thick-set, rough-and-ready and full of habit, surmounted by a round head whose graying hairs indicate his years near fifty, and an open, prominent face, clean shaven, with whiskers of the [Horace] Greeley fashion, and whose characteristic expression of worldly wisdom was enhanced by his marked way of surveying the questioner, jury and people with his head tipped gently back on his broad shoulders.

The following day when Bassett was recalled, he described aspects of the dam's design that he considered defective. He had warned the mill owners that the gravel foundation on the west wall would leak but they said they would "risk it." The slope of the reservoir side of the embankment was too steep, and he had told Clement, Clark, Dimock, and Hayden that the inside slope should be 3:1. Hayden responded that they would have to fix it next year. The *Republican* quoted him as he recalled what he said at the time: "If they raised the water on that bank as it was," he said, "he wouldn't give a dollar for all the property in the valley."

Jury foreman Parsons questioned Bassett about the details of his work as they compared it with the evidence at the dam ruins. Bassett was adamant: The wall was built into a three-foot trench and the organic material was cleared from the soil within thirty feet of the wall, as called for in the specifications. Parsons asked Bassett to account for the fact that there was organic matter in the soil within five or six feet of the wall. Bassett's normally short, blunt answers turned rambling and evasive. After several vague attempts, Bassett relented: "I 'spose it was left there." Asked to show any evidence of a trench, he said there wasn't any, the flood had washed away all traces. Dr. Trow delved deeper. How did Bassett, believing that the trench had washed away, account for the fact that the stumps and natural earth rested on ground level with the foundation? A tired reporter concluded: "Finally, after the most wearisome repetitions of the question, Mr. Bassett was driven to say, 'I can't tell, sir.'"

The morning after Bassett's second appearance on the stand, his partner, Emory Wells of Northampton, was called. Like Bassett, he said that at first he took orders from Fenn, and, after Fenn left, he took them from directors Clark, Dimock, and Clement. Sometimes Spelman complained that they were digging too deep for the wall's foundation. Wells took direction from Gardner whenever he gave any, which was rarely. The directors asked Wells and Bassett to do work the following year, to add dirt to the banks to increase the slope. Bassett declined because of other business. Wells testified that he did some of it.

On the morning of Friday, May 29, before Bassett's third time testifying, the jury went up to the dam ruins, accompanied by the expert engineers Phineas Ball, Henry Wilson, and George Raymond; Delano; the mill owners; and Daniel Bond, the mill owners' attorney. They spent most of the day investigating how the dam was constructed and testing the materials used to build it. Bassett and Wells answered questions.

The next day, the coroner called Bassett for the final time. "Defiant and combative to the last degree" was how the *Springfield Republican* described him. He acknowledged that the original earth was not removed down to hardpan, but protested that the work suited Fenn or at least Fenn didn't say they should do any more. A juror asked whether the work was done according to the specifications. He said he thought at the time that they had followed the specifications, but now he had seen some muck and fibrous material in the bank, adding defensively that he hadn't seen many roots as big as his finger. He and his partner Wells knew there were springs under the embankment, which they took no steps to divert, unaware of where the springs would travel or how they would affect the dam.

The inquiry turned to Bassett's conscience. Delano recalled that Bassett had testified earlier that he had expressed doubts about the dam's stability because of the steep slope of the upstream bank. Delano wanted to know if he wavered about completing the project because of this fear. Bassett answered "no." Delano went further, inquiring if he knew that loss of property and life would result if the dam failed. He said "yes," he supposed that he did. Bassett confessed that he didn't know that they should have stopped out of consideration for property and life. Dr. Trow queried, "There wasn't a great deal of conscience in that?" and Bassett answered,

"I don't know what you mean by conscience. I don't know why conscience should hinder me. If the dam had to be built, I don't know why we shouldn't just as well build it as anybody else." After a short discussion about grouting, during which he allowed that it was never completely impervious to water and said he didn't know that the specifications required it to be so, Bassett was asked if he had a right to build a dam he knew to be unsafe. "I don't know but I have, if they want such a dam," he replied emphatically.

At the end of his testimony, he confessed that he expected the dam to go within the first year if it was left as it was built, but added quickly that he had meant to have made more money on it. The directors put extra faith in him and Wells, and the mill owners paid for it. Bassett and Wells were paid $23,600 and, after expenses, made $2,500 to $3,000 apiece for six months' work, an enormous sum, when a skilled brass worker made only about $250 in the same period.

Later that afternoon, Dimock was recalled to respond to similar questions about responsibility. In a soft, cautious manner he corrected earlier testimony by William Skinner, who had said that he heard him "cuss Bassett and Wells up hill and down" when referring to the contractors. Dimock admitted to swearing about them, not to them, when a little more than a year after the dam was finished, he found that the dam was slumping and leaking. Delano asked Dimock if he "confessed" that the mill owners did wrong in leaving the dam as it was. Dimock replied that he didn't mean to confess anything of the sort: "no one was perfect."

Delano pursued what Dimock knew about the quality of the work. He never had any idea that the grouting was so bad, he said, as he only saw how one or two stones were laid. Bassett and Wells never told him the dam would leak. He did not know they laid the stone on gravel and he would not have hesitated about digging deeper because of the expense. Mr. Fenn never expressed any distrust of the specifications to him, nor did Clark mention such distrust on Fenn's part.

On the subject of the reduction of the pipe size, Dimock was adamant that the pipe's only purpose was to regulate the supply of water, not to relieve pressure in an emergency. It was not useful to avert danger of overtopping since no rainfall would raise the reservoir as much as four feet unless it was empty. A ten-inch outlet pipe would suit fine. In the event that the dam was about to break, no outlet would have been of any value. Delano asked why the reservoir company supplied the gatekeeper with a horse. Dimock saw no need for a horse, saying "if he had a dam so weak as that, he would tear down the dam." The jury concluded his examination with questions about responsibility, which the *Springfield Republican* quoted:

> Dr. Trow asked 'Do you believe that any mill owners would have accepted the risk of his property had he known how it was built, as now revealed?' Mr. Dimock answered, 'No.' Capt. [a military title from the pre–Civil War local militia] Parsons asked 'Did you not have every opportunity of knowing how it was built?' but did not get a straightforward answer.

Dimock stepped down.

Although Dimock and the other mill owners would not admit to knowing how the dam was built or that it posed a hazard, the coroner brought forth several villagers who testified that they were aware of its instability and its potential hazard from the start. These men knew they lived beneath a dangerous dam, and after it failed, they were happy to state that they had seen the signs all along.

Gaius O. Wood, a clerk at the Henry James woolen mill, reported that the general sense of the insecurity of the dam was so great that many people left their homes at times of high water. He admonished Spelman for being so unaware of the importance of Cheney's arrival—implying that Spelman should have anticipated such a panicked visit by Cheney—that he would argue with Cheney long enough to delay him.

John W. Belcher, a livery owner in Williamsburg who had repaired the dam, corroborated Wood. The *Springfield Republican* summarized Belcher's testimony:

> Everybody was afraid of the dam till within a year or two. He [Belcher] had sometimes alarmed his neighbors below to such an extent that they removed their goods and the mill girls their trunks and taken to the hills, as far down as Skinnerville, where he had known everybody to remove everything from their homes.

Even Bassett and Wells's subcontractors testified they foretold the dam's failure. Justin Cook of Northampton, who had been employed by Bassett and Wells to excavate the ground and build up the earth walls, guessed he hadn't removed the organic matter from the soil quite as thoroughly as he should have. At one time, he had shared his feeling of insecurity because of water coming out near the gate pipe. He had heard Emory Wells himself express doubts one day when the two were coming back from Williamsburg while the dam was under construction. In Cook's words, Wells "didn't think it substantial enough."

The most damning testimony about the extent of the reservoir company's knowledge came from Joel Hayden's sons, Thomas and Joel Jr. On the last day of the inquest, when the coroner called Joel Jr. to the stand, it was an eerie moment. He so closely resembled his father, with the same distinguished presence, that those who had known his father may almost have wanted to believe it was him. When Delano asked what his father had thought of the dam, he reluctantly admitted that his father was scared of it. Trying to shield his father's integrity by pleading his timidity in his old age, Young Joel was forced by Delano, whom both he and his father knew well, to admit the depth of his father's fear. When Delano asked why his father went up to the dam in the middle of the night, Hayden supposed that he went for the same reason that he would sometimes go over to the brass works: to make sure it wasn't on fire. Delano countered that the brass factory was across the street from his father's home, while the reservoir was five miles up in the hills. "No," Hayden said, he only went up on rainy nights. He didn't think it would ever break.

Joel Hayden Sr.'s grave distrust of the dam was confirmed by Young Joel's brother, Thomas S. Hayden, who operated the Haydenville tobacco mill. Looking much like his younger brother, Thomas testified that his father had driven up to the Williamsburg dam in rainy weather late in the evening perhaps ten times and once asked Thomas to make the drive for him. Then, about a year ago, he had heard his father remark that he had never felt so secure about the dam as then. If his father gave a reason, Thomas didn't mention it in his testimony.

The jury turned its attention to the county commissioners, who had inspected and passed the dam. Commission chairman Elisha Brewster of Worthington testified that in 1867 the commissioners talked freely and informally with the directors as they walked around the dam together, discussing the source of leaks, whether they needed to be plugged, and how that might be accomplished. With none of the contractors invited, the stockholders referred to the written specifications, explained the construction themselves, and offered no history of any "weak spots." The commissioners saw no reason to doubt the mill owners' account. Brewster testified that he, at the time, had misgivings about the wall and said that he wouldn't have accepted it if he had known its character.

Delano asked commissioner Elisha Edwards of Southampton if he had any experience in dam building. No, came the reply, but he assumed that the commissioners knew as much about it as any three men. Later in the inquest, Delano exposed former commissioner Justin Thayer's limited knowledge of water, leaks, and dams by forcing him to admit that "they all were in doubt, as to where the water observable on the outside of the dam came from." The commissioners recommended repairs and returned to inspect the dam again in 1868 when they approved it. One of them wrote in their record book: "in the judgment of the Commissioners, [the Williamsburg dam is] sufficiently strong and substantial to resist the action of the water under any and all circumstances which may reasonably to be exposed [expected] to exist."

On June 5, the American Society of Civil Engineers sent a committee of three of the most famous engineers in America—James B. Francis of Lowell, Theodore Ellis of Hartford, and William E. Worthen of Pittsburgh—to investigate the disaster. Their findings, which were presented at the society's meeting, were the most thorough contemporary report of the failure, one with which today's engineers would generally agree.

"Usually more is to be learned from one failure than many successes," the report began. They found that "the remains of the dam indicate[d] defects of workmanship of the grossest character." The dam had at least seven problems that could have contributed to the failure. First, the banks were made of gravelly soil extracted from the hillsides that had little binding character and would not puddle. Second, the grout and mortar used to bind the wall was of "very bad" quality. Poor workmanship on the wall left grout that had "not completely filled the cavities." Third, roots from the site and bank materials had not been removed. The remaining problems were in the design. Fourth, requiring nothing more than to find a secure bottom for the wall to rest on, as though it were a building or bridge abutment, ignored the vital function of the wall, which was to prevent passage of water under it. Fifth, it was expected that the embankment would prevent water from leaching under the base of the wall, but the bank was to be of tamped earth which, even if it had been perfectly made, could not have stood up to the pressure of water in the reservoir. Sixth, the slope wasn't great enough; it should have been at least 2:1 on the downstream side and 2½:1 on the upstream side. Finally, the top of the wall should have been at least five feet below the crest to be protected from frost.

While the immediate cause of failure was difficult to determine with certainty, the engineers conjectured that "water found its way under the wall" east of the pipe, which caused the bank on the downstream side to saturate and slip. The wall was then unsupported and "yielded to the pressure on the upper side," which made a breach that was rapidly enlarged by the escaping water and the falling parts of the wall.

William Worthen added his own assessment. At the meeting of the Society he described the dam before and after the failure, referring to a clay model of the dam and showing specimens of the rock, mortar and grout, and hardpan. He summed up: "Men were employed who were ignorant of the work to be done, and there was nothing like an inspection, although money and life depended upon it. I do not believe, however much we are an evolved species, that we are derived from beavers; a man cannot make a dam by instinct or intuition."

The mill owners had gambled and lost. They knew the dam was inadequately designed and poorly constructed, and despite many warnings about its condition, they couldn't, or wouldn't, stop using it or tear it down. Their engineering ignorance and their shared need for waterpower allowed them to believe that it might actually be safe. The reservoir company had sole control over what course of action to take, and the directors had two options. The first was to acknowledge its inadequacies and pay to tear the dam down, lose their investment, suffer some embarrassment, and find more capital to build another one, reducing their available waterpower until a new dam could be erected. The second option was to stay the course, maintain the present dam, patch it, hope that it held, and minimize their liability in case it broke. In the absence of regulation, their consciences were their guides, and their consciences favored their own self-interest and the interests of maintaining harmony among the directors.

Members of the reservoir company consistently deferred to those who professed to have more knowledge in a particular area. When William Clark suggested they hire the railroad engineer to design the dam, they went along. When Clark suggested a surveyor and architect to look over the work, they agreed. When Hayden's former business partner Samuel Williston recommended contractors who had never built a reservoir dam, they followed his advice. When the contractors suggested that they lay the foundation of the west wall on gravel, they hemmed and hawed and complied. When he was there, Hayden went along, too. Maybe he thought the politically wise thing to do was to acquiesce to others, worry in private, and fix the dam later. Maybe he felt some guilt over not having been personally in charge of the construction of the dam and thought it was his responsibility to fix it. Maybe, too, he was a little vain, confident that he could fix this one. To tear it down would be to admit defeat. The characteristics that made a good manufacturer—self-confidence, technical know-how, can-do attitude, decisiveness, and cost-consciousness—were precisely the wrong attributes for a dam overseer.

For members of the reservoir company, it was easier to participate in the collective delusion that the dam was reparable than it was to challenge the status quo. It was more palatable to throw small sums of money at the project than to pay a huge sum to start over. As the group made each repair, complacency set in. The owners became accustomed to worrying about the dam, to repairing, to thinking that another patch was what was needed, they just hadn't hit upon the right spot yet. Then, as each prediction of failure turned out to be a false alarm, any warning about the dam became like the boy who cried wolf. Hayden actually convinced himself it was secure. It had stood the test of time. Then he convinced the others. In a slow accumulation, a kind of rolling rationalization with a momentum all its own, they gradually accepted the weak dam as strong enough. They were accustomed to living with its insecurity just as the villagers grew used to living with fear of its failure. The villagers inquired of the mill owners about the dam's safety, speaking as individuals, but when the mill owners offered assurances, the villagers took no further action. There was a line they could not properly cross; to protest or take collective action against their local patriarchs would have been unthinkable. The Williamsburg dam was the valley's sleeping giant that no one wanted to believe would awaken.

Wright adjourned the inquest on May 29 after seven days. He and the jury planned to reconvene in three weeks on June 18 to review testimony written up by the court reporter and, possibly, to recall some witnesses. They expected to deliver a verdict soon afterward.

CHAPTER 7

THE VERDICT

FIVE days after the inquest adjourned, on June 3, 1874, workers digging for button mill machinery on William Quigley's meadow in Leeds discovered the body of a tall boy, his arms wrapped around a thick timber. Someone ran to Ross's store at the top of the village to find Henry Sharpe, who had been working there as he waited for news of his sixteen-year-old brother Arthur. Will Tunnicliff was the last person to see Arthur alive, thrashing in the stream, crying for help after being swept out of Warner's button mill. But Will couldn't reach Arthur and watched helplessly as he sank into the current. Henry looked at the body, which was in bad condition. He knew it was Arthur by the shortness of one leg and by the clothes he was last seen wearing. Arthur Sharpe was the one hundred thirty-fifth victim found.

Four others were still unaccounted for. The body of seven-year-old Rosa Wilson of Haydenville would be located under a barn in Leeds a week later. Her father, who had brought the family from Canada six years earlier, was the family's only survivor; he had already buried Rosa's mother, Margaret, and Rosa's two sisters, ten-year-old Matilda and five-year-old Margaret. The second unrecovered victim was Julia Patrick of Leeds, seventeen years old and Canadian-born, whose body would be found two weeks later, lodged against a tree beneath the stone bridge in Leeds. The third, Canadian Augustus Laney, had been a sawyer at the button mill where his job had been to slice thick ivory nuts into thin buttons. According to coworker Fred Howard, Laney "was last seen holding on the fence just above the wooden shop and was probably struck by a timber as many were." Fred lamented that Laney "was one of the best Frenchmen in the place." His body would be found in Leeds July 17, two months after the flood, the last one recovered. The fourth missing victim was six-year-old John Fennessey of Leeds; his body was never located.

There was no published official death toll, no single roster of victims. Newspapers revised their totals daily, ranging them from 135 to 150, as they added and dropped names. The *Hampshire Gazette* put their final total at 145, the *Springfield Republican* at 144, and the *Springfield Union* at 140. The names on the published lists varied, the spelling was irregular, and the newspapers often counted incorrectly. While the *Springfield Union* asserted that there were 140 dead, it listed only 136 names. The Williamsburg and Northampton town clerks, who inscribed the names of those who died in their town in tall ledgers, listed all but a few of the victims. Their numbers, plus a few from trusted sources, add up to 139.

The same day that Arthur Sharpe's body was found, general talk flowed through the valley that something ought to be done to honor the flood's heroes, who had become national celebrities. During the last two weeks in May and the first two in June, Americans couldn't pick up a newspaper or magazine without encountering the Mill River disaster and the stories of George Cheney's and Collins Graves's rides. Graves saw himself on the cover of the May 20 issue of the *New York Daily Graphic*, which featured an artist's rendering of him racing down a mountainside, lashing his horse vigorously as he twists in his saddle to glance back at the foggy tower of water looming behind. The caption read, "Collins Graves. The Heroic Milkman Alarming the Villagers, The Hampshire Flood." Two weeks later, *Harper's Weekly* magazine, with a circulation of about 160,000, presented portraits of Cheney and Graves on the cover, along with a sketch of Cheney, switch in hand, speeding away from the crumbling dam. Inside, a two-page bird's-eye view of the valley captured the geography and the wasted buildings in such detail that it looked like a sketch from an aerial photograph. The accompanying article concluded with a tribute to the heroes:

> It must not be forgotten that the disaster would have been tenfold more terrible but for the bravery of CHENEY and GRAVES who spread the alarm through the valley just in advance of the flood. We give their portraits on our first page. CHENEY was a soldier in the Twentieth Army Corps, and served with credit and honor through the whole war.

Graves and Cheney earned some cash from their celebrity. Graves drove sightseers to the dam for a fee. He was offered $50 to exhibit himself at Holyoke but refused. Cheney stayed in Williamsburg, rode the same horse to farm laboring jobs, and sold stereographs of the flood. The papers reported that Cheney and his horse went on exhibition in Connecticut with a Holyoke man, but Cheney denied it. Myron Day did not appear in any of the magazines, perhaps because the writers and artists focused on the relay of the news from Cheney to Graves.

Beginning the day after the flood, photographers drove tall, boxy wagons, which served as mobile darkrooms, into the valley to record the destruction. They took stereophotographs by using small compact cameras with two short parallel lenses that snapped two pictures of the same scene at the same time, inches apart, much the way one's eye would see the image. The photographs would later be paired side by side on a card approximately three-and-a-half by seven inches, and viewed through a special viewer called a stereoscope. Making use of the principle of binocular vision—that each eye records a slightly different image that is then fused with the other by the brain—the stereoscope had two small lenses for viewing the two photographs at the same time. Seeing the scenes in stereo produced the illusion of being in the space, a much more immediate effect than that made by two-dimensional pictures. By the 1840s stereophotograph viewing was a world-wide craze, the first universal system of visual communication before cinema and television. Most middle- and upper-class homes owned a hand-held or tabletop stereoscope and an assortment of cards on such topics as Niagara Falls, the Civil War, the Swiss Alps, and the Great Chicago Fire.

Within a week or two after the flood, at least eight companies offered for sale four hundred images, sold in sets, at an average price of twenty-five cents per dozen. The gap in the dam, the site of Spelman's button mill, Main Street in Williamsburg with crosses marking the former location of houses, Skinnerville flat, and Quigley's house in Leeds were favorite subjects. There was only one image of a victim. A somber group of men look down on the body of a woman stretched out on a wooden door, her leg broken, the men ready to carry her to a morgue. Images of Cheney on the porch of the gate-keeper's cabin and Graves posing in his milk wagon added the heroes' narrative. The humble heroes looked like ordinary men, with untrimmed hair brushed back from their faces and their modest clothes smoothed.

Readers couldn't get enough of the Mill River disaster, with its tales of valor and despair, of man against nature, and nature against civilization. The publication that assured Cheney's and Graves's celebrity was the forty-eight-page booklet amply titled A *Full and Graphic Account of the Terrible Mill River Disaster, Caused by the Breaking of a Reservoir in Hampshire County, Mass., May 16, 1874, with Full Details of the Loss of Life and Property at Williamsburg, Skinnerville, Haydenville and Leeds,* published within three weeks of the flood. This wildly popular booklet, which drew heavily from the *Springfield Republican*'s coverage, told the thrilling aspects of the flood story through the heroes' actions and summarized the rest. These booklets were inexpensive enough for Graves's cover image to have graced the parlor table of most homes in New England.

A *Full and Graphic Account* concluded with three poems reprinted from newspapers about the heroes' deeds, accompanied by their portraits. With biblical and literary images familiar to nineteenth-century Americans, the poems immortalized the heroes as larger-than-life figures.

"George Cheney's Warning at the Breaking of the Dam," reprinted from the *New York Graphic*, begins with the narrator urging Cheney on as he rides ahead of a shrouded, icy-breathed Death figure, the pale horseman of the Apocalypse:

Ride! Cheney, ride! For close beside,
On a ghostly galloping steed,
Is a grizzly shade, in a shroud arrayed;—
Death rides behind thee! Speed!

The flood was the Mill Valley's own miniature apocalypse.

"The Ride of Collins Graves," a twenty-five-stanza poem by Sidney Dickinson of Amherst, also used images of a race with a pale rider within a narrative verse rife with strained rhymes and poetic clichés. The first stanza sets the scene in the verdant valley, "dressed in spring-time's bright array," down which "comes a horseman, breathless and pale." The first rider is Cheney, who sinks to the ground astride his exhausted horse and cries to the people gathered around:

Curious, laughing, or dreading the worst—
"Flee for your lives! The reservoir's burst!"

Graves hears Cheney's message and picks up the ride:

His hat is gone—his hair in the wind
Streams back from his earnest face,
And turning his head he glances behind,
Yet never relaxes his pace.
He sees the tossing of shattered beams,
And hears in the tumult the dying screams

Of those o'er whom the torrent has gushed,—
An instant more and their shrieks are hushed,
And faster he urges his race.

The poem concludes by praising Graves as a hero for the ages, in a league with Paul Revere and Civil War hero General Philip Henry Sheridan.

Heroes were popular topics for nineteenth-century American poetry. Beyond the literary appeal, which tended to ennoble the subject, magnify the peril, and preserve the deeds in a conventional, memorable form, broadside poetry about the flood's heroes also helped survivors recast the awful event into something to celebrate. Such poems easily summarized and romanticized the tragic events and never mentioned responsibility. By turning the flood into a death figure or a wild animal, they pitted human strength against the brute force of the water and focused on those who dared to race against it. While the heroes could not defeat the water or force it into submission, they could alert people to move from its path, giving survivors a measure of success and control in the face of disaster. Telling and retelling the heroes' narrative were steps in rebuilding the community.

As poetry and popular literature inflated their brave deeds, the heroes became easy targets for reporters scrounging stories. Five days after the flood, one enterprising *Boston Globe* reporter wrote: "It is an ugly task to prick this bright bubble" of the heroes "but it must be done for the blessed sake of truth!" From unnamed sources, he cobbled together another version of the famous rides. Cheney, who was "not over bright," was so frightened that his only thoughts were to seek help from his employer, Spelman. Graves was so slow-witted and unwilling to face danger that he had to see water first and be told several times to head downriver to Haydenville. The editorial page highly praised the journalist:

> One or two poets got the start of the reporters and tried to immortalize them, but in this utilitarian age, when the prosy reporter has displaced the imaginative minstrel, it will be impossible to keep up the illusion and send these riders down the stream of time with . . . Paul Revere.

The *Springfield Republican* angrily shot back at the *Globe* reporter, accusing him of having an "unhealthy hankering for originality" and making a "malicious snatch at their [heroes'] laurels." "Graves and Day are not apocryphal heroes—and the poets may sing on," blared the *Republican*.

In response, *The Boston Globe* sent an unnamed member of the editorial staff to the Mill Valley "to ascertain the exact facts." He arrived in Williamsburg on a Sunday morning, eight days after the flood, and found Graves at church. As the writer waited outside, he chatted with townspeople, none of whom had a bad thing to say about the man they described as a "likely" fellow, an honest and hardworking milk peddler. While the townspeople's stories about Graves's ride differed in detail, they all praised him for starting promptly and driving speedily. When the church doors opened and villagers poured out, a man the *Globe* writer had been chatting to called out "Colly." A tall, slim, youthful man, about thirty-five, with gray-streaked brown hair and a thick moustache, walked over and talked openly about his new status. Graves admitted that his sudden notoriety saddened him. Neighbors teased him about the poems and pictures in newspapers and magazines. Fueled by *The Boston Globe*, others chided him for being a false hero. What hurt most, he said, was that some Williamsburg inhabitants blamed him for not spreading the alarm in his home village to save his own friends and neighbors. Graves said he was so sure that others would warn the village after he left to warn Haydenville that he never gave it another thought. He was shocked, he said, when he learned later that so many in Williamsburg had perished. Although he knew in his heart that he had done his best, it was hard to be condemned, especially by neighbors. The next day, the *Globe* sheepishly retracted its condemnation of Graves and suggested that readers evaluate the truth of the hero tales themselves. The cloud over Graves's heroism would follow him the rest of his life.

Despite the *Boston Globe* articles and the controversy they generated, most of the valley's residents wanted to participate in a public gesture of appreciation before too many honors were bestowed by outsiders. The *Boston Transcript* reported that an unnamed Bostonian had presented Collins Graves with a silver-based lamp with the words FLY TO THE HILLS etched on the glass globe. For nineteenth-century Americans, publicly honoring heroes with ceremonies, speeches, awards, tributes, and the dedication of plaques and statues were familiar civic events. Henry C. Hayden, a distant cousin of Joel Jr., a Boston businessman and a well-known poet whose collection sold well all over New England, offered the proceeds from a benefit reading to be held at the Northampton town hall on Saturday night, June 13. Tickets were fifty cents each, with no reserved seats and no free tickets. "A rare treat to hear Mr. Hayden read," the *Northampton Free*

Press chimed. A short, fat, and jolly man in his late forties with the pronounced Hayden nose, Henry Hayden handed Skinner $102 after the con-
cert to spend on the heroes as he saw fit. With the promise of more to come,
Skinner commissioned Tiffany & Co., the New York jewelers, to design
four gold medals, one each for Cheney, Graves, Myron Day, and Jerome
Hillman. While no poetry had been written about Day and Hillman, the
Springfield Republican exclaimed that Day's "close quarters with death" as
he raced through the gorge qualified him for a medal. Hillman's biggest
supporter was Joel Hayden Jr., whose letter to the editor of the *New York
Tribune* told how Hillman saved lives at the brass works:

> Sir: There is one fact connected with the disaster of Saturday last that
> seems to have escaped general note, and that is that Mr. Jerome Hillman
> of Skinnerville followed Collins Graves to this place, leaving his own
> home and family, his wife being one of the victims swept away by the
> flood: and it is to him that we are indebted more than to any one else, for
> the alarm being given to our operatives and citizens, thereby saving many
> lives. He rushed into our works and rang the bell.
>
> J. Hayden
> Haydenville, Mass., May 22, 1874

There would be no medal for twelve-year-old Jimmy Ryan of Williamsburg,
who had raced the family wagon downriver to warn his father and brother
at the brass factory. The guard at the factory gate, Benson Munyan, would
later assert that Jimmy arrived before Hillman or Graves and that young
Ryan should be credited with saving the brass workers. While it can never
be settled who was first, it was clear that it took Ryan, Graves, and Hillman
to convince the brass workers to evacuate. Perhaps Jimmy was too young to
have his role taken seriously enough for a medal to be made for him.

How Skinner came to head the heros' fund is uncertain. Skinner was
undoubtedly indebted to Graves for saving his life and those of his workers,
but perhaps, too, valley residents were savvy in persuading Skinner to lead
the hero campaign, hoping that Skinner, still undecided about where to
rebuild his factory, would respond to the strong tug of community ties and
resolve to stay in Skinnerville. Or, perhaps Skinner was politically astute. If
he had felt a sting of dishonor after the inquest, he might have seen the fund
as an opportunity to reassert his role as community leader. Whatever the
reason, the financially ruined mill owner could draw on the generation of

goodwill he had built up and marshal his influence, his wide circle of con-
tacts, and his sophisticated taste to benefit the community.

As valley residents discussed the heroes' fund, they also talked about the
condition of the Goshen dams on the West Branch. In early June, fifty-one
men petitioned the county commissioners to inspect the dams, citing as an
example of their concern a stream as large as "the face of a watch" bubbling
up from under the west end of the upper dam. The mill owners went along
with the inspections to quell public fears. On the morning of June 11, the
county commissioners and members of the reservoir company, followed by
interested townsfolk and a *Springfield Republican* reporter, rode up to
Goshen to inspect the dams. The commissioners and the mill owners were
well acquainted. Two of the three county commissioners—Elisha Edwards
of Southampton and Justin Thayer of Northampton—had inspected the
Williamsburg dam seven years earlier while in office; one commissioner,
S. M. Cook of Granby, was a new member. They had invited Emory Davis,
who had designed the upper dam, but he couldn't attend and the commissioners sought no substitute engineer. W. R. Holliday of Northampton, who
had built the upper dam, was there. The group had no sooner arrived at the
upper dam and marveled at the sunshine lighting up the green hills and
blue reservoirs when a cluster of dark clouds rolled over the hills to menace
them with showers all day.

When the commissioners looked at the upper dam, which had been in
use for a year, they were astounded at how unfinished it appeared, as though
workers had walked away in mid-job. Water lapped against the bare
upstream bank while a load of stone, enough to riprap the inside bank to
prevent erosion, was heaped on the top of the dam. No grass was planted on
the bare downstream bank to bind the soil and prevent erosion. A narrow,
unevenly dug dirt trench, not wide enough to carry off the water in heavy
rains, served as the wasteway. For all its sloppiness, it was a massive structure—14 feet high and 528 feet long, almost the length of two football
fields, end to end, and 80 feet thick at its base. The core of puddled earth—
dirt and clay mixed with water and compacted—was ten feet thick at the
bottom, sunk into rock. While puddle cores were commonly used, they
required extreme care and close supervision to ensure the layers were
tamped tightly and smoothly. Now covered with earthen banks, it was
impossible to tell how carefully it had been made.

The commissioners then turned their attention to the watch-sized stream on the dam's west end. The reservoir company insisted that the stream was the result of saturation by rain, while locals argued that the leaks, which had always been there, were evidence of reservoir water making its way through the earthwork. Back and forth the two parties debated. The argument escalated when W. R. Holliday, the builder, remarked offhandedly, "We put in frozen earth here, last fall, before we got through." The villagers charged Holliday with knowingly compromising the dam by using earth they couldn't compact. The builder and the reservoir directors adamantly defended the materials and workmanship until finally, the reservoir directors backed off. They didn't need to win the argument; they simply needed to keep the dam in use, so they offered to fix the leak. The commissioners assented. Tension dissipated as everyone agreed that there was no immediate jeopardy because there was so little water in the reservoir.

Finished with the inspection of the upper dam, the party traveled a mile down the valley to the lower Goshen reservoir, built by Joel Hayden Sr. in 1852. Water jetted from the gate pipe that penetrated the 528-foot-long bank. Its strength was its core. A row of four-inch-square timbers, tongue-and-grooved together and driven on end into hardpan, were sandwiched between two masonry walls that were supported by banks of mica slate decomposition mixed with hardpan and built in layers, each as hard as roadbed. The base was 60 feet thick and the top was 40 feet, more than twice the thickness of the Williamsburg dam. The county commissioners thought this twenty-two-year-old dam was a very solid structure, the safest dam on the Mill River. Their only concern was that, if the upper dam broke, the lower dam wouldn't be able to handle the overflow.

The party's last stop was the Searsville reservoir, a small, eighteen-acre pond, a mile and a half north of Williamsburg village. It had been built in the 1850s by three men who owned several small Searsville factories on the West Branch. In the 1870s, its owners gave it to the Mill River and Williamsburg Reservoir Company to use and repair. The reservoir company used it but never repaired it. After inspecting the dam the commissioners agreed that while it did not appear safe, it posed little danger compared with the larger dams upstream. The day over, the county commissioners scheduled a time to reconvene to write up a list of repairs.

Four days after the commissioners' inspection, with tension still high about the Goshen dams, Goshen gatekeepers Tim Lyman and Charles Barrus took the opportunity to lay some ground rules by addressing the villagers through the *Hampshire Gazette*. Still smarting from the near-violent treatment they received after the flood by villagers who wanted the reservoirs drawn down, Lyman wrote:

> Hereafter no order from Tom, Dick, or Harry, will open the gates, and that if he or any one else, wishes the gates opened, they must first get an order from one of the directors of the Co., also, that threats do not pass current at this bank.

Barrus was equally clear:

> I now hold the key to the gate, subject to the order of Mr. Clement and the proper authorities, and shall neither raise nor shut the gate unless under extraordinary circumstance and that not by threats of violence or mob-law.

When the county commissioners filed their report in late June, it contained no surprises. They pronounced the older or lower Goshen reservoir "in good and safe condition," and recommended only that a wing wall be added to the west end of the dam; this had been Henry Wilson's suggestion when he viewed it earlier. However, the upper dam—"not being sufficiently strong" to resist the water under normal circumstances—required massive rebuilding. The commissioners ordered the core of the newer dam to be rebuilt on the same design as the older dam, with a five-foot-wide ditch to be dug down three feet into the hardpan several feet behind the existing wall. Four-inch-square pilings were to be sharpened on one end, driven into the hardpan, tongue-and-grooved together, and then held in place by courses of grouting and concrete mixtures topped with "closely rammed" layers of puddling material. Then they were to raise the top of the dam three feet above the wasteway and cover the downstream slope with pasture soil, which they were to plant with grass and oats and fence to keep cattle off until the grasses took hold. They were instructed to grade the inside slope with a 2:1 ratio and pave it with one-foot-thick stones "compactly placed." Massive changes were also required of the Searsville dam, whose center wall was to be removed and rebuilt. A month after the commissioners' report, the reservoir company advertised for sealed proposals for repairs to the Searsville and upper Goshen dam. The contract was awarded a week later to Emory Davis. His contractors, partners Sumner and Fuller of Holyoke, began work on the upper Goshen dam in mid-August and on the Searsville structure a month later.

A week after taking charge of the heroes' fund, on the one-month anniversary of the flood, William Skinner received the design for the medals from Tiffany & Co. The solid gold pieces, about the size of a silver dollar, were to be inscribed with the words MILL RIVER RESERVOIR DISASTER, MAY 16, 1874. Engraved upon the reverse, wreathed in laurel, was to be the name of the recipient with the word *courage* above and *humanity* beneath. Cheney's and Hillman's medals would bear on the face a horseback rider at full speed, while Graves's and Day's would show a man driving a wagon ahead of a torrent, lashing his galloping horse. With Skinner's approval, Tiffany & Co. began making the medals. A week later, a party of seventy-five local men, who vowed that Skinner would not "go back on them," surprised the mill owner by showing up at his house for a work "bee," equipped with eight pair of oxen and six teams of horses to spend the day clearing and leveling his property. Their work demonstrated their appreciation for his efforts on their behalf and their desire for him to stay. The *Springfield Republican* commented that Mr. Skinner had so many warm friends that "the work has been done with a right good will."

But Skinner had no real hopes of rebuilding. He had only a section of his old dam, no canal, and, with the factory site stripped to a rocky plain, no soil in which to dig a new foundation or canal. If he were to remain in Skinnerville, he would have to use steam and he couldn't afford the high cost of freighting in fuel to run the steam engines. So Skinner considered Philadelphia, Brooklyn, Worcester, and Holyoke, among other places, and took a long trip to visit all of them.

In the end, Skinner couldn't pass up the Holyoke Water Power Company's offer. Their inducement included a $6,000 mill site and water power rent-free for five years, money at 7 percent interest to erect the factory and connect the machinery, the opportunity to buy the mill and site in five years for the original cost, and one whole city block for his house lot. For working capital Skinner would cash in his $20,000 endowment life insurance policy, which had matured that year. On June 27, William Skinner composed this letter, which Samuel Bowles, the editor of the *Springfield Republican*, published two days later.

> *To the Editor of the Republican.* I write to say I have fixed upon Holyoke as my future place of business. I have examined various places and found none that offer such inducements as this place. Cheap and reliable water

power is to a manufacturer what good rich land is to a farmer. He can get good returns for his labor. And I take this means of expressing thanks to my friends in Worcester, Springfield, and Northampton for the sympathy and interest they have expressed in my behalf, and the desire they have evinced that I should, if forced to make a change, locate among them. I consider the competition is too great to allow me to run my business by steam. And to my dear old friends in Williamsburg: I leave you with a heavy heart after spending so many happy and prosperous years among you but my "poverty and not my will" compels me. And may the good old town soon recover from the sad calamity now resting upon it, is the desire of

WILLIAM SKINNER

On the morning after he signed the contract, fifty men began clearing the Holyoke factory lot.

The valley was saddened but not surprised. A correspondent named M.P. from Goshen wrote to the *Hampshire Gazette:* "We are . . . sorry to hear that Mr. Skinner has concluded to leave his old spot, where he has made a handsome fortune, and gained for himself a good name which no flood can wash away."

If M.P. took the news in stride, others didn't. An unidentified reader from a hill town near Williamsburg ranted that his neighbors had forgotten that the future of the mills was everyone's business:

While you have buttoned up your pocket, others more far-seeing have made him [Skinner] such inducements that he cannot afford to stay where he has made himself an honored man, a father and brother to his whole village . . . Three hundred men may read this article who could well afford to set every wheel in motion on Mill River have given him the inducements to stay . . . The towns in this county, west of a line drawn north and south at the intersection of the Goshen and Chesterfield roads in Williamsburg, cannot do a more sensible thing than to voluntarily tax themselves, if it is a legal possibility, to the amount of thirty thousand dollars, and give it, in favor of rebuilding the destroyed district . . . The proportion of our [farmers'] produce sold in Williamsburg and Leeds is enormous . . .

Then he raged at the mill owners:

Citizens of the county, they, like all others, owe a duty at home. Their business and their property have been made in our midst, and this should have all the weight that it is entitled to. It should be a very grave reason that causes them to abandon their hundreds of operatives, who have grown up under their protection, and are now so anxiously awaiting further developments.

The blistering commentary may have been too late to affect Skinner's decision, but it spurred local business leaders to redouble their efforts to convince Hayden and Warner to stay. On July 3, Hayden agreed to accept the offer from the Northampton businessmen, the county commissioners, and the railroad and committed to rebuild the brass works in the valley.

Three days later, a group of Northampton capitalists stepped in and together loaned Warner the remaining $20,000 at 6 percent interest that he needed to rebuild his button factory. The principals in Warner's newly formed company, whose investments totalled $41,000, were familiar faces in valley industries: Alfred Critchlow, Warner's father-in-law, was the factory's previous owner and a founding member of the reservoir company; Horatio Knight was Samuel Williston's business partner; and A. Lyman Williston, John Payson Williston's son and Samuel's nephew, was a prominent investor in the Greenville Manufacturing Company (cotton) in Florence, the First National Bank in Northampton, the Hampshire Savings Bank, and the Florence Savings Bank. The factory's principal building would be brick, two stories high, and 32 by 130 feet. The packing, storehouse, and offices would be combined in another structure. Fred Howard must have been overjoyed. He was probably one of the fifty neighbors who, a week later, met for a day to clear Warner's factory grounds.

Of the twenty-nine mills, shops, and stores that were damaged or destroyed by the flood, twenty-two were reopened locally. Henry James had already started up his woolen mill in Williamsburg using steam. Soon after, his workers redug his old channel so the river could power his machinery. The valley's economy remained largely unchanged as local mill owners continued in charge and most of the workforce stayed. Only Skinnerville ceased to exist.

That summer a sign of hopefulness sprouted at the end of the flood route. Shoots of grass pushed aside a thin layer of gravel to spread small soft green patches on sections of the Florence meadows. Farmers hoped that the verdant display meant that some fields hadn't suffered permanent damage, but most knew that the loss of alluvial topsoil meant that their fields, the most expensive acreage in the valley, would never again approach their predictably large harvests. This year they would have to wait to see what the earth yielded. Against this backdrop of the promise of renewal came the verdict of the coroner's inquest.

While Skinner, Hayden, and Warner decided the futures of their factories, coroner's inquest jurors Enos Parsons, George Hubbard, Silas Hubbard, Hiram Nash, William Trow, and John Mayher deliberated over who was responsible for the failure of the Williamsburg dam that caused John Atkinson's death. For several days the jurors failed to agree on a verdict—"every member holding an opinion of his own" as the *Springfield Republican* characterized it—until finally each juror was instructed to write out his own verdict. Four jurors completed the task. The two who hadn't—they may have been absent or chose not to do it for some other reason—were assigned to merge the four draft verdicts into a single document. By the end of a day, these unnamed jurors had written a single statement. After a lawyer adjusted their language, the jury revised it. Finally, the committee adopted the verdict, which they handed to a copyist whose neat handwriting filled eight pages. The jurors signed it July 3, nearly six weeks after the disaster. The Springfield, Boston, and New York newspapers published it with no commentary on the Fourth of July, amid articles about holiday picnics, horse races, balloon ascensions, boating trips, and fireworks.

The verdict found that John Atkinson came to his death by drowning during a "sudden rise or overflow" of the Mill River "caused by the breaking away" of the Williamsburg reservoir dam. The break was the result of the "great and manifest delinquency of the several parties who were concerned in originating, planning, constructing and approving [the reservoir] for use." The verdict named five parties responsible:

I. *The Delinquent Legislation.* The verdict read that the "Commonwealth through its law makers assumed a large share of the responsibility" when it granted corporate powers and privileges to the reservoir company for the construction of a dam above villages with "no other guarantees for the security of life and property below than such as might depend on the self interest or will of a private citizen." Further, the statute was designed to "repel rather than invite careful scrutiny of works," a reference to the clause that required a person who calls for an examination of the dams to pay the cost of the proceeding if the dam is found to be safe. The verdict pleaded for prompt action to ensure the security of such projects in the future.

II. *As to the Proprietors of the Reservoir.* The jury's judgment was that the proprietors cared "far less for the safety and security of the lives and property of the inhabitants below the dam, than for reducing the cost of construction to the minimum figure." The building committee was particularly responsible because they had no experience and either ignored or partially followed the advice of the engineers. When signs of weakness appeared in the dam, "they either but half applied the remedy or ignored the danger altogether." Finally, the vote to consult counsel and to take steps to relieve individual liability in case the dam broke was "speaking evidence that self interest and not the welfare of the community dictated the action of this company."

III. As to the Engineers. Their work reflected poorly on both the employer and the employee. The dam was "without an hour's attendance of a competant [sic] and watchful engineer" from the groundbreaking to the job's completion. Fenn yielded "his own judgment on points of safety" to accommodate the requirements of his ignorant employers. As unqualified as he was, Gardner was "the only superintendent or engineer" in attendance after Fenn's departure, and he ought to have been more thorough.

IV. As to the Contractors. The contractors were "guilty of great and manifest delinquency." By the jurors' own observation, the work of preparing the ground, laying the wall, and making the grout was not performed according to specification. These deficiencies coupled with the "large profit confessedly made on the job" are evidence that Bassett and Wells "did not faithfully execute the work contracted for."

V. As to the County Commissioners. Their duty was of the "gravest character," and they had full power to take any steps necessary to thoroughly examine and test the reservoir, including the authority to call in engineers and other experts. The evidence at the dam site shows that "their examinations were not thorough nor in conformity to the spirit of the law," and their actions were a "superficial discharge of a most important duty."

To the jury's credit, they overlooked personal interests and associations and found fault with mill owners, commissioners, and legislators, many of whom were their friends, business associates, and peers. The verdict was unanimous except that Hiram Nash, a former legislator from Williamsburg, dissented on the first paragraph concerning the legislature because he didn't believe that lawmakers should be held responsible for situations, like the flood, that they never could have imagined at the time they wrote the laws. He would later say that he wished he had reserved blame on the county commissioners, too, because, as he told the *Hampshire Gazette*, "they adjudicated on a dam that, according to the evidence presented them, was safe." The verdict mandated no indictments. No one was charged with a crime and no civil suits were carried out. In the end, no one paid a dime for the disaster.

The verdict accurately and thoroughly described how the five parties abrogated their duties and caused the disaster, and it pinpointed the central problem with the state-sponsored system of dam construction and maintenance—that it relied on the personal ethics of the dam owners, designers, builders, and inspectors. When the participants neglected their moral responsibility to build a safe structure, there was no mechanism to check their actions.

If the verdict's breadth was its strength, it was also a weakness. It spread blame so thinly it stuck to no one. The *Hampshire Gazette* compared it to "the sermons of the old-time divines—it covers many points and has many heads." With the responsibility "so widely and evenly" distributed "nobody will feel especially hurt." After six weeks of voluminous daily flood coverage, the newspapers had little more to say. The *Springfield Republican* summed up: "The public rendered its verdict on the Mill River disaster a long while ago, and the formal finding of the coroner's jury . . . comes too late to excite any more than a languid interest. They have come to very much the same conclusions . . . as the larger jury of the public has already reached."

Survivors didn't react, protest, storm anyone's house, or hang anyone in effigy. No one called for the resignation of county commissioners or legislators. If villagers gossiped or fumed about hostile actions they would like to take against mill owners, engineers, and contractors, the papers didn't mention them. Rather than expressing malice or powerlessness, villagers were shocked to think that their local manufacturers had caused the flood. Preaching a week after the disaster, the Reverend Kimball said that this was a time "when the very foundations seem to be washed away." It was a time when the moorings of their paternalistic society were jolted, when their world teetered, but stood. In the end, the mill owners, who impressed them as self-made men, and to whom they were indebted for the churches, schools, and social institutions they had created, could not be cast out as evil men. Evildoers did not wear silk vests, attend church, join the Masons, fight local fires, or chair flood relief committees. If the status of the mill owners was reduced or lowered, and if they were humbled or chastened, it wasn't by much. The valley's social foundations may have shuddered, but they were steady and strong enough to build upon again.

The valley accepted the verdict, and so did the nation. Americans in 1874 lived in a complacent moral climate in which steam engine explosions, bridge and building collapses, and train collisions occurred with alarming frequency. While Americans saw the Mill River flood as a terrible calamity, it was but one incident out of thousands for which no one was held accountable. Mark Twain and Charles Dudley Warner satirized such blamelessness in *The Gilded Age*, published in 1873, the year before the Mill River flood. To win a steamboat race in what began as a friendly rivalry, a captain overtaxes his engine, and the boiler explodes, sending more than a hundred passengers—most dead—into the Mississippi River. Twain and Warner conclude the incident:

> A jury of inquest was impaneled, and after due deliberation and inquiry they returned the inevitable American verdict which has been so familiar to our ears all the days of our lives—"NOBODY TO BLAME."

Twain's own brother was killed in 1858 in a similar Mississippi River explosion, for which no one was named responsible.

The Boston Globe labeled the flood "not an accident but a crime" and called upon the next session of the Legislature to enact laws that would require strict accountability for all mill owners, contractors, and elected officials. Similarly, *The New York Times* summed up by calling the event "a gross and criminal evasion of law and trifling with life and property." Then it charged: "Now let us see what Massachusetts will do about it." The Legislature would take up the challenge the following year.

But next year would be too late. Eleven days after the verdict, two reservoir dams piggybacked on Middlefield Brook in Middlefield, fifteen miles west of Williamsburg, burst on a rainy Sunday afternoon. On July 14, 1874, Harry Meacham, who lived about a quarter mile away, went down to the upper reservoir, a thirty-acre pond, to check on the water level. Reassured that the water level was still a few feet from the top, Meacham turned to leave when, out of the corner of his eye, he saw a large chunk of the upper dam slide away. He jumped on his horse and rode to Blush Hollow, the village below. Broadcloth mill owner Sumner Church didn't believe him but instructed Meacham to warn the valley as a precaution. Meacham raced down the hollow, while another man set off to warn another downstream village. As riverside dwellers grabbed a few items, water overtopped and crumbled the upper dam, sending a huge volume into the lower reservoir, which held for only a moment until its dam broke. A torrent like the one on Mill River roared through the valley, taking out the Church Brothers mill, a stave factory, a gristmill, several houses, and roads. Thanks to Meacham's warning, no one was killed, although several survivors made dramatic escapes. Lost property totaled $330,000, one third the damage caused by the Mill River flood. One of the biggest losers was the Boston and Albany Railroad with nearly $100,000 in washed-out roadbed and destroyed bridges. The flood stranded two hundred carloads of freight in Chester, southeast of Middlefield, until the company dispatched 250 men to repair the track. It took them two days.

Lawmakers were dumbstruck at this latest disaster. The poor conditions of reservoir dams were beginning to hamper the state's economy. By the end of 1874, $1.4 million was lost due to reservoirs; $1.25 million in Hampshire County in the Mill River and Middlefield disasters, $48,000 in Hampden County in floods not named, and $105,000 in losses to the Boston and Albany and New Haven and Northampton railroads. So great was the threat of floods to railroad track that half the railroad companies required their engineers to examine the condition of the reservoirs along their line. Concerned that waterpower and industry were suffering from the haphazard development of reservoirs, the Legislature appointed a new committee to examine the condition of the state's reservoirs. The committee proposed a statewide hydrographic survey to understand the waterpower available and the best means to develop it. Legislators could see that the troublesome condition of the state's reservoirs taxed the state's economy and that something needed to be done about it.

By the time Skinner received the design for the heroes' medals in June, he had said good-bye to many of his former workers. At the end of May, he presented twenty young women each with $100 and a trunk filled with clothing before striking their names from the relief list. Eight or ten Haydenville families prepared to leave, several returning to Canada. At Leeds, a half dozen families and many more single persons were, as the *Springfield Republican* called it, "disposed of" and crossed off the relief rolls. Many left the village.

Skinnerville dissolved into a scattering of houses along the road that hugged the river. Thaddeus Bartlett set his farmhouse upright at the south end of the village and resumed farming. John Coogan repaired his house near Haydenville, ready for when the brass works reopened. Salmon K. Wait moved his store from the top of Skinnerville to Williamsburg village, where he would be assured of more business.

With Hayden's new promise to rebuild, shop owners in Haydenville rebuilt as well. Haydenville Savings Bank received new deposits and made rebuilding loans, elevating real estate prices to a satisfactory level. The iron bridge at Joe Wright's Brook was repositioned. A fifty-ton boulder exposed by the flood (originally deposited by a glacier) at Gleason and Bisbee's slaughterhouse was cut into door and window caps and windowsills for the new brass works. By January, Hayden received a large contract to supply plumbing goods for a new hotel in San Francisco.

Four fifths of the valley businesses, large and small, that the flood had demolished were erected again in their original locations. Hayden's iron foundry and gas works, William Adams's gristmill, and Spelman's button shop were not reestablished, but Adams's flour mill was rebuilt by Williamsburg son Levi Bradford, who owned the Searsville flour mill.

Several factories reopened with alternate power supplies. The Nonotuck silk factory at Leeds installed a new steam engine; they would rebuild the dam later. Henry James also turned to steam to reopen his woolen mill, housing his male employees in tents on the grounds. The Emery Grinding Wheel Company threw a dam across Roberts Meadow Brook, which ran along the side of their factory. By August, George Warner had built walls for a new engine and boiler house so that he could run by steam until the river could provide power. Below the mills, July's hay harvest on the Florence meadows was pronounced a "dead failure." In September, Samuel A. Bottum tried plowing deep to mix the flood's deposit with original soil. Some of the deposit was silt, but most was sand and gravel.

Upriver the financial future looked bleak for the Haydenville Church. Before he died, Hayden Sr. intended to leave it $20,000 but never did, and typically Hayden and Skinner paid about half the operating expense, but they would no more. In Williamsburg, Madison Culver, a well-to-do black-smith who lost his home and shop, received money from the relief com-mittee. He accepted, then left "under a cloud," not to resume business locally. The hard feeling against him came because the relief money was intended to keep artisans such as Culver in town.

The relief committee continued to accept donations throughout the summer. Skinner, Hayden, and the other members of the finance commit-tee developed a new policy for aid distribution, granting money directly to individuals, rather than to the village committees to purchase goods for those in need. The new system was hotly debated; some argued that the suf-ferers weren't sensible enough to purchase their own goods while the finance committee insisted they ought to be trusted to buy what they need-ed. Over the summer, the committee met with sufferers individually to assess their needs and give them their due. Along with the individual grants, the finance committee voted to pay all bills for labor and coffins, which totaled $2,000. By the end of the summer, on August 31, Skinner and Hayden and the committee closed the relief accounts, retaining a total of $10,000 in the account through the winter for people still in need.

With $100,000 in hand from the state Legislature, the Hampshire County commissioners—two of whom, Elisha Edwards and Elisha Brewster, had approved the Williamsburg dam—acted swiftly to rebuild the roads and bridges. From July through November, Williamsburg and Northampton officials contracted for stonework for bridge abutments, the purchase of wooden and iron bridges, the building and repair of roads, and the construction of a river wall. The commissioners ignored the legislative stipulation that they contract the work to experts and organized their own work crews to do some of the labor themselves. By Christmas, they had accomplished the reconstruction, accounted for all their expenses, and given back almost $10,000 to the state. Northampton, angry that the state had given it such a small sum, resolved at its June town meeting that its representatives to the Legislature should be instructed to present a bill at the earliest possible moment to reimburse the town for the expenditures of rebuilding bridges and roads.

Summertime called for vacations, and local papers kept readers abreast of comings and goings. Nonotuck Silk Company president Samuel Hill traveled to Colorado to enjoy the exhilarating air. Some of the Skinner family went to the beach. Enos Parsons, the jury foreman, rode the train to Detroit and the Michigan lakes, but was forced to take a roundabout route because the reservoir break in Middlefield had wiped away a section of the Boston and Albany Railroad tracks.

On Tuesday evening, November 10, the largest crowd ever gathered at Cosmian Hall in Florence, standing room only, to honor the flood's heroes. Paid for by the proceeds from Henry Hayden's poetry reading and by the mill owners, who split the remaining cost ten ways (so that no one paid more than $25), the gold medals had been ready since September, when they were placed on exhibit at Tiffany & Co.'s New York store.

Alfred Lilly, a trustee of the Florence Free Congregational Society and a major contributor to the construction of Cosmian Hall, presided in the ornate new theater and lecture hall in the brick Romanesque building topped with a bell and clock tower. The evening began with selections by the Sewing Machine Company Band, a forty-member band and orchestra recently returned from Montreal, where they had received rave reviews. A

choral group sang. Then Cheney, Graves, Hillman, and Day—a gatekeeper, a milkman, a laborer, an express driver—were called to stand beneath
the gilded proscenium arch. The *Hampshire Gazette* described their
appearance on the platform:

> They were welcomed with enthusiastic applause, and for a time they
> were the observed of all observers. Their demeanor, in this trying posi-
> tion, was at once modest, tranquil, and gentlemanly. The Rev. E. G.
> Cobb of the Congregational church, Florence, made the presenta-
> tion . . . of the medals [which] was accomplished in a most happy and
> felicitous manner, and they were received with a modesty and dignity
> becoming the unassuming men whom destiny made the leading actors in
> that fearful drama of the Mill River valley, on the morning of May 16th.

After short addresses by Reverend Cook of the Methodist Church and
Charles Burleigh, head of the Free Congregational Society, the evening
concluded with vocals by the Florence Musical Society and instrumentals
by the Sewing Machine Company Band. Like other civic ceremonies of the
nineteenth century, the evening was pleasingly predictable, a tribute to the
valley's unchanged social order. While Cheney, Graves, Hillman, and Day
were the heroes of the evening, mill owners such as Lilly were still the
guardians of tradition and the pillars of the community.

The heroes took home their medals nestled in the dark green velvet lining
of the black leather cases made to hold them. The disaster had spun their lives
around. Cheney had lost his job. Graves had lost many friends, and his home
village was largely in ruins. Hillman had lost his wife and home. Day had lost
his sister, a brother-in-law, and three nieces. And now they were heroes.

If William Skinner had been in the audience, he would have driven twelve
miles from his new home in Holyoke. A month earlier, on October 2, the
family had "pulled up stakes," as Will termed it in his diary, and left the Mill
Valley. What they could salvage, they carted away. For the mill, they recovered the ruins of the water turbines and machinery. The Skinnerville house
was taken apart piece by piece, loaded onto carts and pulled by oxen to
Holyoke, where it was reassembled on the corner of Cabot and Pine Streets,
on a hill high above the factory. William Fenno Pratt, the architect who had
originally designed the house, and Clarence Luce were in charge of reconstructing and remodeling the house. In Holyoke, work gangs had already

dug the canals to connect the river to the new mills, using the earth from the excavations to fill in the low areas on the site of the new factory. On November 16, young Will Skinner cheered: "They began to make silk in Holyoke by starting up a few winding frames." In December, Skinner began spinning silk for spooled twist, and by January he employed seventy-five workers. His optimism running high, he installed machines to produce the silk braid used by New York and Boston custom tailors for binding the edges of men's suits and frock coats. It was instantly profitable. Among the workers were some from Skinnerville.

Any smudge on the mill owners' characters was faint and short-lived. Later that month, Lilly and Dimock were reelected directors at the Nonotuck Silk Company. That winter, Skinner was tapped to be a director of Northampton National Bank. The Republican party continued to place its candidates in office. That fall, Henry James was elected to the State House, and Isaac Stone was sent to the United States House of Representatives from the First Hampshire District. Elisha Edwards, the chairman of the county commissioners, was reelected to the same position in 1876. In 1877, the reservoir company's attorney, Daniel W. Bond, was elected district attorney for Hampshire and Franklin Counties. The flood had enhanced the political careers of the mill owners by showcasing them as sympathetic figures who suffered a great loss but were strong and energetic enough to restore their businesses.

Five days before Christmas, seventy children skated on the pond above Hayden's new mill dam at the brass works (built in the same location as the old one that washed away), when the dam suddenly collapsed. All the children scrambled off the ice safely. Panicked workers telegraphed downriver to warn the factories in Leeds and Florence that a huge volume of water was headed their way. Evacuated factory workers stood on the riverbanks to watch the swell, but most of the water was easily trapped behind empty mill dams in Leeds. Hayden's three-month-old dam had been designed by an engineer and constructed by Delaney and Sons of Holyoke, a well-respected firm that had built other mill dams on the Mill River. The contractors replaced the dam. The Massachusetts Legislature, which had already appointed a committee on reservoirs to inspect the state's reservoir dams, dispatched the committee to the Mill Valley to determine the cause of the failure. They concluded that sand taken from the river bottom to grout the joints in the masonry was of such a weak composition that when ice loosened some of the covering stones (which were not adequately fastened to the body of the dam), water penetrated the poor-quality grouting and toppled the structure. By the end of 1874, weary of dam failures, the Legislature vowed to take up the question of safe reservoirs in the new year to make sure such disasters and near-misses never happened again.

CHAPTER 8

CHANGE

O N an October morning five months after the flood, Lewis Bodman and Emory C. Davis, a Northampton civil engineer, welcomed to the Northampton town hall the Massachusetts Legislature's new committee on reservoirs. Charged with collecting facts and reporting on the condition of the state's reservoirs, the committee was in town for a public meeting to gather ideas for legislation that would prevent such a disaster from recurring. Two of the legislators on the committee, Henry Wilson of Boston and C. A. Shaw of Groveland, were engineers. The other senators and representatives in attendance were B. C. Currier of Newburyport, Z. Fay of Chelmsford, and Z. C. Wardwell of Groveland. Only Wilson had served on the legislative committee that investigated the disaster to determine aid for the Mill Valley. The mill owners were invited; Lewis Bodman of Williamsburg was there. A reporter from the *Hampshire Gazette* captured the discussion.

Davis had so many ideas of his own on the subject of dam safety that he had drafted a bill, which he was anxious to present to the committee. Since the flood, Davis's business had boomed as the valley discovered the value of an engineer. Hayden had hired him to survey the brass works site to determine the size and location of the new buildings. The county commissioners selected him to oversee the reconstruction of Williamsburg roads and bridges, and the reservoir company awarded him the contract to repair the Goshen and Searsville dams. Davis was also in charge of rebuilding the roads and dams in Middlefield. To help with his increased workload, he took as a partner a recent graduate of the Chandler Scientific Department at Dartmouth.

Davis was the first to speak. He proposed that county commissioners be required to submit to the state a report on the condition of their county's reservoirs every year. Each April and May, with the help of "competent engineers," they would inspect the reservoirs in their counties and then serve each reservoir proprietor, if necessary, with a list of repairs to be executed promptly, the repair work to be supervised by a "proper person." A "competent engineer" was a common designation for someone knowledgeable about engineering practices, while a "proper person" might be an engineer or simply an informed, conscientious overseer. According to Davis's plan, the expenses of the engineer and the designated overseer would be reimbursed from the state budget. County commissioners would be required to approve all new dam construction plans and specifications. If, during the construction process, the work was found not to be done according to specification, the commissioners would have the power to appoint an inspector to oversee the work. Finally, Davis suggested that the state Supreme Court have the power to suspend the use or construction of any defective dam.

The reservoir committee thought Davis's plan granted too much power to the county commissioners, who might easily be corrupted by powerful corporations attempting to control their election as well as their selection of an engineer. Henry Wilson repeated his opinion that commissioners weren't competent inspectors. In the case of the Williamsburg dam, he said, the Hampshire County commissioners had suggested ineffective repairs— so much so that they added only "rubbish" and "not one iota of strength." In other words, the commissioners' involvement provided the appearance of a competent examination that lulled some into believing that the dam was safe. An ineffectual inspection was worse than no inspection.

In the middle of Wilson's rant about county commissioners, Alfred Lilly of the Nonotuck Silk Company walked into the room. When it was his turn to speak, Lilly protested that the mill owners had been abused and wrongly judged by the people and the press. He stated that the repair work upon the Williamsburg dam was done at an expense of $10,000 and that Joel Hayden Sr.—whose opinion he trusted—was satisfied that the repairs were strong enough. Hayden was the gold standard for dam safety in the valley. The work was done by the mill owners in the same way they did all their work— "trusting to the word and wisdom of others." Lilly then recounted the detailed history of the design and construction of the dam, defending the choice of earth as a building material, which he believed that even Wilson would advise. The meeting that was supposed to be about the future bogged down in the past. Wilson couldn't help attacking past mistakes and Lilly couldn't stop defending them.

Finally, Lilly got to the topic of new legislation. He said he favored making a new law that would place authority for safe construction of reservoirs somewhere, but he didn't know where. He added that he wasn't particularly concerned how the new law worked since his company could use steam power. Perhaps he meant that if new regulations were too stringent, the Nonotuck Silk Company might bypass them by using steam exclusively.

Lewis Bodman offered his ideas. He thought that reservoir company directors should be held personally liable for damages resulting from building imperfect reservoirs. The honorable thing was for the owners to be responsible for their own dams. Someone else argued that mill owners with factories below reservoirs were already, in effect, liable to heavy damages, because broken dams caused mill owners to lose all or most of their property. If anyone countered this argument by suggesting that someone ought to pay for the property not owned by the manufacturers, the *Gazette* didn't mention it. Bodman added that a special commissioner, someone more independent and unprejudiced, ought to be appointed to look after the reservoirs, rather than county commissioners. If he was suggesting that a Massachusetts employee take charge of dams, then he was one hundred years ahead of his time.

After debating such questions as limits on the size of reservoirs and the necessity of wasteways large enough to divert water away from slumping dams, the meeting concluded. No one had questioned the value of reservoirs or suggested that they were too dangerous to build; reservoirs were essential to the state's economy and would remain. Davis agreed to draft his legislation and submit it to the committee. The meeting concluded at midday.

The Mill River flood occurred at a time when most Americans believed a man's economic success was determined by his own hard work, perseverance, ambition, and good morals. Only in a laissez-faire economy could moral men reap the fruits of their labor. Regulation, they reasoned, would cheat the worthy man by redirecting his wealth to slackers and dishonorable people; regulation bore the taint of class legislation or socialism. In addition, laws that controlled or shackled a corporation in the business of economically developing the nation and building public works would hamper progress that would benefit all.

In spite of America's anti-regulation mind set, Massachusetts had become a national leader in passing reform legislation. A factory law of 1867 provided that no child under the age of ten should be employed and no child under fifteen should work longer than sixty hours in one week. The Legislature created a Bureau of Labor Statistics in 1870 and passed laws on water pollution that same year. By 1874, the state had established commissions on railroads, hospitals, asylums, libraries, charities, and penal institutions to regulate some of their operations. Two weeks after the flood, Acting Governor Talbot signed into law the ten-hour workday for women and children in certain industries. But the state's new regulations weren't always effective because they were rarely enforced. Without a strong tax base (the state depended chiefly on a property tax) or a civil service to enforce regulation, most often if no one brought a lawsuit or complained of a violation, nothing was done. Still, many states new to large-scale manufacturing looked to Massachusetts's examples in social policy, commercial regulation, and health and public safety because, as an industrialized state, Massachusetts already had a long history confronting problems related to industrialization. Into this climate—defined by a Massachusetts Legislature that was willing to pass regulatory statutes that it didn't have the ability to enforce—came the new debate over how to ensure the safety of reservoir dams.

As the committee considered new legislation, they examined existing dams. The day after the October 1874 public meeting in Northampton, Davis, the committee on reservoirs, and Acting Governor Talbot traveled up to the Goshen dams to view the repairs that the county commissioners had ordered three months earlier and had passed. They, too, were satisfied with the dams. In January 1875, when the committee completed its study on the safety of reservoir dams, the Goshen dams were not among the twenty-six reservoirs statewide that the committee named "unsafe." In that report, the committee praised only a few dams: the log dams on the Connecticut River at Holyoke and Turner's Falls and the stone dams on the Merrimack at Lowell and Lawrence, which they declared "works of the highest engineering."

With so many potentially faulty dams, entrepreneurs hoping to make a buck offered a rash of reservoir alarm inventions. One inventor proposed an automatic electrical device that would ring a bell in the gatekeeper's cabin when it detected a sudden shift in the structure of a dam or a dramatic change in reservoir volume or stream flow. A writer to the *New York Tribune* suggested that cannons languishing in the U.S. arsenals after the Civil War could be placed at reservoirs and at ten- or fifteen-mile intervals below, so that in case of a dam break the gatekeeper could blast a warning that would be relayed down the valley by cannon fire. Another writer suggested stringing telegraph wire from a reservoir to the village below so that a gatekeeper could tap out a warning to the station downstream. The Mill River and Williamsburg Reservoir Company took no notice of these ideas.

One year after the disaster, in May 1875, after intense debate on the role of engineers, the Massachusetts Legislature passed "an act to provide for the supervision of the construction and maintenance of reservoirs and dams." The first draft had called only for county commissioners to review plans for new dams. Then a phrase was added requiring that plans be "drawn by a competent hydraulic engineer of not less than five years' experience," a far more stringent requirement than either Emory Davis or Henry Wilson had proposed. Later it was crossed out. The final bill called for the county commissioners simply to approve the plans, inspect the work in progress, and "appoint an inspector" if it appeared that the plans and specifications were "not faithfully adhered to." The inspector was granted the power "to order [the dam's] discontinuance" if not constructed correctly. The county commissioners could select whomever they thought competent to do the job, or they could do it themselves. After a dam was erected, inspections could still be called for by concerned citizens, other mill owners, or town officials, but now they had to be done "with the assistance of a competent engineer," who would advise on the alterations required to make it secure. As before, noncompliant mill owners were to have their reservoir water drawn down or their dam removed by the commissioners' orders. There was no longer a penalty for being a watchdog; now the reservoir companies would have to pay the cost of dam inspections. Finally, if the commissioners accepted the dam as safe, the mill owners might still be held criminally liable for the loss of life and property resulting from a dam break. "No order, approval, request or advice of the county commissioners" shall change dam owners' "liability for the consequences of their illegal acts, or of the neglect or mismanagement" of those working for them, the law stated.

Subtle changes in the language of the laws governing dam building showed that the Legislature now understood the destructive power of large reservoirs. Laws prior to 1875 mentioned only that the "breaking of a mill or reservoir dam" might cause damage to a "mill or other property" or to "roads or bridges." After the Mill River flood, statutes mentioned "loss of life" as well as property. With the passage of this 1875 law, the Legislature had taken some first steps toward governmental responsibility for the safety of the public, a change that would take generations to complete.

Other New England states revised their laws in response to the Mill River flood. Three days after the flood, the lower house of the Connecticut

Legislature adopted a resolution to appoint a commission to determine if new laws were necessary to protect life and property from possible reservoir damage. One legislator suggested that a new law ought to require every reservoir in Connecticut to be under the supervision of a civil engineer. Within seven months of the flood, Rhode Island appointed its own commission to review its dams. In February 1875, Maine authorized its governor to appoint a "competent and practical engineer" to inspect reservoirs and dams during August and September (the months when volume in the reservoirs might be low) if the governor had been petitioned by the town's selectmen, assessors, or county commissioners where the dam was located. A petition from an ordinary citizen would not warrant an inspection. Reservoir owners were to make repairs as required. A Vermont statute, in 1876, called for a judge to appoint a commission of three "competent engineers" to examine a suspect dam upon petition. A few years later Connecticut went further. An 1878 law established a board of civil engineers to supervise all existing dams and to review the plans and construction of new reservoirs. By 1882, Rhode Island created the position of commissioner of dams and reservoirs to be filled by a civil engineer who was to make a thorough inspection of every dam and reservoir in the state "as often as may be necessary to keep himself informed" on their condition. Other New England states took a stronger message from the disaster than did Massachusetts.

Massachusetts dam reform inched forward. An 1893 law allowed the county commissioners to use their "discretion" in deciding whether to direct a "competent engineer" to make an examination, or to conduct the investigation themselves. It was not until 1901 that Massachusetts strengthened the role of the government and of engineers. Falling just short of required inspections, the new statute authorized county commissioners to inspect the reservoir and mill dams in their areas once in a three-year period "if in their judgment the public good requires it." The commissioners could either conduct the inspections themselves "with the aid of a competent engineer" or hire engineers, who would submit written reports to them. In determining and directing repairs to be made, commissioners were required to solicit the advice of an engineer. Commissioners were required to inspect the work in progress on a new dam.

It was not surprising that it took so long for Massachusetts dam laws to change; their precepts were embedded in eighteenth-century ideas about water that promoted economic development, even to the extent of sacrificing the sanctity of private property. After the passage of the 1795 mill act (an amendment of a 1713 act), if a land owner, a farmer for instance, could

prove that the flowing of the stream over his lands because of a dam erected by a mill owner did damage, that farmer could bring an action for damages. But the dam owner would only have to compensate the farmer; he
didn't have to stop overflowing the farmer's land. The development of mills,
for board sawing, grain grinding, or manufacturing had taken precedence
over crop or meadow land. By 1854, the charters of many reservoir companies authorized them to create reservoirs by flooding lands owned by another and to provide compensation, and an 1869 statute extended the privilege
to all reservoir companies. Once a dam was built at a large capital commit-
ment, the owners were usually, but not always, accorded substantial immunity from culpability.

Up to and beyond the time of the Mill River flood, capitalism and
calamity had gone hand in hand as occasional accidents and even disasters
were understood to be part of the unavoidable and necessary cost of industrial development. But by the turn of the twentieth century, capitalism and
calamity were starting to be decoupled. In the first two decades in the early
twentieth century, in what has been called the Progressive Era, the locus of
control over dams in Massachusetts slowly shifted from private to public
hands, and the emerging engineering profession acquired at least a sup-
porting role where previously it had had none.

Despite reform, there were many more dam failures in Massachusetts,
although no other was as deadly as the Mill River flood. In 1875, a dam
break in Athol cost $3,000 in property loss and shut down a cotton and
hosiery mill for two months. The following year, the Lynde Brook reservoir
dam in Leicester, near Worcester, gave way after it had been leaking at a
rate of 48,000 gallons per day. Ten years later, in 1886, a reservoir dam collapsed in East Lee, in Berkshire County, killing a half dozen people and
costing $80,000 in damage to paper mills. The eleven Berkshire County
paper manufacturers who held interests in the dam had never bothered to
establish an association or become incorporated. Their "meetings" consisted of conversations at the general store during which some agreed to contribute money to the project and others promised labor. The Middlefield
reservoir dam, which had been rebuilt after it broke in July 1874, was overtopped in the spring of 1901 after a week of heavy rain, washing out the
same valley it had ruined twenty-seven years earlier.

Dam oversight in Massachusetts was transferred from the counties to the
state in 1970 when the Massachusetts Legislature placed the operation of
county-overseen dams with the state's commissioner of public works. (It has
since moved to other offices within state government.) The transfer was the

result of political pressure after the March 1968 failure of the Lake Lee dam, in far western Massachusetts, which killed two and damaged $15 million in property. The report on the cause of the failure prepared for the county commission said that the dam's concrete core was not impervious to water, as was required in the design, and the dam was not "keyed" into the soil base adequately.

In the forty-eight years after the Mill River flood, between 1874 and 1922, there were seventy-nine significant earthen dam failures, or partial failures, in the United States, making dam breaks the most common engineering failure. Major reasons for failure included overtopping due to inadequate spillways (data on rainfall and stream runoff were meager); the existence of piping or a flow of water through the dam; and an inadequate foundation that allowed water under or through the dams. By mid-twentieth century, scientific research in such areas as soil mechanics, geology, meteorology, and hydrology changed long-held rule-of-thumb practices, making dams safer.

On Sunday, May 16, 1875, one year after the Mill River flood, Reverend John Gleason ascended the pulpit at the Williamsburg Congregational Church to deliver his sermon on the flood's anniversary. He was dark-haired, thin with sunken cheeks, a hooded brow, and a long moustache that hid his mouth. He began by lamenting that the once sweet waters "which had caused the busy hum of industry to sound through the valley, became very bitter to us. They brought death . . . destruction . . . and desolation" because of man's carelessness and cupidity. He sympathized with the congregation that the image of the flood has "so often intruded upon our thoughts by day, and reproduced itself in our dreams at night, that if life were lengthened to a thousand years . . . the event would still be vivid to our minds." He continued, "The snows of winter concealed for a time some of the effects of the flood, but now its track is made prominent by contrast with the increasing verdure on either side." His real message came at the end when he warned the mill owners about the Goshen dams on behalf of thousands of nervous valley dwellers. It was springtime and the Goshen reservoirs were full. If a disaster recurs, he promised, "there would not again be that leniency and charity of judgment, but the whip of justice would be seized by private hands and the lash applied by private judgment, amidst the approving amens of an indignant community." If Massachusetts law couldn't provide justice, citizens would. Joel Hayden Jr., Lucius Dimock, William Clement, and the other mill owners could have read his warning in Monday's *Springfield Republican,* where his sermon was published.

Three hundred yards from the church, Main Street and the land along it remained a dreary wasteland of sand and rocks, still pocked here and there, and heaped with stacks of rubbish and wreckage that resembled monuments or sculptures to the tragedy. No one had the heart or strength to move them. Residents lobbied for a new town hall; they had recently thought the town hall too cramped, and now they didn't like meeting in a room that had been a morgue. A block away, things looked brighter. Spencer Hannum and Hiram Hill had restored their houses, the first ones struck in the village. Patrick McGowan built a new home on Village Hill, several hundred feet above the flood line, where the center of the old village had stood. Some of Spelman's workers were employed by another local button factory. The town coffers hurt badly. Williamsburg's net worth, which included Haydenville's, dropped by one quarter, while the total value of the town's personal estates plummeted the same amount, and real estate values fell 22 percent—not surprising since sixty-seven dwellings, 16 percent of the total, no longer existed. Farmers who felt the pinch sold off horses, cows, and sheep.

Downstream, Haydenville's progress in rebuilding had slackened. Three or four houses remained upended or on their sides near the mangled gas works. Just the previous week, the first hundreds of the ten million bricks needed for the brass works had been laid. A few months earlier, Hayden had received a large contract to supply plumbing goods, ornamental brass work, steam valves, and earthenware sinks for a grand new hotel in San Francisco, but he was already behind on the order. Laborers packed "as thick as sardines" in the old wooden buildings couldn't get the work done fast enough, even with the aid of two new sixty-horsepower steam engines. The replacement for the mill dam that had failed last December hadn't been started. Hayden had hoped to move into the new brass works by July, but it was evident that he wouldn't make it. Near the depot, on a new street, three small houses, four to seven rooms each, were being erected for families who had lost everything, paid for in part by the relief fund at a cost of $800 to $1,200 for each.

Leeds showed only slight improvement. Wrecked structures rested on the rock-strewn and gullied main street like twisted abstractions of buildings, left there by residents who had rebuilt on higher ground. With no chapel, Sunday school and other religious services were held in the depot. Nonotuck Silk Company, enjoying prosperous times, planned a boardinghouse for forty or fifty workers on the same spot as the one the flood washed away. Three Leeds widows, with thirteen children between them, had depended on the relief committee for survival the past year and would again this year from a fund of $2,800 managed by John Otis, who furnished support at $450 per year for the three families. The money was expected to aid the families for about six years, probably until some of the children were old enough to support their families.

Further downstream, debris still littered much of the Leeds and Florence meadows even though twelve hundred wagon loads had already been removed. The members of the Florence Congregational Society, who themselves had benefited from the kindness of faraway strangers after the Mill River flood, sent $350 in cash and six barrels of clothing to the grasshopper sufferers in Kansas and received a warm thank-you letter. Meanwhile, Joel Hayden Jr. hired Boston and Northampton architect Clarence Luce, who had designed the new brass works, to update his Northampton home by wrapping a long curved porch around its colonial frame and erecting a two-story addition.

While the villages slowly recovered, Hayden and the other mill owners looked for more waterpower. Companies like Clement and Hawks were often interrupted and lost productivity because the water level was so low. So, the reservoir company instructed Springfield civil engineer Phineas Ball, who had testified at the inquest as an expert, to draw up plans for an earthen dam to replace the Williamsburg dam. His design called for a core wall of 14-inch-thick concrete, a 24-inch diameter gate pipe, and slopes of 2.5:1 on the downstream side and 2:1 on the reservoir side. The new dam would incorporate the ruins of the old dam, absorbing the old embankment inadequacies and all. Following the requirements of the new law, the reservoir company submitted the plans to the county commissioners, who approved them in July 1875. Survivors didn't object to rebuilding the dam as long as it was secure. Only a lone voice protested the factories' use of waterpower, but not the reservoir specifically: "the material prosperity of this valley is closely connected with the *factory* . . . yet men and women with any humanity left in them, also have an idea that it is possible to pay too great a price for a few years of this prosperity. The valley had been 'looted' long enough." The lone dissenter was ignored.

But the mill owners didn't have the money for the new dam, which was dependent upon the sale of $40,000 in first mortgage bonds, which many of the mill owners could not afford. The Goshen dams would have to be filled to their limits to satisfy their water needs.

In the summer of 1875, the reservoir company raised the height of the old Goshen dam a few feet by stretching flashboards—wooden planks attached to iron rods driven into the dam—across the top of the dam. Tempers flared again. Unusually heavy August rains filled the reservoirs until the excess ran down the wasteways. But this time, there were frequent anonymous threats of destroying the dams. From Toledo, Ohio, Lewis Bodman's son, Lewis H. Bodman, wrote to his father about a visiting Williamsburg man who rumored that his neighbors back home "were so frightened about the Goshen reservoirs all the time that some of them wanted to go up and *blow them up*." The reservoir company, Bodman's son asserted, needed to gain the valley's credibility by recognizing the permanent feeling of insecurity. They should have opened the gates to draw the reservoirs down, but instead, they added "fuel to the excitement" by "ordering on the flashboards." Bodman's son concluded, "I don't wonder they *threatened the reservoirs* if such management continues while the water is high." He added that he didn't think threats of violence would have any effect. The reservoir company made no statements to ease tension. The dams never broke and no one blew them up.

Blowing up dams wasn't unheard of. In the previous one hundred fifty years, farmers occasionally and intentionally damaged mill and reservoir dams that overflowed their crops and grazing land or interfered with the numbers and migration of fish in the stream. In 1859, fifty New Hampshire farmers used axes and iron bars to attack a Lake Winnipesaukee dam owned by the Boston Associates group of mill owners, who used it to control the Merrimack River, which provided power to their mills in Lowell and Lawrence. Farmers attempted to blow up another dam on the same river. A century earlier, Rhode Island farmers broke down dams that obstructed the passage of fish along the rivers. In 1875, concerns for personal safety were a new reason for wanting to destroy dams. Those who considered striking down the Goshen dams would have found the penalty was up to five years in prison or a fine of up to five hundred dollars.

Gradually, the fear of the Goshen dams subsided, but not before Reverend Gleason requested dismissal from the Williamsburg Congregational Church because his family could no longer bear to live in the track of the Goshen reservoirs. Every night before bed, they prepared to leave their home at a moment's notice. Before Gleason departed, he returned one quarter of his annual salary of $375 to the church. He had offered it after the flood, and the church society had finally accepted.

No individual victims of the Mill River flood filed civil suits; they knew
they had little chance of compensation. According to the *Boston Daily Advertiser*, in the first few days after the flood, there was some talk "about
bringing heavy suits for damages against the corporation of mill owners
who built the reservoir, but as nearly every man in the company is ruined,
it would be a good deal like the old proverb of suing a beggar." They
weren't likely to win. Few laws at the time protected workers and citizens,
and it was a hardship to hire lawyers, pay fees, and risk paying costs if the
suit failed. Of those in this period who did make a tort claim—a suit charging a civil wrong or injury resulting from interpersonal conduct—about 90
percent lost their cases because courts tended to favor promotion of economic growth over satisfaction of claims by individuals harmed by industrial expansion. Many courts sought to pinpoint a single negligent act or
locate one responsible agent, but when they were unable to identify the act
that set the chain in motion that led to disaster, they decided no one was to
blame. Other courts identified so many contributors that they named no
one accountable. As a result, tort claims were quickly quashed so they did
not siphon precious capital away from business expansion. By the end of
the nineteenth century, though, pressured by labor unions and public disgust over such tragedies as the Mill River flood, states established laws to allow victims of industrial accidents and disasters to be protected and
compensated. But in the period from about 1830 to 1890, when industrialization was in full swing, citizens were vulnerable. Protective legislation
became more common in the 1890s and was widespread by 1900.

A review of Hampshire County court cases reveals that none of the reservoir
company members, contractors, engineers, or county commissioners were
sued for damages over the Mill River flood. However, there are two puzzling
entries in the court records. William Clement's firm, the Clement and Hawks
Manufacturing Company, and Joel Hayden Jr. each sued the Mill River and
Williamsburg Reservoir Company in March 1875 "in an action of tort," but
never defined what the cases were about. The suits were never pursued; the
October 1879 court record reported for each case that the "plaintiff is non-
suited" and the "defendant defaulted under the 54th rule of this Court," which
stated that inactive cases were to be dismissed unless there was a reason to the
contrary. Hayden and Clement simply let the cases drop, probably because it
would be an expense to pursue and there was little chance of recovering damages from other mill owners suffering financial burdens after the disaster.

While no landmark cases grew out of the Mill River flood, the historic event and its aftermath still contributed to a change in Americans' attitude about the greater meaning of such disasters by galvanizing public opinion against self-interested capitalists. Up through the mid-nineteenth century, most Americans had viewed entrepreneurs as exemplars who risked personal fortunes to develop the national economy by harnessing rivers, building railroads, inventing machinery, and erecting factories. These men accomplished what government hadn't and their success entitled them to such high social standing and moral leadership that no one thought them capable of wrongdoing. By the end of the century, after repeated disasters and scandals, Americans realized that moneymakers were not necessarily moral beings. By the time the Johnstown flood occurred in 1889, the level of scorn heaped upon the industrialists and bankers who owned the failed dam was high. Even so, the Johnstown victims didn't collect a dime in damages either. In one case tried in Pittsburgh, the hometown of some of the members of the South Fork Fishing and Hunting Club that owned the dam, the jury found them not guilty, despite overwhelming evidence to the contrary.

One hundred years after the Mill River Valley flood, the prospects for victims to recover damages had changed dramatically. One Saturday morning in February 1972, a mining company's refuse pile of coal waste, which dammed Buffalo Creek in West Virginia, collapsed and sent a floodwave of water and sludge down a narrow valley, killing 125. A group of 625 survivors of the Buffalo Creek flood sued the Pittston Company for $52 million. Pittston settled out of court for $13.5 million—the plaintiffs not only received $5.5 million for property damage and wrongful-death claims but also won $8 million for mental suffering. In this groundbreaking case, survivors, most of whom had never been touched by the murky floodwater, collected damages for psychological harm because their lives and communities had been disrupted by a man-made disaster.

A year after the flood, Joel Hayden Jr. struggled to keep the brass works afloat. Financially overextended, Hayden stalled on payments to carpenters, masons, painters, and bricklayers engaged in building the new factory. A dozen fed-up tradesmen filed claims that were eventually paid. Hayden's lawsuit against the reservoir company, which was later dropped, was an attempt to alleviate his financial woes. The reconstruction of the brass works dragged on until October 1875 when two hundred employees moved into the new building, designed to accommodate six hundred. Hayden's economic gloom continued through winter 1876 when he reduced the cotton mill employees' wages by 5 percent, the cotton mill overseers' paychecks by 20 percent, and the brass-factory workers' wages by 15 percent. After a three-day strike, some brass workers agreed to the reduction while others left Haydenville. The cotton-mill workers accepted the decrease. The next year, debt-ridden Hayden, Gere & Co. dissolved. Collins Gere withdrew from the partnership, leaving Hayden and Sereno Kingsley to reorganize under the name Joel Hayden and Company. But the losses were so great that the company reorganized again in 1878 under the name the Hayden Company (and later the Haydenville Company), this time without Joel Hayden. He had left the firm for Lorain, Ohio, where he founded the Joel Hayden Brass Works with Amasa Stone, president of the Lake Shore Railroad, and other influential Cleveland capitalists. Hayden built up the small rural town of Lorain by purchasing broad tracts of land on which he constructed houses and encouraged workers to erect their own, the way his father had developed Haydenville. About 1890, Hayden severed his connection with the Ohio company; he may have been forced out by his partners.

He first returned home to Northampton. His fortune dwindled. By 1905 he had moved to Boston. The next year, the bank had foreclosed on his large Northampton house, which was operated as a hotel. In 1912, when he was seventy-five and infirm, his oldest son, Joel III, died of pneumonia at age forty-three. Joel Jr. tried to gain access to the estate by breaking his son's will, which, written two years earlier, left nothing to his father. Before he wrote the will, Joel III had transferred $30,000 in property to his long-term love, an attractive and charming widow named Georgie McCabe who worked in a corset shop in Boston's Back Bay. It was said that his family opposed any alliance outside their social circle, and so he saw Mrs. McCabe secretly for twenty-five years. In the court papers, Joel Jr. contended that his son had been of unsound mind and addicted to drugs. Joel Jr. lost the claim and died penniless six years later in 1918. At the end of his life, he may have been aided financially by his sister Isabella, who had been willed money from their sister Jenny for the "care of brother Joel."

Although Joel Hayden Jr. left the Mill Valley, more than two thirds of the 122 men who had appeared on the 1870 census as brass-mill workers were still laboring there in 1880. Andrew Breckenridge, forty-six, whose home had been destroyed by the torrent, brought his twenty-year-old son Thomas into the factory. Brass finisher Michael Ryan stayed with the brass works, and his three sons, Jimmy, Philip, and William, took jobs there, too, when they became old enough. Pattern maker George Blanchard celebrated his sixtieth birthday at the factory. Skinnerville widow Sarah Wrisley, whose twisted house was returned to its original site, boarded two brass workers. After suffering economic difficulties in the 1890s depression, the Hayden-ville Company was purchased in 1899 by Christian J. Hills and his four brothers, Albert, Henry, Reuben, and Jacob, better known in boyhood as Will Skinner's best friend "Dick." All five brothers had grown up a mile from the brass works where their father worked, near where their mother died in the flood. The Hills brothers ran the brass works until they all passed away. The brass works closed in 1954.

The valley's economic recovery was slow, and many factories never bounced back to their former healthy positions. When the flood struck in 1874, the valley's manufacturing economy was in the middle of a gradual transformation in which the older industries of textiles and buttons were being overshadowed by silk and metals. In 1845 the four most profitable products (in rank order) were: buttons, wool, paper, and silk. Twenty years later, silk was second only to metals. By 1886, silk had outstripped all other products with an annual value of almost $1.9 million. Metals were far be-hind with less than a half million dollars in products, and wool, cotton, and buttons no longer topped the list. In the valley, the center for silk was Flo-rence, and for the metal trades, both Florence and Haydenville. But the smaller upstream factories in Leeds, Haydenville, and Williamsburg that made textiles and buttons didn't disappear. If anything, the disaster strengthened the resolve of local men to keep them going as long as they could.

While the flood occurred at the beginning of the end of the age of New England waterpower, it did not provoke a wholesale abandonment of it. Waterpower was still useful, especially for smaller companies. Before the flood, steam represented perhaps a quarter or a third of the power used along the river. The large factories, such as the Nonotuck Silk Company, the brass works, Skinner's silk company, and Warner's button factory, sup-plemented waterpower with steam engines, while the smaller factories used water exclusively. A year after the flood, 57 percent of the valley's power still came from water, but it was more difficult to obtain: The flood had scoured the river and filled it with rubble, rendering it less efficient and useless in some places. As waterpower declined, steam engines became more efficient and easier to operate. By the end of the century, in 1895, steam power finally overtook waterpower, with steam engines furnishing 59 percent of the power, water 37 percent, and new electric motors 4 percent.

In shifting to steam, the Mill Valley was in step with the rest of the nation's growing dissatisfaction with the irregularity and unreliability of waterpower in the railway age when nationwide competition was keener than ever. The shift to steam was part of a gradual concentration of manufacturing in cities where, mostly, waterpower was not available, but railway networks were located. This led to the decline of the numerous small manufacturing centers, like the Mill Valley, in the northeast. In addition, as leadership changed from the hands of older men experienced in waterpower to younger men familiar with steam engines, steam's acceptance increased.

Henry James hung on to his woolen mill until the business failed in 1891. A New Yorker named George C. Cook purchased and operated it for ten years when it then fell back into local hands under Gilbert Bradford, who used it as a sawmill and whose father Levi had purchased the Adams gristmill after the flood. When the Bradford sawmill was destroyed by fire in 1913 and Bradford was unable to finance the rebuilding, a group of local citizens formed a stock company and sold $25,000 worth of shares at $25 each, which kept the business under local control. In Leeds, John Otis's son Harry succeeded him as manager of the Emery Wheel Company.

George Warner rode out his economic loss and held on to his newly reestablished Mill River Button Company for twelve years until the company dissolved and he sold the large brick building to the expanding Nonotuck Silk Company. During most of the time the button mill was in operation, it employed 175 workers—including Fred Howard, who was a foreman—and produced 1,000 to 1,500 gross of vegetable ivory nut buttons daily. A hundred years later, Fred's letters about the flood were found in the attic of a Howard family home on Chesterfield Road in Leeds and given to local historian James Parsons.

In 1879 Lewis Bodman tried to bolster the valley's recovery by investing in a Williamsburg railway, but the scheme failed and Bodman lost almost $6,000. Near bankruptcy at seventy years old, he headed west to Bement, Illinois, where he and his brothers had bought government land a quarter century earlier. Lewis was the last Bodman to leave Williamsburg (his three sons had moved west), where his family had been prominent for over a century. Bodman died in Illinois in 1886 at age seventy-six.

Onslow Spelman started a new button business in the late 1870s when he and a partner built a new stone dam near the site of the old one and outfitted the ninety-foot-long factory with two water turbines. At age sixty in 1882, Spelman sold his share to his partner and became president of a textile mill in Westfield. When he died in 1905 at age eighty-three, his obituary called him "one of the wealthiest men in Williamsburg."

Mary Hill stayed in Williamsburg and wrote a daily diary until 1896, three years before her death at age fifty-one.

William Clement left the valley briefly, then returned to purchase a screw and nail factory in the Bay State village section of Northampton to manufacture cutlery. When he died at age seventy in 1882, the *Hampshire Gazette* referred to him as "a well known and respected Northampton manufacturer."

Twenty-eight years after the flood, in 1902, Walter Carson of the *Boston Globe* wrote a follow-up piece on the lives of the Mill River flood heroes. He found Collins Graves working as a caretaker on the Williamsburg estate of Mrs. Lyman D. James, the wife of the store owner and the sister of Marshall Field, the Chicago multimillionaire. Graves had lived in Williamsburg all his life and described himself as contented and happy. He still cherished his medal. He told the *Globe:* "On the whole I have been treated kindly but there have been those for one reason or another who have subjected me to ridicule and laughed at me largely because of the papers and people have pictured me as a hero . . . I make no claim other than that I did my best." In her will, his daughter left her father's medal to the Meekins Library in Williamsburg.

Carson found George Cheney, at fifty-nine, living in Williamsburg and working as a day laborer when his poor health permitted. Four of his twelve children still lived at home. While still occupied by the Cheney family, the gatekeeper's cabin burned to the ground from a chimney fire in May 1880; his medal was never found.

Myron Day farmed in Northampton all his life. At seventy and supposedly retired, he worked every day, walking to and from his duties stooped over from the waist. Years later, Myron Day's nephew donated his medal to Historic Northampton.

In 1902, Jerome Hillman was already dead. Twenty-one years after the flood, in 1895, on his sixtieth birthday, Hillman committed suicide at his home in Northampton by hanging himself with a wire suspended from a beam in the barn. His wife (he had remarried after his first wife was killed in the flood) came home from church to find a note from him on the kitchen table telling her not to go to the barn alone. Relatives said he had been melancholy for almost a year.

Dam builder Joel Bassett continued to find work. Sixteen months after the flood, he was selected to construct a railroad bridge over the Green River in Greenfield, fifteen miles north of the Williamsburg dam. Eugene C. Gardner was hired as an architect to remodel the Williamsburg Congregational Church, where dozens of flood victims had worshiped.

The year after the flood, Haynes Starkweather lost reelection as Northampton selectman. He had served seventeen successive years in office, longer than any other man. He moved to California, where his three brothers and his son had relocated, and died there in 1895 at the age of seventy-three.

Charles Delano, the questioner at the inquest, remained a prominent Northampton attorney. His practice was lucrative, and he spent his earnings on his large house and property. He died in 1883.

Alfred Lilly, Samuel Hill, and Lucius Dimock grew richer, remaining directors of the Nonotuck Silk Company for the rest of their lives. Of all the Mill Valley industries, silk was the most stable and profitable, the result of manufacturing inventions, a growing trade with Asia, and consumers who demanded more silk. Nonotuck Silk, the region's largest company, enjoyed a fivefold profit increase from 1865 to 1900. The company exhibited at the 1876 Centennial Exhibition in Philadelphia, which showcased American industry; in better times the brass works would have exhibited too. Until the mid-1870s, Nonotuck Silk Company sent its goods only as far as Boston and New York, but soon added distributors in Baltimore, Philadelphia, Cincinnati, Chicago, St. Louis, and San Francisco. In the 1890s, Nonotuck Silk shipped spool silk as far away as France and South America. As business increased, the company expanded into the vacant cotton mill in Haydenville and the button mill in Leeds and, in the 1880s, to a branch plant in Quebec. Plans for a Mexican branch were never executed. By the end of the nineteenth century, half of all wage earners in the Mill Valley worked in a silk mill.

After the flood, Dimock took no chances with the structures he built; in fact, he overbuilt them. In 1880, when he erected a new silk factory in Leeds, he called on Eugene Gardner, the architect who was supposed to have superintended the Williamsburg dam. His design required that the factory rest on a solid rock foundation that formed the riverbed. The basement floor was concrete. Integrated into the five-story, one-hundred-foot-long structure were two waterwheels and two steam engines for reserve power and for heating the plant. His intention was that a flood would not budge the factory. Dimock personally supervised the construction by Connecticut Valley contractors.

Dimock lived out his life on his private Grove Hill estate on a hill in Leeds. The year before he built the new factory, he had hired Gardner to design a large brick Eastlake-style house fitted out with a library, billiard room, and skylit conservatory. From the tower he could see up and down the Connecticut Valley and, on a very clear day, some sites in Connecticut. Dimock had built the house so substantially that the walls were fourteen inches thick and the foundation rested on hardpan. Dimock pumped fresh water from a nearby natural spring into his own reservoir, a pool twenty feet wide and seven feet deep, where it was gravity-fed to his house. In 1876, he donated $10,000, including furniture and fixtures, for the Nonotuck Hall and School-House in Leeds. He later built a dance hall in Leeds for workers. He spent twenty-five years, from 1869 to 1894, as a member of the Northampton board of water commissioners, helping to establish the town's water system. When he died in 1906 at age eighty, the *Hampshire Gazette* lamented, "his death removes another of the older and more prominent men of the city . . . he was a man of excellent judgment."

Samuel Hill continued his interests in reform politics and in education. In 1876, he opened his home to what is now the oldest endowed kindergarten in the United States. For the first year or two, until he built a school, classes were held in his parlor. In his will he funded the Hill Institute, which today operates the kindergarten and adult education classes.

Alfred Lilly gave $35,000 to the president of Smith College to build the Lilly Hall of Science, the first building at a women's college for the sole purpose of teaching of science. The building was dedicated in 1886. Two years later, Lilly built the Lilly Library for the citizens of Florence. When he died in 1890, his will provided that his estate be left to the trustees of the Florence kindergarten for educational purposes.

In Florence, paternalism continued through the early years of the twentieth century. In 1901, the Nonotuck Silk Company owned fifty-seven workers' houses and continued to encourage home ownership. Young women received room, board, and supervision of their conduct in a boardinghouse. Lectures, concerts, and dances that were sponsored and chaperoned by the company were held in the community hall. Even near bankruptcy, Joel Hayden Jr. continued some informal work habits, as when he shut the factory for a morning so everyone could attend the wedding of one of the brass contractors. The persistence of paternalism yielded little union organization in the Mill Valley.

In the early 1920s, the Nonotuck Silk Company merged with the Brainerd and Armstrong Company of New London to form the Corticelli Silk Company. Aggressive cost-cutting measures shored up the company during a rough period later in the decade. Business improved for a short time but failed during the Great Depression when it merged with a competitor that moved its operation to Connecticut. The company's Leeds and Florence property—mills, tenement houses, cottages, vacant land, and offices—were sold at public auction.

After the flood, silk mills prospered in Holyoke too. The Skinner name continued to be synonymous with top-quality silk, and William Skinner regularly enlarged the factory until his company became known as the largest and best of its kind in the world. One building was one-thousand-feet long, the largest silk mill under one roof in the world. His trademark was the words "Skinner's Satin" woven into the fabric's selvage. Skinner drove to the mill each morning at 6:45, greeted people at the entrance, unlocked the door, and rode back home for a large breakfast. Ever the natty dresser, he wore linen shirts and black silk ties and his trademark embroidered silk vests. When Skinner died in 1902, his sons Will and Joseph took over and enjoyed prosperity especially during the teens, twenties, and the World War II period. Several grandsons managed the mill starting in the late 1940s until Skinner Silk Mills finally closed its doors in 1961. It had been the longest operating family-owned business in Holyoke.

Will Skinner attended Yale College briefly. Two years after the flood, he joined the Skinner silk sales office in 1876 on Broadway and remained head of the office in New York. His signature attire was red silk ties, which he bought by the gross. In the company booklets that showcased his products and company history, he used the flood to illustrate his father's resilient character. William Skinner owed part of his success to the Mill River flood. It catapulted him to a larger scale of manufacturing, which he never could have achieved on the Mill River.

William Skinner was a devoted benefactor to local charities, including Holyoke Hospital, the Holyoke Library, and Mount Holyoke, Smith, and Vassar colleges (three of his daughters went to Vassar). After World War I, his daughter Belle (Ruth Isabelle), who had been eight at the time of the flood, adopted a small war-torn French village, about the size of Skinnerville, and spent her own fortune reconstructing the landscape, schools, and other buildings. Will died in 1947 at the age of ninety. He never married.

The house that Skinner carted in pieces to Holyoke from Skinnerville remained the family home until 1959 when the family deeded it to the city. It is now the Wistariahurst Museum (the house is covered with wisteria vines) on the crest of Holyoke's Beech Street.

In the years following the flood, no one talked much about it. Psychological aftereffects and grief were borne privately and grisly details were held in, too horrible to share. Certainly witnesses carried unbearable guilt about their survival and their inability to save others while some bore the burden of responsibility. No malice was ever shown to those people. The intense community spirit demonstrated in the aftermath continued in the memory of the flood.

Over the years, the description of the cause of the flood has been muted, softened, and even ignored. In the early years, people kept mum on the topic of responsibility, as it was not the style of local history to lay blame or dwell on problems and conflicts. In a chapter on the flood in the *History of Florence* (edited by Charles A. Sheffeld, a grandson of Samuel Hill), Clayton E. Davis attributed the flood to "the defective reservoir." Agnes Hannay, in her exhaustive and excellent 1936 "Chronicle of Industry on the Mill River," mentioned only that "a disastrous flood" in 1874 "hastened the transition from water-power to steam." In an essay in the 1954 *Northampton Book*, Lucy Wilson Benson remarked only that "fears as to its safety" were entertained but that the dam was claimed to be as strong as granite. Williamsburg's 1946 history by Phyllis Baker Deming concluded that "the direct cause of the disaster, aside from the general weakness of the dam, must remain a subject of speculation."

In 1921, on the occasion of the one hundred fiftieth anniversary of the incorporation of the town of Williamsburg, the townspeople staged a historical pageant in ten episodes called *Pages of History*. The final "page," titled "The Flood," began with six men building the reservoir to satisfy the "desire for more power," as the playbill described it. Then characters Cheney, Loud, Graves, Hillman, and Day (Collins Graves was played by his son Frank, and Robert Loud by his son James) gave the warning, which

sent forty citizens, including children and a baby, scurrying offstage to
return moments later draped in black as the mourning procession. In 1946
Williamsburg's one hundred seventy-fifth anniversary pageant featured a
procession of the dead in which three clusters of downcast, black-clothed
people—fifty-seven representing Williamsburg's dead, thirty representing
Haydenville's, and four representing Skinnerville's—paraded across the
open field where the pageant was held. No mill owners were represented in
the pageant and the cause of the disaster was not mentioned.

Some survivors resisted telling their descendants. In 1999, Norman
Graves, a vigorous gentleman in his eighties who lived in his great-
grandfather's house, said that when he was a boy he often asked about the
disaster. "What do you want to know about that for?" was all his grandfather
and great-grandfather would respond. His persistence paid off when his
great-aunt Bertha Graves told him how his great-grandfather, also named
Norman Graves, had rushed into the house shouting, "It's here! Head for
the hills!" Everyone knew what "it" was, so they made it to safety. The
family's carriage shop was washed away but rebuilt. Aunt Bertha then told
the story of how the dam burst, but never said why. Others made sure to
tell the succeeding generations. Williamsburg native Mary Bisbee heard
about the flood from her grandmother, who frequently told how her own
grandmother's sister, Sarah Cowing Bartlett, was the flood's first victim.
Ralmon Black's father took him up to the dam ruins and explained the
flood. Today, Ralmon regularly leads local school groups to the dam site
and down to Haydenville to show students the brass works, the path of
destruction, and the Haydenville Church, which served as a morgue. Inside
the church, on a wall in the sanctuary, hangs a marble memorial tablet that
Joel Hayden Sr.'s daughters placed there two years after his death as a per-
petual reminder of his life and deeds. It reads:

Joel Hayden, born at Williamsburg, April 8, 1798
Died at New York, November 10, 1873
Lieutenant-Governor of the Commonwealth, 1863–66
A life of successful yet untiring industry
An early and constant courage in support of human freedom, and a
    faithful devotion to Christian works.

Haydenville is his most enduring monument.

EPILOGUE

Today if you follow the Mill River from the Connecticut River upstream through Northampton and Florence and further to Leeds, Haydenville, and Williamsburg, the river slips back and forth from one side of the road to the other, usually visible but sometimes hidden behind a row of houses, a warehouse, a dike, or a patch of woods. The hills around the river are forested and hold more water so the river is smaller, with a more regular flow, not often given to spring freshets. The riverbed is silted in so that it is no more than a slow, wide stream that meanders in some spots. In others, it races furiously over rocks, adding motion to the New England villages it traverses. It is picturesque but inconsequential, no longer pumping life blood to the industries, no longer the soul of the villages, and no longer the source of terror.

The Mill River glides quietly into an oxbow of the Connecticut in the midst of the Arcadia Wildlife Sanctuary and within earshot of the interstate that parallels the railroad. The Mill River's course has changed. In March 1936 a record spring flood saw rowboats plying the streets of downtown Northampton, and as part of a subsequent flood-protection plan, the Mill River was diverted to a new channel far south of Northampton center. It now winds through the Pynchon Meadows on its way to the Connecticut River, bypassing the shops and restaurants that crowd Northampton's downtown. The river drifts lazily through the Smith College campus, where it forms Paradise Pond (which used to be a factory millpond), not far behind Lilly Hall. The river slips past Northampton State Hospital, now closed, and through Bay State, a manufacturing village of close-set clapboard houses. The river races and swirls white past William Clement's cutlery factory, now home to a machine shop, a catering business, and a karate studio. The river flows not far from Lilly Library, a brick-and-granite structure with a graceful bay window. Nearby is the Hill Institute, still a kindergarten with evening adult education classes held in the original large gray building. The largest employers in Northampton are no longer the silk mills; they are the Cooley Dickinson Hospital and Smith College. Northampton's population is nearly 30,000, three times larger than it was in 1874.

From a picnic table in Look Park a mile upstream, one can gaze across the Mill River, which borders the park (and feeds the paddleboat pond), on to the Florence meadows, still cultivated farm land. One hundred thirty years ago the fields, the park, and the adjacent golf course were heaped house-high with flood debris laced with battered bodies. In the 1930s, workers digging a children's pool unearthed a large skein of silk there. On the other side of the river, at the Northampton Country Club, in the 1970s, a hunk of buried metal gradually worked its way up from the ground until it jutted out of a fairway. Lodged too deep to pry up and too prominent to cover over, it was dug out and discovered to be a large piece of machinery from an upstream factory; no one could tell which one.

In Leeds the road crosses four bridges, the one at the upstream end a replacement for the bridge that seven silk mill women were crossing when it was swept away and they died. Fred Howard's house on Chesterfield Road, where he wrote his letters to his brother, remains. The button mill site is mostly vacant. The silk mill on Leeds's Main Street is now Leeds Village Apartments, and Dimock's elegant house on what became Yankee Hill has been divided into condominiums. Warner's house stands next door. For a mile through the gorge from Leeds upstream to Haydenville, the road is a narrow shelf carved into the hillside. Here Myron Day felt terror as he raced through the gorge ahead of the flood with no place to go but downstream.

The road and the river are entwined in Haydenville, a smaller and quieter village than it was in the 1870s. If Joel Hayden Sr. came home today he would find his handsome columned mansion watching over the brass works. The red brick main building his son built now houses offices, a fitness studio, and a charter school. As the river falls over the dam behind the factory, it roars so loud that it is hard to carry on a conversation next to it; standing there, it is easy to understand why Joel Hayden Sr.'s uncles tapped this place on the river for waterpower nearly two hundred years ago. Nearby, the High Street cemetery is the final resting place for Joel Hayden Sr., Joel Jr., and Joel III, as well as for five-year-old Robbie Hayden, killed in the flood. The last Hayden in Haydenville was Anna, Joel Sr.'s niece, who died in 1912.

A mile upstream, at the bend in the river, there is no trace of

Skinnerville. The Wrisley and Coogan houses are still there and an electric substation (no longer in use) sits where the Skinner house once stood. The site of the train depot is a sawmill. The last train made its run in 1962.

In Williamsburg, the last industry to be built along the Mill River was the Williamsburg Blacksmith Shop, established in the 1930s on the West Branch. Today, Elizabeth Tiley uses a gas forge and some of her grandfather's tools to turn out colonial-style door hinges, handles, and hooks, which she sells to customers across the country. Around the corner, Onslow Spelman's grand house with the round window has been partitioned into condominiums, but Collins Graves's farmhouse still stands a little south of the village. The town's population is 2,500, only 500 more than it was in 1874. The land is largely wooded so that wild turkeys, bear, and deer are not infrequent sights once again.

At the Williamsburg village center, the former town hall, where the coroner's jury was sworn in over John Atkinson's body, is now the historical society's museum. Displayed here are a portrait of Joel Hayden Sr. and a small collection of flood items picked up along the river over the years: a chest full of black silk thread, wooden spools of wool, and brass castings for water pumps. At a historical society meeting last year, a Graves descendant showed the silver-based lamp that Collins Graves had received as a tribute to his heroism.

If you drive up from the village toward the dam, and walk through woods on the path that once led to Cheney's house—marked only by a small depression beside a shallow ditch that was the wasteway—you will come upon the ruins of the Williamsburg Reservoir dam. For one hundred thirty years, the breached dam has remained mostly untouched except by pines and maples rooting in its banks and chipmunks dwelling in the crevices of the masonry. Stepping from the hillside onto the still perfectly contoured embankment, its size is overwhelming, a long artificial hill drawn like a curtain between two knolls. Crunching dead leaves and pushing aside tree branches, one can walk about one hundred feet along the level crest—still wide enough for two carts to pass—until the embankment abruptly ends. Four stories below trickles a stony brook. Across the chasm where the middle of the dam disappeared, branches of mature trees block one's view of the remainder of the east wall, a wedge-shaped section about thirty feet long. Dried leaves and vines hide the stones, some the size of softballs and others more like basketballs. Some grout and mortar crumbles, while other samples hold tight as concrete.

The two Goshen dams still stand today. They were rebuilt by the

Civilian Conservation Corps in the 1930s with stone walls at their cores and their banks carpeted with thick grass. The state has performed several major repairs since then. The lower reservoir, called the Lower Highland Lake, is lined with private cottages and a 4-H camp. In the summer, the public swims and boats in the Upper Highland Lake, a part of the Daughters of the American Revolution State Forest. The state inspects the dams regularly.

The Williamsburg and Goshen dams were little more than enormous heaps of dirt and rubble that had held back a mountain stream. Yet this rude reservoir system had fueled factories so productive that they shipped goods all over the country. These dams, and hundreds of others like them nestled in the New England hills, had made the American industrial revolution possible.

Today, the state maintains an inventory of nearly three thousand dams in Massachusetts. They exist on nearly every little brook and river around the state, ranking Massachusetts ninth in the country in its number of dams. Most were built between 1850 and 1900, in the heyday of waterpower.

In the first edition the *Hampshire Gazette* published after the flood, Henry Gere wrote:

> It should be the task of some person, historically inclined, to gather up all these [newspaper] accounts from which a very complete record of the whole disaster can be made for the benefit of coming generations; for, as long as these towns and villages shall stand, this will be the greatest event in their histories.

Growing up seventeen miles from Haydenville, I often heard my father tell how the Mill River flood wiped out the Haydenville tin shop owned by Ezbon Sharpe, my father's great-grandfather, and George Ames, my father's great-great-uncle. I never heard any stories of how Ezbon or his fifteen-year-old son Franklin, from whom we are descended, escaped from the shop or their nearby home. It seems no one talked about it. If my father knew why the dam broke, I don't remember him mentioning it.

On May 16, 1999, a sunny Sunday afternoon with lilacs and tulips blooming in the valley, one hundred people gathered to commemorate the one hundred twenty-fifth anniversary of the disaster by dedicating three monuments along the flood route—one each in Leeds, Haydenville, and Williamsburg. "It's about time," people said, "that we do something in memory of the victims."

Norman Graves, the chairman of the Williamsburg Historical Commission, introduced descendants of Collins Graves, Jimmy Ryan, and Jerome Hillman (no descendants of Cheney and Day could be found), and one by one, they were asked to step forward to be acknowledged with applause, not unlike the heroes at the Cosmian Hall tribute. This time Jimmy Ryan was doubly honored; one of his descendants had arranged for a governor's certificate that recognized the "courage and life-saving efforts of James F. Ryan." When the tribute to the victims and heroes was over, the audience was invited next door to the Williams House, where Cheney had warned miller Theodore Hitchcock about the coming flood and Hitchcock rushed off to the mill and his death. Inside the tavern, visitors looked at historical documents and placed orders for photocopies of the *Springfield Republican* "extra" on the flood. Ralmon Black showed Collins Graves's medal (on loan from the Meekins Library). Some asked what caused the flood.

As I write this, Leeds citizens are planning to complete a small memorial park around the monument they erected in 1999. In a spot on the riverbank, cleared of overgrown brush and saplings, soon a bricklayer will pave a pattern of a giant swirl representing the swell of the floodwaters. Set on the swirl will be two granite blocks from the dam at the old Emery Wheel Company. One block will serve as a bench, while the other will lean against it, evoking the flood's destruction. By next summer, visitors will be able to sit beside the water and read the names of those who lived and worked along the river and then one day, without warning, perished.

APPENDIX A: CONTRACT AND SPECIFICATIONS FOR THE WILLIAMSBURG DAM

THIS agreement made this 28th day of June 1865, between the Williamsburg Reservoir Company by their committee, consisting of Messrs. W. T. Clement, Wm. Clark, Jr., and Lucius Dimock, of the first part, and Emory B. Wells of Northampton and Joel L. Bassett of Easthampton, of the second part, both parties residents of the county of Hampshire and state of Massachusetts.

Witnesseth: That said party of the second part, in consideration of stipulations of said party of the first part to be hereinafter set forth to be performed, do hereby contract and agree to grub, clear, thoroughly break up and prepare the ground, construct and complete the earthwork and masonry of a dam for said party of the first part, on land purchased of Simeon Bartlett, in the town of Williamsburg, by said Williamsburg Reservoir company, said dam to be located in such place as the said committee shall direct, all to be done in a thorough and workmanlike manner, and in all respects in strict conformity with the directions, plans and specifications, and to the acceptance of the said committee, or the superintendent employed by the said committee to take charge of the work.

The said Wells and Bassett agree to clear and remove from the ground under the whole embankment all perishable materials, such as trees, stumps, roots, and also to remove all muck and everything of that character, the whole length of the embankment, for a distance of 30 feet each side of the center wall under the highest part of the embankment, and a proportionate width where the bank is of less height. It is agreed and understood that the top of the embankment when finished is to be 43 feet above the original bed of the stream on the center line of said dam, to slope uniformly at the rate of one and one-half feet base to one foot rise on each side; to be 16 feet wide on top, and level from one end to the other. It is also understood that all perishable material, of whatever nature, is to be excluded, and the dam to be built wholly of earth and masonry, the earth to be placed in thin layers, wet and tamped or beaten with a maul for a distance of five feet each side of the center wall. The whole embankment to be built in layers, not exceeding five feet each in thickness, and made as solid as possible. At no time during the progress of the work is the earth to be less than one and a half feet below the top of the masonry until the wall is finished.

For foundations of masonry the said Wells and Bassett further agree to dig trenches three feet deep, or of sufficient depth to give a firm, hard and secure bottom for the masonry to rest upon, and which will not allow the masonry to settle.

The said Wells and Bassett also agree to build a good rubble wall through the center of the dam longitudinal therewith, the top to be 42 feet above the original bed of the stream on the center line of the dam, to be two feet thick, uniformly level and increase in thickness downward with a batir of one inch per foot, making the thickness, at 45 feet from the top, five feet nine inches. The whole wall to be well banded, laid in a substantial and workmanlike manner, and except from 10 to 15 feet from top downward, to be well grouted with the best of hydraulic lime and sand. From the top downward 10 or 15 feet (the exact distance optional with the committee), may be laid in mortar with 25 per cent of quick lime mixed with 75 per cent of hydraulic lime, instead of being grouted. The wall is to be a thoroughly solid one, except an opening for the passageway of a trunk or iron pipe to be put in by the committee at a proper time during the progress of the work.

The said Wells and Bassett further agree to build a wall for a trunk or iron pipes to rest upon, for an outlet through said dam. Said wall at the upper end to be grouted where possible for a distance of 30 feet from the face, and the same for 20 feet at the lower end or outlet. The whole of the wall, except the wings, and face wall at the upper end to be good rubble masonry. The face wall and wings at the upper end are to be split dimension stone.

It is further agreed by the said Wells and Bassett, to complete the dam on or before the 25th day of December 1865, and all masonry laid after frost shall be kept covered and protected so as to insure the same permanence as if laid earlier in the season.

It is understood and agreed by both parties to this contract that if the committee are compelled to reduce expense for want of money, it shall be done by reducing the height of the dam.

It is further agreed that the said Wells and Bassett are to be allowed all the facilities and privileges for constructing the dam that are granted by Simeon Bartlett to the Reservoir company for the same purpose.

It is further understood that should the amount of earth embankment exceed the estimated quantity, viz., 24,000 cubic yards, such excess is to be paid for at the rate of 36 cents per cubic yard; if it falls short, a deduction at the rate of 36 cents per cubic yard is to be made. And if the masonry varies from the estimated amount, viz., 1800 cubic yards, a like variation at the rate of $6.50 per cubic yard is agreed upon.

It is also agreed that the work is to be measured as a finished dam, deducting the masonry from the earth work. It is further understood that there shall be an estimate, on or about the first of each month, of the work done the preceding month, and for the work done 80 per cent paid to the said Wells and Bassett on or about the 10th of every month, and the remaining 20 per cent is to be retained by the said committee until the said dam is completed and accepted by said committee, and when so accepted the said Wells and Bassett are to be paid the full amount.

It is agreed by the party of the first part in consideration of the faithful performance and fulfillment of the foregoing stipulations hereinbefore mentioned to pay the party of the second part the sum of $21,000 for the estimated amount, viz., of earth 24,000 cubic yards, of masonry 1800, the price subject to be increased or diminished from $21,000 as the number of cubic yards vary from the estimated amount as before mentioned.

Source: This text of the contract for the construction of the Williamsburg Reservoir dam was published in the *Springfield Republican*. The contract was never signed. SDR, May 25, 1874, p. 5.

APPENDIX B:
LIST OF FLOOD VICTIMS

T H E R E was no official death toll published. For my total of 139, I have relied on the death records of the towns of Williamsburg and Northampton and on newspaper accounts of the circumstances of deaths not recorded in the towns' Vital Statistics. Augustus Laney doesn't appear in the Vital Statistics of either town, but I have included him because Fred Howard, a trusted source, described the circumstances of his death in a letter. Laney's name also appeared on several newspaper lists as Alexander Lanier.

NAME	AGE	PLACE OF BIRTH	OCCUPATION
WILLIAMSBURG			
Williamsburg Village			
1. Mary Josephine Adams	36	Williamsburg	Keep House
2. William Adams	7	Williamsburg	
3. William H. Adams	51	Pittsfield, Mass.	Miller
4. George Ashley	16	Leverett, Mass.	
5. John Atkinson	48	England	Wool Mill
6. Saloma Bartlett	55	Hatfield, Mass.	Keep House
7. Sarah Bartlett	24	Worthington, Mass.	Keep House
8. Spencer Bartlett	74	Williamsburg	Farmer
9. Carrie Birmingham	7	Hinsdale, Mass.	
10. Henry Birmingham	47	England	Supt., Wool Mill
11. Laura Birmingham	43	Hinsdale, Mass.	Keep House
12. Lillie Birmingham	16	Hinsdale, Mass.	
13. Mary Birmingham	20	Hinsdale, Mass.	Teacher
14. Frederick Burr	34	England	Fireman
15. Mary Brennan	62	Ireland	
16. Michael Burke	61	Ireland	Wool Mill
17. Michael Burke	9	Williamsburg	
18. Annie Burke	5	Williamsburg	
19. Jennie Burke	8	Williamsburg	
20. Mary Carter	23	Canada	

21. Caroline Chandler	39	Albany, N.Y.	Keep House
22. E. Mary Chandler	8	Greenbush, N.Y.	
23. Viola Colyer	4	Gill, Mass.	
24. Eliza Downing	28	Ireland	
25. Edmond Downing	1	Whateley, Mass.	
26. Johanah Downing	54	Ireland	
27. Theodore Hitchcock	34	New Lebanon, N.Y.	Miller
28. Epaphro Hubbard	56	Williamsburg	Farmer
29. Elbridge Johnson	38	Feeding Hills, Mass.	Physician
30. Mary F. Johnson	32	Oakland, Md.	Keep House
31. Charlotte Johnson	4	Williamsburg	
32. Edward Johnson	8	Williamsburg	
33. Mary H. Johnson	6	Williamsburg	
34. Lucretia Johnson	67	Unknown	
35. Annie Kingsley	25	New York	Keep House
36. Elizabeth Kingsley	60	Becket, Mass.	Keep House
37. Lyman Kingsley	1	Williamsburg	
38. Nellie Kingsley	3	Williamsburg	
39. Electa Knight	80	Williamsburg	
40. Archie Lancour	21	Canada	Wool Mill
41. Susan Lamb	54	Leverett, Mass.	Keep House
42. Mary Ann McGee	14	Williamsburg	Servant
43. Frank Murray	53	Ireland	Wool Mill
44. Mary Murray	53	Ireland	Wool Mill
45. Alexander Roberts	42	Somersworth, N.H.	Railroad Engineer
46. Caroline Roberts	37	Somersworth, N.H.	Keep House
47. Nettie Roberts	3	Worcester, Mass.	
48. Olivet Roberts	1	Williamsburg	
49. Elizabeth Scully	8 mos.	Williamsburg	
50. John Scully	3	Williamsburg	
51. Mary Scully	26	Ireland	Keep House
52. Sarah Snow	76	Williamsburg	
53. James Stephens	49	England	Wool Mill
54. William Tilton	3	Williamsburg	
55. Jeremiah Ward	71	Buckland, Mass.	Stone Mason
56. Emma Wood	21	Williamsburg	Keep House
57. Harold Wood	1	Williamsburg	

Skinnerville Village

58. Eli Bryant	77	Chesterfield, Mass.	
59. Joseph Hayden Jr.	5	Williamsburg	
60. Sarah Hillman	42	Northampton	Keep House
61. Christina Hills	46	Germany	Keep House

Haydenville Village

62. Rosa Bissonette	22	Canada	
63. Joseph Bissonette	9 days	Williamsburg	
64. Francis Brodeur	20	Canada	Brass Works
65. Stephen Kiely	57	Ireland	
66. Mary Kiely	59	Ireland	
67. Mary Hogan	50	Ireland	
68. John Kaplinger	73	Germany	Shoemaker
69. Margaret Lablone	54	Canada	
70. Mary Macy	50	Canada	
71. Agnes Miller	10	Holyoke, Mass.	
72. George Miller	8	Holyoke, Mass.	
73. William Miller	1	Williamsburg	
74. Edmond Mockler	55	Ireland	
75. Georgianna Nafroyze	14	Canada	
76. Mary Norris	50	Ireland	
77. Ilocrain Pouzee	14	Canada	
78. Isabelle Pouzee	22	Canada	
79. Nayerene Pouzee	11	Canada	
80. Theresa Pouzee	45	Canada	
81. Teresa Tafor	45	Canada	
82. Freddie Thayer	1	Williamsburg	
83. George Thayer	5	Williamsburg	
84. Johanah Williams	22	Ireland	
85. Margaret Wilson	49	Canada	
86. Matilda Wilson	10	Canada	
87. Rosa Wilson	7	Canada	
88. Margaret Wilson	5	Williamsburg	

NORTHAMPTON

Leeds Village

89. Mrs. Nicholas Bagley			
90. Carrie Bonney	16	Northampton	Button Mill
91. Isaac Braulette	19	Canada	
92. Osina Braulette	16	Canada	
93. Louis Napoleon Braulette	15	Canada	
94. Meline F. Braulette	38	Canada	
95. Victor Braulette	1	Northampton	
96. Eliza Carpenter	16	Canada	
97. Clara Clancy	1	Northampton	
98. George Clancy	3	Northampton	
99. Annie Cogan	23	New York	Teacher
100. Grace Cogan	20	Wisconsin	Student
101. Jane Cogan	42	Northampton	
102. Samuel Davies	30	England	Button Mill

103. Terence Dundan	10	Northampton	
104. Ellen Dunlea	72	Ireland	
105. Amos Dunning	78	Northampton	Farmer
106. Ellen Fennessey	80	Ireland	
107. Andrew Fennessey	40	Ireland	
108. Ellen Fennessey	40	Ireland	
109. Nellie F. Fennessey	11	Northampton	
110. Elizabeth Fennessey	36	Ireland	
111. Katie Fennessey	3	Northampton	
112. John Fennessey	6	Northampton	
113. Annie Fitzgerald	7	Northampton	
114. Bertha Fitzgerald	unk.	Northampton	
115. Charles Fitzgerald	20	Northampton	
116. Jane Fitzgerald	38	Ireland	
117. Lottie Fitzgerald	4	Northampton	
118. Thomas Fitzgerald	10	Northampton	
119. Bridget Hannum	7	Ireland	
120. Edward Hannum	4	Northampton	
121. John Hannum	2	Northampton	
122. Michael Hannum	5 mos.	Northampton	
123. Mrs. Edward Hannum	28	Ireland	
124. Mrs. Hurley	63	Ireland	
125. Ralph Isham	31	Brooklyn, N.Y.	Bookkeeper
126. Alexander Laney	unk.	Canada	Button Mill
127. Patrick O'Neille	35	Ireland	
128. Charles Patrick	24	Canada	
129. Julia Patrick	17	Canada	
130. Mary Patrick	56	Canada	
131. Mary Patrick	23	Canada	
132. Mary Rouse	12	Canada	
133. Charles Ryan	4	Northampton	
134. Sarah Jane Ryan	21	England	
135. Arthur Sharpe	17	England	Button Mill
136. Sarah Shaughnessy	38	Ireland	
137. Eveline Sherwood	18	Northampton	
138. T. F. Vaughan	40	Canada	
139. Mary Woodward	20	unk.	Silk Mill

Source: Vital Statistics, vol. 4 (1861–1900), Williamsburg Town Hall, Williamsburg, Mass.; Registry of Deaths, vol. 5 (1873–1875), Northampton City Hall, Northampton, Mass.; U.S. Census: Population, 1870; Fred Howard to brother, June 7, 1874.

APPENDIX C: VERDICT OF THE CORONER'S INQUEST

A N inquisition taken at the Town Hall in Williamsburgh in the County of Hampshire, on the twentieth day of May in the year one thousand eight hundred and seventy-four and continued by adjournment at the Court House in Northampton in said County on the 25th, 26th, 27th, 28th, 29th, & 30th days of said month of May & on the 13th, 29th, & 30th days of June & 2d & 3d days of July in said year before Ansel Wright one of the Special Coroners of said County of Hampshire, upon the view of the body of John Atkinson there lying dead, by the oaths of the Jurors, whose names are hereunto subscribed, who, being sworn to inquire on behalf of said Commonwealth, when, how, and by what means said Atkinson came to his death, upon their oaths do say that said Atkinson came to his death by drowning in Mill River in said Williamsburgh on Saturday the 16th day of May 1874 at about eight of the clock in the forenoon during a sudden rise or overflow of said Mill River caused by the breaking away of the dam of the Williamsburgh Reservoir situated on said Mill River in Williamsburgh about three miles North-East from the upper village of said Town and belonging to the Mill River and Williamsburgh Reservoir Co. And the Jurors further say that the breaking away of said dam was the natural and inevitable result of the great and manifest delinquency of the several parties who were concerned in originating, planning, constructing and approving for use the said dam and Reservoir, not excepting the Legislature itself under whose authority the Reservoir Company acquired its chartered privileges.

I. THE DELINQUENT LEGISLATION

In the judgment of the Jurors the Commonwealth through its law makers assumed a large share of the responsibility for this disaster when in 1865 it granted a charter to William Skinner, Joel Hayden, Lewis Bodman and others with full corporate powers and privileges for the construction of a dam 45 feet in height flowing a basin of 104 acres holding about 600,000,000 gallons of water and overhanging at an altitude of from 350 feet to 800 feet, eight prosperous villages within a distance of eleven miles the nearest being three miles distant with no other safeguards or guarantees for the security of life and property below, than such as might depend on the self interest or will of a private citizen. Indeed our Statute law as it has stood for many years has been calculated to repel rather than invite a careful scrutiny of works like the Williamsburgh Dam, for while it provides that any person who fears the destruction of his property or of a highway from an unsafe reservoir may call out the County Commissioners for an examination, yet if his fears are not indorsed by the Commissioners he is to be inulcted [*sic*] with the costs and expenses of the whole proceeding.

In view of the utterly inadequate legislation on this subject and the desolation and ruin in the case before us, it is to be hoped the Legislature if it cannot provide indemnity for the past, will at least by prompt and stringent action ensure security for the future.

II. AS TO THE PROPRIETORS OF THE RESERVOIR

In the judgment of the Jurors while it is evident that the Proprietors as a body consulted far less for the safety and security of the lives and property of the Inhabitants below the dam, than for reducing the cost of construction to the minimum figure; nevertheless they cannot but regard those owners who acted in the capacity of a building committee as especially responsible for the breaking away of the dam. They had little or no experience in similar undertaking; they adopted the plan upon which the structure was built because of its low price; they either entirely overruled or but partially followed the advice of the Engineers whom they consulted in points vital to the strength of the dam, from parsimony or some other unaccountable motive they were led at an early stage of the work wholly to dispense with the services of the only Engineer in their employ at all competent to superintend and guard the construction at all points. When in the progress of the work signs of insecurity in the earth work were pointed out to the committee such as the action of hidden springs and the sloughing of the banks; they either but half applied the remedy or ignored the danger altogether; and finally the recorded vote of the proprietors that counsel should be consulted and all necessary steps taken for relieving the owners from individual liability in the case the dam should fail and damage and disaster follow, is speaking evidence that self interest and not the welfare of the Community dictated the action of this Company.

III. AS TO THE ENGINEERS

In the judgment of the jurors there was no engineering connected with the work which does not reflect equal discredit on the party employing and the party employed. The only Engineer by profession employed was Lucius Fenn who upon his own admission regarded himself as but the mere Attorney or Agent of the Proprietors, yielding his own judgment on points of safety and accommodating his specifications for the dam to the requirements of his unskilled employers.

The specifications moreover as finally drawn by him were ambiguous in terms and defective in details: they failed to require the constant supervision of the work by a competent engineer, and were entirely inadequate for a substantial and durable structure. Mr. Fenn's services *such as they were* terminated with the location of the dam, the draft of specifications and some slight attention to the preparation for the superstructure. Mr. Eugene C. Gardner who succeeded him, (by profession a Surveyor and Architect) had no experience or fitness as an Engineer; and as a witness before the Jury, claimed, that he was employed merely to compute from time to time the amount of work done and payments due. The Jurors find however that he was the only Superintendent or Engineer after Mr. Fenn employed for any purpose by the Proprietors, and they further find and declare as their judgment that the entire active work on the Dam from the first breaking of ground for the foundation to the completion of the job was without an hour's attendance of a competent and watchful engineer.

IV. AS TO THE CONTRACTORS

In the judgment of the Jurors the Contractors were guilty of great and manifest delinquency in executing the work required of them, even under the specifications as drafted. The space required by the Specifications to be cleared of all soft earth roots and vegetable matter, within thirty feet each side of the central wall down to a hard foundation was found (upon a view taken by the Jurors in the presence of the Contractors) permeated with fragments of roots, rootlets and fibrous substance throughout much of the original swamp bottom as it was left by the Contractors.

The surface Soil was here removed only to the depth of a single furrow; more than this the laying of the foundation of the central wall with large boulders supported by small pinning stones resting on the original soft earth and the imperfect grouting, with excessively poor grout of large sections of the wall sometimes 20 feet long by five feet high and five feet wide from a grouting box stationed at a single point; all these with many other evidences of want of thoroughness in preparing the foundations and erecting the superstructure of the Dam, corroborated by the large profit confessedly made on the job, satisfy the Jurors that the Contractors Joel L. Bassett and Emory B. Wells did not faithfully execute the work contracted for according to the true intent of the Specifications.

V. AS TO THE COUNTY COMMISSIONERS

As to the County Commissioners who lent their approval to the structure in question.

In the judgment of the Jurors, the Legislature intentionally devolved upon the board of County Commissioners when acting upon such an application as was made in the present case a duty and responsibility of the gravest character. By the Statutes of the Commonwealth the County Commissioners have the fullest power to take all necessary steps for most thoroughly examining and testing a Reservoir Dam. If they are not themselves Engineers and Experts they have authority to call to their aid Engineers and Experts capable of giving them reliable advice. They are expressly authorized to assess the necessary expense of their examination upon the applicant if his application shall prove needless and upon the Proprietors of the Reservoir in case the structure shall be found defective. They have power to tear down, make alterations and make safe, or cause the same to be done by the owners thereof, and the Statutes give the Supreme Court full jurisdiction to compel the Proprietors to comply with every requirement of the County Commissioners. The Jurors are therefore unable to view the action of the County Commissioners in examining and accepting this Reservoir Dam in any other light than as a Superficial discharge of a most important duty. The Statute contemplates a most thorough examination and inquiry and the testimony of the Commissioners makes it apparent that no such examination or inquiry was made; no evidence was taken concerning the work, except such as was given by the Proprietors who were present. The contractors were not called or inquired of, as to how and in what manner the dam was constructed; no Engineers having skill and experience with such structures were examined to aid the Commissioners in arriving at a right and safe decision, in short though they made three separate views of the dam, and ordered specific repairs; the evidence shows that their examinations were not thorough nor in conformity to the spirit of the law; and with these facts before the Jury they are forced to conclude that not a little of the responsibility for this terrible disaster rests with these officers.

In testimony whereof, said Special Coroner and Jurors of this inquest have hereunto set their hands the third day of July aforesaid. Hiram Nash one of the Jurors aforesaid dissenting from so much of said verdict as refers to the Legislature.

[Signatures]

Ansel Wright, Special Coroner

Jurors

Enos Parsons, Foreman

Hiram Nash

Geo. W. Hubbard

John Mayher

W. M. Trow

S. G. Hubbard

Source: Inquest on the body of John Atkinson, May–June 1874. Filed in Hampshire County Superior Court, July 31, 1874, Hampshire County Courthouse, Northampton, Mass.

NOTES

ABBREVIATIONS
BG *Boston Globe*
HG *Hampshire Gazette & Northampton Courier*
NFP *Northampton Free Press*
NYT *New York Times*
SDR *Springfield Daily Republican*
SDU *Springfield Daily Union*
WRC Williamsburg Reservoir Company
WCS William Cobbett Skinner

PROLOGUE
2. "reminds one forcibly": *SDR*, May 30, 1874, p. 5.
2. their dialogue went like this: A complete record of the inquest comes from contemporary newspapers, such as the Boston, New York, and Springfield dailies which printed detailed summaries of the previous day's testimonies. Their reports included the appearances and demeanors of the most important witnesses, abstracts of the testimony, some verbatim exchanges, and transcriptions of relevant documents, interrupted only occasionally with the editor's or reporter's opinions. I have relied mostly on the *Springfield* (Massachusetts) *Daily Republican* and the *Springfield Daily Union* because their reports were the most complete, averaging 5,500 words per day for each of five days. The original inquest transcript cannot be found.
2 "Mr. Hayden says": *HG*, May 26, 1874, p. 1.
3. "testimony with reluctance": *SDR*, June 1, 1874, p. 5.

CHAPTER 1: THE MILL VALLEY
6. In Massachusetts in the early 1870s: Louis C. Hunter, *Waterpower in the Century of the Steam Engine, History of Industrial Power in the United States*, vol. 1 (Charlottesville, Va: University Press of Virginia, 1979), especially pp. 119, 130–31, 179–80.
7. One geologist later estimated: Hunter, *Waterpower*, p. 511. For a discussion of upstream storage reservoirs see Hunter, *Waterpower*, pp. 509–13.
8. The hills and valleys: Agricultural products of the Mill Valley from *Statistical Information Relating to Certain Branches of Industry in Massachusetts for the Year Ending May 1, 1865* (Boston: Wright & Potter, State Printers, 1866), p. 317. In 1865, Williamsburg residents sold 1,700 cords of firewood.

9. make the stream flow work for everyone: Massachusetts law on waterpower from Edward R. Kaynor, *Dam Policy in Massachusetts* (Amherst, Mass: Water Resources Research Center, University of Massachusetts, 1979), pp. 9–10; Theodore Steinberg, *Nature Incorporated: Industrialization and the Waters of New England* (New York: Cambridge University Press, 1991), pp. 25–32; and Morton J. Horwitz, *The Transformation of American Law, 1780–1860* (Cambridge, Mass: Harvard University Press, 1977), pp. 47–53.

10. Compared to other large Massachusetts manufacturing centers: *The Statistics of the Wealth and Industry of the United States, Ninth Census of the United States (1870)* (Washington, D.C.: Government Printing Office, 1872), p. 528.

11. Hayden was born into: Josiah Hayden and Hayden family history from Donald Bradford Macurda, *Josiah Hayden of Williamsburg, Massachusetts (His Antecedents and Descendants)*, vol. 1 (Privately published: 1984), pp. 353–407; Phyllis Baker Deming, *A History of Williamsburg in Massachusetts* (Northampton, Mass.: Hampshire Bookshop, 1946) pp. 8–11.

14. "When your heart gets up": Macurda, *Josiah Hayden*, vol. 1, p. 357.

15. "the largest and most extensive of its kind": Henry S. Gere, ed., *An Historical Sketch of Haydenville and Williamsburg* (typescript prepared from *Hampshire Gazette* articles published in the early 1860s), p. 6.

16. "Began poor": Abner Forbes, *The Rich Men of Massachusetts*, 2d ed. (Boston: Redding & Co., 1852), pp. iii–vii.

20. Mary Hill: Hill lived 1848–1899. Her diaries for the years 1866–1896 are in the collection of the Williamsburg Historical Society, Williamsburg, Mass.

21. "Nothing happens of any account": WCS Diary, January 21, 1874, collection of the Williamsburg Historical Society. Will was named for English political writer William Cobbett, whom his father greatly admired.

23. "Dick and I had a good time": WCS Diary, January 3, 1874.

23. Most of Will's social life: Social institutions and community outings—church socials, skating and sleighing parties, and picnics—brought youth together so love could bloom on neutral ground where friends and family were nearby but not in direct oversight of the actions of courting couples. Unmarried men and women, singly or in groups, frequently called at one another's homes in the evenings or on weekends for spontaneous gatherings, nominally watched over by parents. See Karen Lystra, *Searching the Heart: Women, Men and Romantic Love in Nineteenth-Century America* (New York: Oxford University Press, 1989); Ellen K. Rothman, *Hands and Hearts: A History of Courtship in America* (New York: Basic Books, 1984); and Peter Ward, *Courtship, Love, and Marriage in Nineteenth-Century English Canada* (Montreal: McGill-Queen's University Press, 1990).

24. "got hold of one of their hands": WCS Diary, March 22, 1874.

26. Critchlow imported several hundred tons: *Historical Register and General Directory of Northampton* (Northampton, Mass: Gazette Printing Co., 1875–76), pp. 88–89.

28. Northampton Association of Education and Industry: Christopher Clark, *The Communitarian Moment: The Radical Challenge of the Northampton Association* (Ithaca, N.Y.: Cornell University Press, 1995).

29. In 1860, the Nonotuck Company: Statistics from Clark, *Communitarian Moment*, fn. 42, p. 259.

29. "Then if I were in your situation": *Memorial: Alfred Theodore Lilly* (Florence, Mass: Bryant and Brothers 1890), p. 17.

33. Reservoirs were part of the chain of progress: For information on the prevailing

view that industry was good for all, see Carl Siracusa, *A Mechanical People: Perceptions of the Industrial Order in Massachusetts, 1815–1880* (Middletown, Conn: Wesleyan University Press, 1979), pp. 58–74.

CHAPTER 2: BUILDING THE WILLIAMSBURG DAM

34. For $1,500, Spelman secured an easement: Hampshire County Registry of Deeds, book 223, pp. 299–300, 303–304, 332–33; book 225, pp. 10–11.

35. "True economy": Hampshire County Registry of Deeds, book 223, pp. 533–34.

35. "to be final and never altered": Hampshire County Registry of Deeds, book 223, pp. 533–34.

37. "What you want is to construct a wall": *SDU*, May 25, 1874, p. 5. William Clement described Stewart Chase's proposal at the inquest.

38. "for the purpose of constructing and maintaining a reservoir": Williamsburg Reservoir Company charter, *Acts and Resolves Passed by the General Court of Massachusetts in the Year 1865* (Boston: Wright & Potter, State Printers, 1865), p. 549. Manufacturers on the Mill River who were not members of the reservoir company reaped the benefits of the increased supply, but the reservoir company was in charge of the rate and when it flowed. Hunter, *Waterpower*, pp. 140, 148–49.

38. Monday, May 8, 1865: The minutes of the May 8, 1865, meeting (and subsequent meetings) of the Williamsburg Reservoir Company are in the WRC Record Book, 1865–1872, Forbes Library, Northampton, Mass.

39. "We can fix it afterward": *SDR*, May 29, 1874, p. 5.

40. "in a substantial and workmanlike manner": Fenn's specifications for the dam were published in the *SDR*, May 27, 1874, p. 5.

40. In 1865, Massachusetts laws: *General Statutes of the Commonwealth of Massachusetts, 1860* (Boston: William White, 1860), chap. 149, pp. 754–61.

40. "free to build a dam of sawdust": *SDR*, May 28, 1874, p. 4.

41. On July 15, 1865, Wells and Bassett began construction: For a description of how the dam was built I have relied on the coroner's inquest testimony of Emory Wells, Joel Bassett, William Clement, and Lucius Dimock as printed in the *SDR* and *SDU* during the period May 25–30, 1874, and conversations with Ralmon Black and Eric Weber on October 28, 2003, and with Tom Famulari on November 5, December 17 and 23, 2003.

42. "risk it": *SDU*, May 27, 1874, p. 3.

42. "wouldn't give a dollar": *SDR*, May 28, 1874, p. 5.

43. "W. T. Clement and William Clark Jr.": *SDU*, May 21, 1874, p. 5.

44. "would not trust this work": *SDR*, May 29, 1874, p. 5.

46. "Men and horses sent to work on new reserv.": Otis G. Hill Diary, April 11, 1867, collection of the Williamsburg Historical Society, Williamsburg, Mass.

46. "sweep everyone on its way": *SDR*, May 19, 1874, p. 5.

48. "We occasionally have a freshet": *New York Tribune*, May 19, 1874, p. 1.

48. "I am gone": *HG*, November 11, 1873, p. 2.

48. "like a father": *HG*, November 18, 1873, p. 2.

CHAPTER 3: THE FLOOD

53. "For God's sake, George": *SDR*, May 26, 1874, p. 5. From Elias Cheney's testimony at the coroner's inquest.

55 Gleason remembered Cheney and Spelman's exchange: *SDR*, May 26, 1874, p. 5. From John Gleason's testimony at the coroner's inquest. Gleason's story didn't differ from Cheney's recollection of the conversation.

56. "George, what's the matter?": *SDR*, May 26, 1874, p. 5. Cheney and Collins

Graves's conversation as recalled by Collins Graves at the coroner's inquest.

56. "seemed to burst all at once": *SDR*, May 26, 1874, p. 5. Elizabeth Cheney's description of how the dam burst is taken from the coroner's inquest. She was the only person to see the dam break.

62. "A great mass of brush, trees, and trash": Reminiscence of Eugene E. Davis, who witnessed the disaster as a boy in Florence, quoted in Deming, *History of Williamsburg*, p. 282.

62. William Adams's sawmill and gristmill: A casualty of the Panic of 1873 and facing bankruptcy, Adams had sold the sawmill and gristmill six months before the flood. He also disposed of his house, horses, cow, three rental houses, a slaughterhouse, eighty-seven acres of land in Williamsburg, and a personal estate of $1,640. In neighboring Chesterfield, his home town, he sold a fifty-acre parcel. At the time of his death, he owed $16,000 to a total of twenty-eight different people. Hampshire County Registry of Probate, William H. Adams, docket 166-49, Northampton, Mass.; Williamsburg Tax Lists, 1873, 1874; U.S. Census, 1870: Population Schedule.

63. Sarah Snow, near the house: Sarah Snow's daughter was the only one of her four children living in Williamsburg. Her three sons had scattered to Brooklyn, New York City, and Ohio. The son in New York would be instrumental in securing relief aid. U.S. Census, 1870: Population; Hampshire County Probate, Docket 250-15; *HG*, May 19, 1874, p. 2.

65. "in its [the flood's] presence": *SDR*, May 18, 1874, p. 4.

66. Eight of the houses belonging to the James mill: James mill employees Frank and Mary Murray and Archie Lancour also died. *HG*, May 19, 1874, pp. 2, 4; Vital Statistics of Williamsburg, 1874; Vital Statistics of Northampton, Registry of Deaths, book 5 (1873–1875), City Hall, Northampton, Mass.

66. "twelve-year-old son, Jimmy": Ryan later recalled that he was twelve at the time. Census and family records indicate that he was either twelve or fourteen. Newspaper clipping, 1924, in Wheeler, comp., "Records of Haydenville."

68. $300,000 in business each year: *BG*, May 19, 1874, p. 5.

68. "in ten years we shall be shipping silk": William Skinner, quoted in *HG*, June 30, 1874, p. 2.

70. home of bookkeeper Nash Hubbard: This large house had been the Skinner family home before William Skinner built the mansion.

70. Now, her home and livelihood: Other Skinnerville structures destroyed were: Andrew Breckenridge's home, located between Bartlett's and Wrisley's; the homes of James Forsyth, Jerome Hillman, Mr. Van Vechten, Mr. Thomas, and that of Mr. Smith, the depot master; two boardinghouses managed by Fred Hillman; a two-family house occupied by Mr. Hubbard and Mr. Adams; and houses belonging to Jacob Hills, Christian Kaplinger, George Warner, Alvan Bradford, and Joseph Hayden. *SDR*, May 18, 1874, p. 5.

72. "It won't be down here for four days": *Boston Sunday Globe*, December 21, 1902. Graves recalled Wentworth's words twenty-eight years later.

72. "Once he looked behind": *New York Tribune*, May 18, 1874, p. 1.

73. "We had waited but a very few minutes": "Real Hero of Mill River Flood," newspaper article from unnamed source (dated 1924) in Charles Wheeler, comp., *Records of Haydenville*, vol. 2, Forbes Library, Northampton, Mass.

73. Hayden's mansion, now vacant: Hayden's widow had not inherited the house; she moved away with their six-year-old daughter.

74. "like a pyramid of sugar": *SDR*, May 18, 1874, p. 5.

75. Pierce Larkin's grocery: Like most other small property owners, Pierce Larkin had invested his entire fortune ($10,000) in his real estate and livelihood—two stores and a house. He had barely enough time to escape with his wife, two daughters, and two horses before the water washed his stores and house away, leaving him penniless. *HG*, May 19, 1874, p. 2; *SDR*, May 19, 1874, p. 5.

80. Meanwhile, in Humphrey's house: Humphrey's sister-in-law, Mrs. Bagley, who was visiting from Fitchburg, was standing on the porch when the flood swept her away. *HG*, May 19, 1874, p. 2; *SDR*, May 18, 1874, p. 5.

81. Fred wrote a firsthand account: Fred Howard letter to an unnamed brother (undated but written between May 16 and May 24, 1874). Letters of Fred Howard, Private Collection, Leeds, Mass. I have modernized the punctuation to make the letters easier to read.

82. ". . . all this time other houses": Fred Howard to brother, May 16–24, 1874.

84. "The red blacksmith shop": Fred Howard to brother, May 16–24, 1874.

89. The body was never found: A week after the flood, the body of a four-year-old girl washed ashore in Middletown, Connecticut, where the river bends southeast. The body was thought to be one of the missing flood victims, but it was determined to be that of a girl from Cromwell, Connecticut, a few miles upstream from Middletown, the victim of a local accident. The child on the mattress was never identified. *SDR*, May 30, 1874, p. 5; June 1, 1874, p. 4.

CHAPTER 4: THE AFTERMATH

92. Ten-year-old George Roberts: George Roberts story remembered by Jimmy Ryan of Haydenville in 1924, in newspaper article of unnamed source in Wheeler, comp., *Records of Haydenville*.

94. "not a tear was shed": *NYT*, May 18, 1874, p. 1.

95. "In these 'extemporized morgues'": *SDR*, May 5, 1874, p. 8.

96. "We worked all day Saturday": Fred Howard to brother, May 16–24, 1874.

98. "as electrifying as eloquent": *Boston Evening Journal*, May 18, 1874, p. 2.

98. to start a relief fund: Mill Valley residents reacted to the flood like typical disaster survivors, according to research by sociologists and psychologists who study people's reactions to disasters. Like survivors of hurricanes, tornadoes, and earthquakes, the Mill Valley survivors took care of themselves and their families and then began assisting others: first by aiding casualties and then by restoring services, such as clearing roads and repairing railroad track. Contrary to a commonly held belief, disaster victims do not go through a period of being so stunned and shocked that they cannot help themselves and those around them. Rather, they get to work immediately, as loosely knit groups cluster around natural leaders who organize work, then settle back into the community without notice or commendation. The first day or two—called the emergency period—is characterized by altruism, euphoria at having survived, a breakdown of social barriers, and the mutual reinforcement of a shared loss. Typical conflicts and competition among community members and groups are set aside as they work toward shared goals of rescue and relief. Kathleen J. Tierney, "Social and Community Contexts of Disaster," in *Psychological Aspects of Disaster*, ed. Richard Gist and Bernard Lubin (New York: John Wiley and Sons, 1989), pp. 20–21, 24; Beverley Raphael, *When Disaster Strikes: How Individuals and Communities Cope with Catastrophe* (New York: Basic Books, 1986), pp. 63–73; Joseph B. Perry Jr. and Meredith David Pugh, *Collective Behavior: Response to Social Stress* (St. Paul, Minn: West Publishing Co., 1978), p. 121.

98. six *Springfield Republican* newspaper reporters: Since it wasn't customary for

nineteenth-century newspapers to use reporters' bylines, the journalists' names are unknown except for William J. Denver.

99. Bodman told the history of the dam: *SDR*, May 18, 1874, p. 8; *NYT*, May 18, 1874.

100. "The Williamsburg Reservoir": Telegram printed in *NYT*, May 17, 1874, p. 1.

100. "I noticed that the men": WCS Diary, May 16, 1874.

100. "When I arrived at the house": WCS Diary, May 16, 1874.

103. "We will telegraph if we need anything": *SDR*, May 19, 1874, p. 4.

103. "To the Hon. H. G. Lewis": Telegram from D. B. Carr.

104. circulated petitions to the Massachusetts Senate: "Petition of Selectmen of Williamsburg and Northampton and Eighty-six Others Asking Relief," May 18, 1874, Massachusetts State Archives, Boston.

105. "Eventful day!": Mary Hill Diary, May 16, 1874.

105. "it's all over now": Fred Howard to brother, May 16–24, 1874.

106. "Notice—Having decided to rebuild": *HG*, May 19, 1874, p. 2.

107. "Something that was once human": *SDR*, May 21, 1874, p. 5.

107. "At almost every hour": *HG*, May 19, 1874, p. 1.

108. "Into Williamsburg": *SDR*, May 18, 1874, p. 8.

108. deluge of curiosity seekers: The flood created a booming business for railroads and hotels, which were "filled to overflowing." *SDR*, May 18, 1874, p. 8; May 19, 1874, p. 5; *HG*, May 26, 1874, p. 2.

109. Through the Associated Press wire service: *St. Louis Post-Dispatch*, May 19, 1874; *Daily Picayune* (New Orleans), May 17, 1874; *Atlanta Constitution*, May 17, 1874; *Times* (London), May 18, 1874; *San Francisco Chronicle*, May 17, 1874; *Daily Rocky Mountain News* (Denver), May 17, 1874.

111. "I went over [to Warner's]": Fred Howard to brother, May 16–24, 1874.

111. "Arose at seven or after": Mary Hill Diary, May 17, 1874.

112. "To George K. Snow": Telegram from *BG*, May 19, 1874, p. 5.

112. "no disaster since the Chicago fire": *SDR*, May 21, 1874, p. 5.

112. "Sir: Please urge the people": Telegram from *New York Tribune*, May 18, 1874, p. 12.

114. "The whole train of seventeen passenger cars": *Boston Morning Journal*, May 19, 1874, p. 2.

115. "Telegrams were recd Monday": Fred Howard to brother, May 16–24, 1874.

117 Survivors would have remembered: There were other dam failures within survivors' recent memories. In the 1830s, in West Becket, in the Berkshire Hills of western Massachusetts, a large reservoir near the Otis town line called Thames Pond spilled over the dam, washing away a barn along with a cow, a wood turning shop, gristmill, and sawmill. In 1810, Long Pond in Glover, Vermont, overran a temporary dam made to change its outlet and damaged property along its seventy-five-mile course to Lake Memphremagog. In 1847, hours after completion, the Holyoke dam across the Connecticut River gave way, killing no one. *SDR*, May 18, 1874, p. 4; *SDU*, May 18, 1874, p. 2; *Boston Daily Evening Transcript*, May 7, 1850, p. 2, May 9, p. 2; *Boston Recorder*, April 17, 1840, p. 3; Hunter, *Waterpower*, p. 206.

118. "Indeed the more intelligent people": *SDR*, May 19, 1874, p. 5.

118. "the responsibility probably rests": *SDR*, May 18, 1874, p. 4.

118. "They built the reservoir": *SDR*, May 18, 1874, p. 4.

118. Its editor Samuel Bowles: Bowles most certainly knew members of the reservoir company. He and Joel Hayden Sr. supported Amherst College. Bowles and William

Skinner were strong supporters of the Greeley-Brown presidential ticket. As a Dickinson family friend, Bowles made the *Springfield Republican* the first publisher of poems of Emily Dickinson. Stephen G. Weisner, *Embattled Editor: The Life of Samuel Bowles* (Lanham, Md.: University Press of America, 1986), pp. xi, 34–36, 120.

119 "It is said": *Boston Daily Advertiser,* May 18, 1874, p. 1.

119."There can be no doubt": *Worcester Spy,* May 18, 1874, p. 2.

119. "one case out of hundreds of thousands": SDR, May 19, 1874, p. 4.

119. "It is time there is a": SDR, May 19, 1874, p. 4.

119. "We drive our railway trains": *New York Tribune,* quoted in SDR, May 19, 1874, p. 6.

120. "committee of sufficient force and prestige": SDR, May 19, 1874, p. 4.

120. "a jealous fear among the village": NYT, May 19, 1874, p. 1.

120. Village men immediately protested: For many years the school year was shorter in Florence than it was in the rest of Northampton. With Alfred Lilly as spokesperson, Florence requested a larger school appropriation to extend the Florence school year. But each time the question came before the Northampton town meeting, Northampton cried that these were "hard times" and they couldn't afford it. Fed up, Lilly waited until the appropriation for street lighting of Northampton came up for action and then urged that if these were such "hard times" that a longer school year could not be afforded, then there were no additional monies to support improvements to streetlights. That session, funds were not appropriated for additional lighting, but soon a longer school term for Florence was approved. *Memorial: Alfred Theodore Lilly,* p. 19.

123. "the popular feeling against him": HG, May 19, 1874, p. 1.

123. "Arose at seven": Mary Hill Diary, May 18, 1874.

CHAPTER 5: REBUILDING

124. Massachusetts Legislature's special committee: Sources for their visit to the valley are *Boston Morning Journal,* May 20, 1874; NYT, May 20, 1874, p. 8; SDR, May 20, 1874, p. 5; BG, May 20, 1874, pp. 1, 4; *New York Tribune,* May 19, 1874, p. 5.

128. Joel Hayden Jr.: Macurda, *Josiah Hayden,* p. 440.

129. "what a fortunate thing": from article by "John Paul" in the *New York Tribune,* reprinted in *History of the Mill River Disaster: A Full and Graphic Account* (Springfield, Mass: Weaver, Shipman, and Co., 1874), pp. 33–34.

129. "Mill Street, 17 lives": SDU, May 29, 1874, p. 3.

130. "the evidence of their fulfillment": NYT, May 20, 1874, p. 8.

132. "Look here, if you want to know": BG, May 20, 1874, p. 4.

132. "he could not regard [the flood] as an accident": NYT, May 20, 1874, p. 8.

132. "such work is homicide": *Boston Morning Journal,* May 21, 1874, p. 2.

132. his "father was always in fear": HG, May 26, 1874, p. 1.

133. an itemized list: BG, May 20, 1874, p. 4.

134. "Nobody can call to mind the miles": SDR, May 20, 1874, p. 5.

134. Massachusetts Legislative Committee: Meeting reported in *Boston Morning Journal,* May 22, 1874, p. 1; *Boston Daily Advertiser,* May 22, 1874, p. 1.

136. "precedent in this state for the grant": "Report of the Joint Special Committee on the Petition of the Selectmen and Other Citizens of the Towns of Williamsburg and Northampton," House of Representatives, Boston, Mass., May 28, 1874.

138. "It took considerable red tape": HG, May 26, 1874, p. 1.

139. "The excitement of the week before": BG, May 27, 1874, p. 1.

139. "It grows worse every day": Fred Howard to brother, May 16–24, 1874.

139. "Warner of course lost the most": Fred Howard to brother, May 16–24, 1874.

140. "buy a farm wholly on credit": *NFP*, June 6, 1874, p. 3.

142. In the 1870s, Holyoke was undergoing an economic expansion: *SDR*, July 10, 1874, p. 6; August 7, 1874, p. 6; Constance Green, *Holyoke, Massachusetts* (New Haven, Conn.: Yale University Press, 1939), pp. 142–43; William F. Hartford, *Working People of Holyoke: Class and Ethnicity in a Massachusetts Mill Town, 1850–1960* (New Brunswick, N.J.: Rutgers University Press, 1990), p. 9.

143. "It is not a light undertaking": *HG*, May 26, 1874, p. 1.

144. "Hayden, Gear and Company": WCS Diary, June 21, 1874.

144. "To the Associated Press": *Boston Morning Journal*, May 21, 1874, p. 2.

146. "send what you wish to give": *NFP*, June 6, 1874, p. 4.

147. For some workers, the allowance: *NFP*, June 13, 1874, p. 2; Agnes Hannay, "Chronicle of Industry on the Mill River," *Smith College Studies in History* 21, nos. 1–4 (1935–1936), 94. Wages are based on 1875 figures.

148. "seems to us to perfectly understand": *SDU*, May 21, 1874, p. 3.

148. a total of 566 persons: Each day for two weeks after the flood, the newspapers listed donors to the relief fund at a rate of about a dozen or more each day. *SDR*, May 20, 1874, p. 4; May 21, 1874, p. 5; May 22, 1874, p. 5; May 25, 1874, pp. 4–5; May 28, 1874, p. 4; May 30, 1874, p. 4; June 16, 1874, p. 6; November 18, 1874, p. 6; November 17, 1875, p. 6.

149. "did not go back to school": WCS Diary, May 18 and 19, 1874.

149. "Since I missed the train yesterday": WCS Diary, May 22, 1874.

149. "Did not know I was so popular": WCS Diary, May 26, 1874.

149. "Went to church in the forenoon": WCS Diary, June 21, 1874.

149. "Father does not intend to build here again": WCS Diary, May 20, 1874.

150. "Everyone had sympathy": WCS Diary, June 5, 1874.

150. "Father and Mother went to Holyoke": WCS Diary, June 13, 1874.

150. "Father has not yet decided": WCS Diary, June 20, 1874.

151. "Oh! it is dreadful": Mary Hill Diary, May 31, 1874.

Chapter 6: The Inquest

152. He chose John Atkinson: Inquest on the body of John Atkinson, filed July 31, 1874, Superior Court Records, Hampshire County, Northampton, Mass.

152. "find and certify, when, how": *General Statutes of Massachusetts, 1860*, chap. 175, sec. 9, p. 849.

152. "some of the most intelligent": *SDR*, May 21, 1874, p. 5.

152. "excellent reputations for intelligence": *BG*, May 26, 1874, p. 1.

153. "Do you solemnly swear": *General Statutes of Massachusetts, 1860*, chap. 175, sec. 4, pp. 848–49.

154. "It's the dam we are trying": *Boston Morning Journal*, May 21, 1874.

155. "capitalists and manufacturers are so thoroughly": *New York Tribune*, May 19, 1874, p. 1.

155. Hampshire County courthouse: When a court session was about to begin, someone watched from the courthouse bell tower until he saw the judge and lawyers coming across the street, then rang the bell. The courthouse was torn down in 1886 and the new dark, stone one, still in use today, was built on the same location. Jacqueline Van Voris, *The Look of Paradise: A Pictorial History of Northampton, Massachusetts, 1654–1984* (New Canaan, N.H.: Phoenix Publishing, 1984), p. 65.

156. "running year in and out": *SDR*, May 26, 1874, p. 5.

156. "as big as a man's arm": *SDR*, May 26, 1874, p. 5.

156. "Have you said": *SDU*, May 25, 1874, p. 3.

157. "Don't be a damn fool": *Springfield Sunday Union and Republican*, May 29, 1929. The newspaper quote was "Don't be a d— fool."

157. When the jurors returned: The afternoon began with Robert Loud, Oliver Everett, and James B. Gleason describing their activities of the morning of May 16. After the first few witnesses who told about the events of the dam break and flood, there seemed to be no logical sequence to the order of the witnesses.

157. "An electrical stir and thrill": *SDR*, May 26, 1874, p. 5.

157. "a young man": *SDR*, May 26, 1874, p. 5.

158. "an air of business-like resolution": *SDR*, May 26, 1874, p. 5.

158. "I *was* a mill owner in Williamsburg": *SDR*, May 26, 1874, p. 5. All of Spelman's quotes in the next seven paragraphs are from this source.

159. "Moved that one be added:" WRC Record Book, p. 17.

160. "restless in every limb": *SDR*, May 26, 1874, p. 5.

160. "he owned a share": *SDR*, May 26, 1874, p. 5.

161. ". . . it was moved that": WRC Record Book, p. 20.

161. "owning [a] mill or other property liable": *General Statutes of Massachusetts, 1860*, chap. 149, secs. 47–52, pp. 759–60.

162. "ill adapted": *Worcester Daily Spy*, May 19, 1874, p. 2.

163. "tall, erect, formal": *SDR*, May 27, 1874, p. 5.

165. "It looks as if the main earth": *NYT*, May 27, 1874, p. 5.

165. "Not for a moment": *NYT*, May 27, 1874, p. 5.

165. "whom he trusted": *SDR*, May 30, 1874, p. 6.

165. "had confidence in the contractors": *SDR*, May 30, 1874, p. 6.

167. "spare, nervous, active gentleman": *SDR*, May 27, 1874, p. 5.

167. "the same that leads a man": *SDR*, May 27, 1874, p. 5.

168. "The [reservoir] corporation": *SDR*, May 28, 1874, p. 4.

168. "Why, we knew it wasn't safe": *SDU*, May 27, 1874, p. 3.

169. "Dimock would cuss and swear": *SDU*, May 28, 1874, p. 3.

169. "I shouldn't build such a dam": *SDR*, May 29, 1874, p. 5.

169. "couldn't think of the expense": *SDR*, May 29, 1874, p. 5.

170. "He [Fenn] was asked if his sense of duty": *SDR*, May 29, 1874, p. 5.

171. "No such work should be constructed": *SDU*, May 29, 1874, p. 3.

172. "to be done in a thorough": *SDR*, May 25, 1874, p. 5.

172. In colonial America: Daniel H. Calhoun, *The American Civil Engineer* (Cambridge, Mass.: Massachusetts Institute of Technology, 1960), pp. viii–xi; John B. Rae, "Engineers Are People," in Terry S. Reynolds, ed., *The Engineer in America* (Chicago: University of Chicago Press, 1991), pp. 35–41; Terry S. Reynolds, "The Engineer in 19th–Century America" in Reynolds, ed., *The Engineer in America*, pp. 10–26.

174. "Mr. Bassett's testimony": *SDR*, May 27, 1874, p. 5.

174. "If they raised the water": *SDR*, May 28, 1874, p. 5.

175. "Finally, after the most wearisome repetitions": *SDR*, May 28, 1874, p. 5.

175. "Defiant and combative": *SDR*, May 28, 1874, p. 5.

175–76. "There wasn't a great deal of conscience": *SDR*, June 1, 1874, p. 6.

177. "Dr. Trow asked": *SDR*, June 1, 1874, p. 6.

177. "Everybody was afraid of the dam": *SDR*, May 30, 1874, p. 6.

178. "didn't think it substantial enough": *SDR*, May 29, 1874, p. 5.

179. "they all were in doubt": *SDR*, May 27, 1874, p. 5.

179. "in the judgment of the Commissioners": Records of the County Commissioners, December 1, 1868, vol. 7 (March 1868–June 1871), Hampshire County Commissioner's Office, Northampton, Mass.

179. "Usually more is to be learned from one failure" and all quotes in next three paragraphs: James Francis, Theodore Ellis, and William Worthen, "The Failure of the Dam on the Mill River," *Transactions of the American Society of Civil Engineers*, vol. 3 (1875), pp. 118–22.

Chapter 7: The Verdict

182. "was last seen holding on the fence": Fred Howard to brother, May 16–24, 1874.

183. There was no published official toll: For my total of 139, I have relied on the death records of the towns of Williamsburg and Northampton and on newspaper accounts of the circumstances of deaths not recorded in the towns' Vital Statistics. Augustus Laney doesn't appear in the Vital Statistics of either town, but I have included him because Fred Howard, a trusted source, discussed his death in a letter. Laney's name also appeared on several newspaper lists as Alexander Lanier. Fred Howard to Brother, June 7, 1874.

183. "It must not be forgotten": *Harper's Weekly*, June 6, 1874, p. 474.

184. They took stereophotographs: Alan Trachtenberg, *Reading American Photographs: Images as History* (New York: Hill and Wang, 1989), pp. 16–17.

184. At least eight companies offered for sale: W. B. Miles and Company of Springfield marketed eighteen different "Views of the Great Disaster," while J. A. French and Company of Keene, New Hampshire, marketed forty "Stereoscopic Views of the Great Disaster on Mill River, in Hampshire County, Massachusetts." Knowlton Brothers of Northampton saw the local flood as a chance to move into the larger markets. They offered 118 different images, then manufactured them at such a large scale that they could sell them for one dollar per dozen. *NFP*, July 4, 1874, p. 2.

185. This wildly popular booklet: Most nineteenth-century disasters were commemorated with similar booklets. In ninety-six pages, *An Authentic History of the Lawrence Calamity* told the tale of the collapse of the five-story Pemberton Cotton Mill in Lawrence, Massachusetts, in 1860. It included the names of the seventy-six killed and the fourteen missing in the fire that consumed the ruins, the report of the coroner's inquest, and abstracts of sermons on the subject.

185. "Ride! Cheney, ride!": "George Cheney's Warning at the Breaking of the Dam," no author, *New York Graphic*, reprinted in *A Full and Graphic Account of the Terrible Mill River Disaster* (Springfield, Mass.: Weaver, Shipman and Co., 1874), p. 40.

186. "Curious, laughing, or dreading": Sidney Dickinson, "The Ride of Collins Graves," reprinted in *Full and Graphic Account*, pp. 41–46.

186. "It is an ugly task": *BG*, May 21, 1874, pp. 1, 4.

186. "One or two poets": *BG*, May 21, 1874, pp. 1, 4.

187. "Graves and Day": *SDR*, May 22, 1874, p. 4.

188. "Sir: There is one fact": *New York Tribune*, May 25, 1874, p. 2.

189. On the morning of June 11: The inspection of the Goshen dams by the county commissioners and all quotes from *SDR*, June 12, 1874, p. 6.

191. "Hereafter no order from Tom": *HG*, June 16, 1874, p. 2.

191. "I now hold the key": *HG*, June 16, 1874, p. 2.

192. "go back on them": *NFP*, June 27, 1874, p. 3.

192. "work has been done": *SDR*, June 24, 1874, p. 6.

192. "*To the Editor of the Republican.* I write to say": *SDR*, June 29, 1874, p. 6.

193. "We are . . . sorry": *HG*, June 30, 1874, p. 2.

193. "While you have buttoned up": *HG*, June 3, 1874, p. 2.

195. The verdict found: Verdict, Inquest of Body of John Atkinson.

196. "they adjudicated on a dam": *HG*, July 14, 1874, p. 3.

197. The verdict accurately and thoroughly described: The jury could have named a scapegoat, but didn't. After the 1860 Pemberton Mill collapse in Lawrence, the coroner's jury pinned ultimate responsibility on Charles H. Bigelow, the chief engineer of the Essex Company, which had erected the collapsed building years earlier. The jury found that Bigelow had allowed malformed cast iron pillars (their condition unknown to him, he claimed) to be used in the mill's construction. The jury found no fault with the manufacturer of the defective pillars. Clarisse A. Poirer, "Aftermath of a Disaster: The Collapse of the Pemberton Mill," in Kenneth Fones-Wolf and Martin Kaufman, eds., *Labor in Massachusetts: Selected Essays* (Westfield, Mass.: Institute for Massachusetts Studies, Westfield State College, 1990), pp. 77–96.

197. "the sermons of the old-time divines": *HG*, July 7, 1874, p. 2.

197. "The public rendered its verdict": *SDR*, July 4, 1874, p. 4.

197. Survivors didn't react, protest: The only surviving private exchange came in the postscript of Fred Howard's letter to his brother in which Fred, enclosing a copy of a local newspaper (he doesn't say which one), advised: "be sure and read what the paper says of Dimock," implying that something uncomplimentary and surprising was written about the Leeds silk factory manager they both knew. Fred Howard to brother, May 16–24, 1874.

198. "A jury of inquest was impaneled": Mark Twain and Charles Dudley Warner, *The Gilded Age: A Tale of Today* (1873; rept. New York: Pengiun, 1994), p. 48. Nan Goodman, *Shifting the Blame: Literature, Law, and the Theory of Accidents in Nineteenth-Century America* (Princeton, N.J.: Princeton University Press, 1998), pp. 13, 66.

198. "not an accident but a crime": *BG*, July 6, 1874, p. 1.

198. "a gross and criminal evasion": *NYT*, July 6, 1874, p. 4.

199. By the end of 1874: *HG*, January 19, 1975, p. 2.

200. "under a cloud": *SDR*, June 24, 1874, p. 6.

202. "they were welcomed with enthusiastic applause": *HG*, November 17, 1874, p. 2.

202. "pulled up stakes": WCS Diary, October 2, 1874.

203. "They began to make silk": WCS Diary, November 16, 1874.

CHAPTER 8: CHANGE

205. A reporter from the *Hampshire Gazette*: The meeting was described in *HG*, October 27, 1874, p. 2. All quotes are from that article.

207. Massachusetts had become a national leader in passing reform legislation: Thomas C. Cochran and William Miller, *The Age of Enterprise: A Social History of Industrial America*, rev. ed. (New York: Harper and Row, 1964), p. 144; Ballard C. Campbell, "Public Policy and State Government," in Charles W. Calhoun, ed., *The Gilded Age: Essays on the Origins of Modern America* (Wilmington, Del.: Scholarly Resources, 1996), pp. 314–18; Donald J. Pisani, "Promotion and Regulation: Constitutionalism and the American Economy," *Journal of American History*, 74 (December 1987), pp. 740–68; Steinberg, *Nature Incorporated*, pp. 227–30; Jack Tager, "Massachusetts and the Age of Economic Revolution," in Jack Tager and John W. Ifkovic, eds., *Massachusetts in the Gilded Age: Selected Essays* (Amherst: University of Massachusetts Press, 1985), pp. 23–24; Sarah Scovill Whittelsey, "Massachusetts Labor Legislation: An Historical and Critical Study," *Annals of the American Academy of Political and Social Science*, supplement to vol. 15 (1901), pp. 10–11.

208. "works of the highest engineering." *HG*, January 19, 1975, p. 2.

209. "an act to provide for the supervision": "Report of Committee on Water Supply and Drainage, April 9, 1875, Massachusetts House of Representatives," Massachusetts State Archives, Boston, Mass.; *Acts and Resolves Passed by the General Court of Massachusetts in the Year 1875* (Boston: Wright and Potter, 1875), chap. 178, pp. 770–72.

210. an 1893 law: An Act Relative to the Examination of Reservoirs, Reservoir-Dams and Milldams by County Commissioners, *Acts and Resolves Passed by the General Court of Massachusetts in the year 1893* (Boston: Wright and Potter, 1893), chap 99, p. 758.

210. "It was not until 1901": *The Revised Laws of the Commonwealth of Mass. Enacted November 21, 1901, to Take Effect Jan. 1, 1902* (Boston: Wright and Potter), chap. 196, sec. 45-46, p. 1697.

211. an 1869 statute: An Act Concerning Reservoir Companies, *Acts and Resolves Passed by the General Court of Massachusetts in the Year 1869* (Boston: Wright and Potter, 1869), chap 383, p. 676.

211. Dam oversight in Massachusetts: Kaynor, *Dam Policy*, p. 12; *Worcester Evening Gazette*, Sept. 18, 1968, p. 24.

212. In the forty-eight years after the Mill River flood: Edward Godfrey, *Engineering Failures and Their Lessons* (privately printed, 1924), pp. 1–29; Joel D. Justin, *Earth Dam Projects* (New York: John Wiley and Sons, 1932), pp. 3–7; Norman Smith, *A History of Dams* (London: Peter Davies, 1971), pp. 212–14.

212. Reverend John Gleason: His sermon was published in *SDR*, May 17, 1875, p. 6.

213. sold off horses, cows, and sheep: The number of cows decreased 43 percent while the numbers of horses and sheep slipped 6 percent and 2 percent, respectively. Williamsburg Tax Lists, 1874, 1875.

214. His design called for: Plan for Proposed Dam at the Williamsburg Reservoir (July 17, 1875), County Commissioners' Office, Courthouse, Northampton, Mass.; Records of the County Commissioners, vol. 8 (September 1871–December 1875), pp. 490–94; *SDR*, July 26, 1875, p. 6.

214. "the material prosperity of this valley": *HG*, July 28, 1874, p. 2.

215. "were so frightened about the Goshen reservoirs": Lewis H. Bodman to Lewis Bodman, August 22, 1875, box 3, folder 64, in Bodman Family Papers, Sophia Smith Collection, Smith College, Northampton, Mass.

215. Before Gleason departed: *SDR*, January 14, 1875, p. 6; November 15, 1875, p. 6.

216. "about bringing heavy suits for damages": *Boston Daily Advertiser*, May 20, 1874, p. 1.

216. By the end of the nineteenth century: Lawrence M. Friedman, *History of American Law*, 2d ed. (New York: Simon & Schuster, 1985), pp. 483–87; Horwitz, *Transformation of American Law*, pp. 69–70.

216. "in an action of tort": By 1879, Clement had moved to Boston and Hayden had left the brass works. Records of Superior Court, Hampshire County, vol. 10, p. 262, cases 9 and 10 (microfilm reel 25), Northampton, Mass.; *Rules of the Superior Court* (Boston: Alfred Mudge and Son, 1874), p. 33.

217. Buffalo Creek in West Virginia: Keith Smith and Roy Ward, *Floods: Physical Processes and Human Impacts* (New York: John Wiley, 1998) pp. 50–51.

218. "care of brother Joel": Macurda, *Josiah Hayden*, vol. 1, pp. 440, 447.

219. The valley's economic recovery was slow: Hannay, "Chronicle of Industry,"

pp. 86, 92, 128–29. By the mid-nineteenth century, only two woolen manufactories remained of what had been a thriving valley industry, and they were forced to change to stay competitive with the larger mills in eastern Massachusetts. In 1868, Lewis Bodman sold his woolen mill, which made satinet and flannel, to Henry James, who began to weave the cheaper, "shoddy" fabric in an effort to keep up profits.

221. "one of the wealthiest men in Williamsburg": *HG*, February 13, 1905, p. 8.

221. "a well known and respected": *HG*, October 10, 1882, p. 2.

221. "On the whole I have been treated kindly": *Boston Sunday Globe*, December 21, 1902.

222. By the end of the nineteenth century: Metals expanded in this era too, although not as much as silk. The Emery Wheel Company opened a branch office in Chicago in the early 1880s. In 1882, William Clement established a cutlery company with a former brass works employee. By 1892, they employed one hundred. Hannay, "Chronicle of Industry," pp. 72, 81, 86, 91–93.

223. "his death removes another of the older": *HG*, September 21, 1880; August 13, 1906.

225. "the defective reservoir": Clayton E. Davis, "The Mill River Flood," in Sheffield, ed., *History of Florence*, p. 193.

225. "a disastrous flood": Hannay, "Chronicle of Industry," p. 91.

225. "fears as to its safety": Lucy Wilson Benson, "Floods and Disasters," in *Northampton Book: Chapters from 300 Years in the Life of a New England Town, 1654–1954*, compiled and edited by Tercentenary History Committee (Northampton, Mass.: Tercentenary Committee, 1954), p. 356.

225. "the direct cause of the disaster": Deming, *History of Williamsburg*, p. 279.

BIBLIOGRAPHY

NEWSPAPERS, MAGAZINES, AND JOURNALS
Atlanta Constitution
Boston Daily Advertiser
Boston Daily Evening Transcript
Boston Evening Journal
Boston Globe
Boston Morning Journal
Boston Recorder
Boston Sunday Globe
Daily Picayune (New Orleans)
Daily Rocky Mountain News
Frank Leslie's Illustrated Newspaper
Hampshire Gazette and Northampton Courier
Hampshire Herald
Harper's Weekly
New York Daily Graphic
New York Times
New York Tribune
Northampton Free Press
St. Louis Post-Dispatch
San Francisco Chronicle
Scientific American
Springfield Daily Republican
Springfield Daily Union
Springfield Sunday Union and Republican
Times (London)
Western Hampden Times
Worcester Daily Spy

MANUSCRIPTS, MAPS, AND PHOTOGRAPHS
Bodman Family Papers, Sophia Smith Collection, Smith College, Northampton, Mass.
County Atlas of Hampshire, Massachusetts. New York: F. W. Beers and Co., 1873.
Delano, Charles. File. Northampton Historical Society, Northampton, Mass.

Everett, Oliver. Diary. 1874. Private Collection, Williamsburg, Mass.

Hayden, Anna. Letter. Undated. Williamsburg Historical Society, Williamsburg, Mass.

Hill, Mary Morton. Diary, 1874. Williamsburg Historical Society, Williamsburg, Mass.

Hill, Otis G. Diary, 1864. Williamsburg Historical Society, Williamsburg, Mass.

Howard, Fred. Letters. Private Collection, Leeds, Mass.

Johnson, Anne. Senior honors thesis on Williamsburg, Massachusetts, Smith College, 1986.

Mill River Disaster. Photograph Collection, Forbes Library, Northampton, Mass.

Mill River Disaster. Photograph Collection, Williamsburg Historical Society, Williamsburg, Mass.

Skinner, William Cobbett. Diary, 1874. Williamsburg Historical Society, Williamsburg, Mass.

United States Geological Survey. Map of Hampshire County, Massachusetts, Nov. 1891. Geography and Map Division, Library of Congress, Washington, D.C.

Walling, Henry F. *Map of Hampshire County, Massachusetts.* New York: H. and C. T. Smith and Co., 1854, 1860.

Wheeler, Charles, comp. *Records of Haydenville.* 2 vols. Forbes Library, Northampton, Mass.

Williamsburg Reservoir Company. Record Book, 1865–1872. Forbes Library, Northampton, Mass.

PUBLIC DOCUMENTS

Act Relating to Mill and Reservoir Dams, chap. 327 (1854). Legislative Background File. Massachusetts Archives, Boston.

Acts and Resolves Passed by the General Court of Massachusetts at a Special Session, 1872. Boston: Wright and Potter, 1872.

Acts and Resolves Passed by the General Court of Massachusetts in the Year 1865. Boston: Wright and Potter, 1865.

Acts and Resolves Passed by the General Court of Massachusetts in the Year 1869. Boston: Wright and Potter, 1869.

Acts and Resolves Passed by the General Court of Massachusetts in the Year 1874. Boston: Wright and Potter, 1874.

Acts and Resolves Passed by the General Court of Massachusetts in the Year 1875. Boston: Wright and Potter, 1875.

Acts and Resolves Passed by the General Court of Massachusetts in the Year 1893. Boston: Wright and Potter, 1893.

Acts and Resolves Passed by the Legislature of Massachusetts in the Year 1840. Boston: Cotton and Wentworth, 1840.

General Statutes of the Commonwealth of Massachusetts, 1860. Boston: William White, 1860.

Hampshire County Commissioner's Office. Records of the County Commissioners. Vols. 7 and 8. Northampton, Mass.

Hampshire County Registry of Deeds. Northampton, Mass.

Hampshire County Registry of Probate. Dockets 166–49, 210–54, 250–25. Northampton, Mass.

Hampshire County Superior Court Records. 1874–1879. Hampshire County Courthouse, Northampton, Mass.

Maine, 54th Legislature Public Laws, Regular Session, 1875.

Massachusetts House of Representatives. A Petition of Selectmen of Williamsburg and

Northampton and Eighty-six Others Asking Relief. May 18, 1874. Massachusetts
State Archives, Boston.

Massachusetts House of Representatives. A Report of Committee on Water Supply and
Drainage. April 9, 1875. Massachusetts Archives, Boston.

Minutes of Meetings of the Governor's Council, 1863, 1864, 1865, 1866.
Massachusetts Archives. Boston, Mass.

Northampton, Massachusetts, Registry of Deaths. Vol. 5. City Hall, Northampton, Mass.

Northampton Cutlery Company. Business Records. University of Massachusetts
Library, Amherst, Mass.

Public Acts Passed by General Assembly of the State of Connecticut in the Year 1878.
Hartford: Wiley, Waterman and Eaton, 1881.

Public Statutes of the Commonwealth of Massachusetts. Boston: Wright and Potter
Printing Co., State Printers, 1886.

Revised Laws of the Commonwealth of Massachusetts, Enacted November 21, 1901, to
Take Effect January 1, 1902. Vol. 2. Boston: Wright and Potter Printing Co., State
Printers, 1902.

Rhode Island General Assembly Acts and Resolves. Adjourned Session, January 1882.

Rules of the Superior Court. Boston: Alfred Mudge and Son, 1874.

Statistical Information Relating to Certain Branches of Industry in Massachusetts for
the Year Ending May 1, 1865, Boston: Wright & Potter, State Printers, 1866.

U.S. Census, 1870, 1880. Population Schedule.

U.S. Census, 1860. Manufacturing Schedule.

Vermont General Assembly. Acts and Resolves, 4th Biennial Session, 1876.

Vermont General Assembly. Acts and Resolves, 6th Biennial Session, 1880.

Williamsburg, Massachusetts, Tax Lists. 1864, 1873, 1874, 1875. Williamsburg
Historical Commission, Williamsburg, Mass.

Williamsburg, Massachusetts, Vital Statistics. Vol. 4. Town Hall, Williamsburg, Mass.

Williamsburgh Town Plan. 1795. Massachusetts Archives. Photocopy in Division of
Geography and Maps, Library of Congress, Washington, D.C.

INTERVIEWS

Bisbee, Mary. Telephone conversation with author. December 31, 2003.

Famulari, Tom. Telephone conversation with author. February 8, 1995; November 5,
2003; December 17, 23, 2003.

Kabat, Robert. Telephone conversation with author. January 15, 1995.

Ryan, Lorraine. Telephone conversation with author. December 20, 2003.

Silva, Rawl. Telephone conversation with author. February 1, 1995.

Tiley, Elizabeth. Telephone conversation with author. January 25, 1995; December
31, 2003.

BOOKS AND ARTICLES

Allmendinger, David. Paupers and Scholars: The Transformation of Student Life in
Nineteenth-Century New England. New York: St. Martin's Press, 1975.

American Society of Civil Engineers. Lessons from Dam Incidents, USA. New York:
American Society of Civil Engineers, 1975.

Amey, Geoffrey. The Collapse of the Dale Dyke Dam, 1864. London: Cassell, 1974.

Appleby, Joyce. Inheriting the Revolution: The First Generation of Americans.
Cambridge, Mass.: Harvard University Press, 2000.

Armstrong, John. Factory Under the Elms: A History of Harrisville, New Hampshire.

North Andover, Mass.: Museum of American Textile History, 1985.

Armstrong, Wilbur B. *The Government in Massachusetts Yesterday and Today.* South Lancaster, Mass.: privately printed, 1940.

An Authentic History of the Lawrence Calamity. Boston: John J. Dyer & Co., 1860.

Barron, Hal S. *Those Who Stayed Behind: Rural Society in Nineteenth-Century New England.* New York: Cambridge University Press, 1984.

Benson, Lucy Wilson. "Floods and Disasters." In *Northampton Book: Chapters from 300 Years in the Life of a New England Town, 1654–1954,* compiled and edited by Tercentenary History Committee, Northampton, Mass: Tercentenary Committee, 1954.

Bisbee, Mary S., Roger A. Bisbee, and Peter B. Banister. *150 Years of Firefighting: A History of the Williamsburg Fire Department.* Williamsburg, Mass.: n.p., 1998.

Blanchard, Michael D. "The Politics of Abolition in Northampton." *Historical Journal of Massachusetts* 19 (1991): 175–96.

Blondheim, Menahem. *News Over the Wires: The Telegraph and the Flow of Public Information in America, 1844–1897.* Cambridge, Mass.: Harvard University Press, 1994.

Bodman, Ellen Fairbanks-Diggs, et al. *The Bodman Chronicle.* Evansville, Ind.: privately printed, 1979.

Boyer, Paul S. *Oxford Companion to United States History.* New York: Oxford University Press, 2001.

Brecher, Jeremy, Jerry Lombardi, and Jan Stackhouse, comps. and eds. *Brass Valley: The Story of Working People's Lives and Struggles in an American Industrial Region.* Philadelphia: Temple University Press, 1982.

Briggs, Peter. *Rampage: The Story of Disastrous Floods, Broken Dams, and Human Fallibility.* New York: David McKay Co., 1973.

Brown, Richard D., and Jack Tager. *Massachusetts: A Concise History.* Amherst, Mass: University of Massachusetts Press, 2000.

Bushman, Richard L. "Farm Security in the Transition from Farm to City, 1750–1850." *Journal of Family History* (Fall 1981): 238–56.

Calhoun, Daniel H. *The American Civil Engineer: Origins and Conflict.* Cambridge, Mass: Technology Press, 1960.

Campbell, Ballard C. "Public Policy and State Government." In *The Gilded Age: Essays on the Origins of Modern America,* edited by Charles W. Calhoun. Wilmington, Del.: Scholarly Resources, 1996.

Carpenter, G. L. "Massachusetts, Haydens and Their Buttons." *National Button Bulletin* 7, no. 6 (1948): 363–66.

Cawelti, John. *Apostles of the Self-Made Man.* Chicago: University of Chicago Press, 1965.

Cendrelli, Daniel A. "Floods from Natural and Artificial Dam Failures." In *Inland Flood Hazards: Human, Riparian, and Aquatic Communities,* edited by Ellen E. Whol. Cambridge: Cambridge University Press, 2000.

Clark, Christopher. *The Communitarian Moment: The Radical Challenge of the Northampton Association.* Ithaca, N.Y.: Cornell University Press, 1995.

———. *The Roots of Rural Capitalism: Western Massachusetts, 1780–1860.* Ithaca, N.Y.: Cornell University Press, 1990.

Clarke, Olive Cleaveland. *Things That I Remember at Ninety-five.* Chesterfield, Mass., 1881.

Cochran, Thomas C. *Frontiers of Change: Early Industrialism in America*. New York: Oxford University Press, 1981.

Cochran, Thomas C., and William Miller. *The Age of Enterprise: A Social History of Industrial America*. Rev. ed. New York: Harper and Row, 1964.

Cole, Arthur Harrison. *The American Wool Manufacture*. Vol. 1. Cambridge, Mass: Harvard University Press, 1926.

Dalzell, Robert F., Jr. *Enterprising Elite: The Boston Associates and the World They Made*. New York: Norton, 1987.

Darrah, William Culp. *Stereo Views: A History of Stereographs in America and Their Collection*. Gettysburg, Penn: Times and News Publishing Co., 1964.

Dean, Charles. "Mills on the Mill River." Typescript, 1935. Forbes Library, Northampton, Mass.

Deming, Phyllis Baker. *A History of Williamsburg in Massachusetts*. Northampton, Mass: Hampshire Bookshop, 1946.

Donahue, Brian. "'Dammed at Both Ends and Cursed in the Middle': The 'Flowage' of the Concord River Meadows, 1798–1862." *Environmental Review* 13, nos. 3–4 (1989): 47–67.

Dublin, Thomas. *Community and Social Change in America*. Baltimore: Johns Hopkins University Press, 1978.

———. "Women and Outwork in a Nineteenth-Century New England Town." In *The Countryside in the Age of Capitalistic Transformation*, edited by Steven Hahn and Jonathan Prude. Chapel Hill: University of North Carolina Press, 1985.

———. *Women at Work: The Transformation of Work and Community in Lowell, Massachusetts, 1826–1860*. New York: Columbia University Press, 1979.

Emrick, Robert P., comp. *Leeds: A Village Within the City of Northampton, Massachusetts*. Edited by James Parsons. Northampton, Mass., 1999.

Engelbourg, Saul. *Power and Morality: American Business Ethics, 1840–1914*. Westport, Conn.: Greenwood Press, 1980.

Erikson, Kai T. *Everything in Its Path: Destruction of Community in the Buffalo Creek Flood*. New York: Simon & Schuster, 1976.

———. *A New Species of Trouble: Explorations in Disaster, Trauma, and Community*. New York: Norton, 1994.

Everts, Louis H. *History of the Connecticut Valley in Massachusetts*. Vol. 1. Philadelphia: privately printed, 1879.

Faler, Paul G. *Mechanics and Manufacturers in the Early Industrial Revolution: Lynn, Massachusetts, 1780–1860*. Albany: State University of New York Press, 1983.

Foner, Eric, and John A. Garraty, eds. *The Reader's Companion to American History*. Boston: Houghton Mifflin, 1991.

Forbes, Abner. *The Rich Men of Massachusetts*. 2d ed. Boston: Redding & Co., 1852.

Foster, David. *Thoreau's Country: Journey Through a Transformed Landscape*. Cambridge, Mass: Harvard University Press, 1999.

Francis, James, Theodore Ellis, and William Worthen. "The Failure of the Dam on the Mill River." *Transactions of the American Society of Civil Engineers* 3 (1875): 118–22.

Friedman, Lawrence M. *A History of American Law*. 2d ed. New York: Simon & Schuster, 1985.

Frisch, Michael H. *Town into City: Springfield, Massachusetts, and the Meaning of Community, 1840–1880*. Cambridge, Mass: Harvard University Press, 1972.

Frizell, Joseph P. "Storage and Pondage of Water." *Transactions of the American Society of Civil Engineers* 31 (1894): 29–54.

Full and Graphic Account of the Terrible Mill River Disaster. Springfield, Mass: Weaver, Shipman and Co., 1874.

Garrison, J. Ritchie. *Landscape and Material Life in Franklin County, Massachusetts, 1770–1860.* Knoxville: University of Tennessee Press, 1991.

Gere, Henry S., ed. *An Historical Sketch of Haydenville and Williamsburg* (typescript prepared from *Hampshire Gazette* articles published 1860–61), reproduced for the Town of Williamsburg by Ralmon Jon Black, 1999.

"Giants of the Earth: The Hayden Family of Williamsburg." Typescript, February 2, 1965. Williamsburg Historical Society, Williamsburg, Mass.

Gifis, Steven H. *Law Dictionary.* 3d ed. Hauppauge, N.Y.: Barron's Educational Series, 1991.

Glassberg, David. *American Historical Pageantry: The Uses of Tradition in the Early Twentieth Century.* Chapel Hill: University of North Carolina Press, 1990.

Godfrey, Edward. *Engineering Failures and Their Lessons.* N.p.: Privately printed. Edward Godfrey, 1924.

Goodman, Nan. *Shifting the Blame: Literature, Law, and the Theory of Accidents in Nineteenth-Century America.* Princeton, N.J.: Princeton University Press, 1998.

Gordon, Robert. "Hydrological Science and the Development of Waterpower for Manufacturing." *Technology and Culture* 26, no. 2 (1985): 204–35.

Gordon, Robert, and Patrick Malone. *The Texture of Industry: An Archaeological View of the Industrialization of North America.* New York: Oxford University Press, 1994.

Green, Constance McLaughlin. *Holyoke, Massachusetts.* New Haven, Conn.: Yale University Press, 1939.

Haltunnen, Karen. *Confidence Men and Painted Women: A Study of Middle-Class Culture in America, 1830–1870.* New Haven, Conn.: Yale University Press, 1982.

———. *Murder Most Foul: The Killer and the American Gothic Imagination.* Cambridge, Mass: Harvard University Press, 1998.

Hammond, Charles. "Concord's 'Factory Village': 1776–1862." *Old Time New England* 66, nos. 1–2 (1975): 32–38.

Handlin, Oscar, and Mary Flug Handlin. *Commonwealth: A Study of the Role of Government in the American Economy: Massachusetts, 1774–1861.* Cambridge, Mass.: Belknap Press, 1969.

Hanna, Frank W., and Robert C. Kennedy. *The Design of Dams.* New York: McGraw-Hill, 1938.

Hannay, Agnes. "Chronicle of Industry on the Mill River." *Smith College Studies in History* 21, nos. 1–4 (1935–1936): 1–142.

Hardenberg, W[illiam] A., and Samuel Baker. *Design of Dams: Irrigation.* Scranton, Penn.: International Textbook Co., 1933.

Hartford, William F. *Working People of Holyoke: Class and Ethnicity in a Massachusetts Mill Town, 1850–1960.* New Brunswick, N.J.: Rutgers University Press, 1990.

Historical Register and General Directory of Northampton. Northampton, Mass.: Gazette Printing Co., 1875–76.

Homespun to Factory Made: Woolen Textiles in America, 1776–1876. North Andover, Mass.: Merrimack Valley Textile Museum, 1977.

Horwitz, Morton J. *The Transformation of American Law, 1780–1860.* Cambridge, Mass.: Harvard University Press, 1977.

Houghton, Walter E. *The Victorian Frame of Mind*. New Haven, Conn.: Yale University Press, 1957.

Howe, Daniel Walker. *The Unitarian Conscience: Harvard Moral Philosophy, 1805–1861*. 2d ed. Middletown, Conn.: Wesleyan University Press, 1988.

———. "Victorian Culture in America." In *Victorian America*, edited by Daniel Walker Howe. Philadelphia: University of Pennsylvania Press, 1976.

Hunter, Louis C. *Waterpower in the Century of the Steam Engine, History of Industrial Power in the United States*. Vol. 1. Charlottesville, Va: University Press of Virginia, 1979.

Jackson, Donald C. *Building the Ultimate Dam: John S. Eastwood and the Control of Water in the West*. Lawrence: University of Kansas Press, 1995.

Johnson, Willis Fletcher. *History of the Johnstown Flood*. N.p.: Edgewood Publishing Co., 1889.

Juravich, Tom, William F. Hartford, and James R. Green. *Commonwealth of Toil: Chapters in the History of Massachusetts Workers and Their Unions*. Amherst, Mass: University of Massachusetts Press, 1996.

Justin, Joel D. *Earth Dam Projects*. New York: John Wiley and Sons, 1932.

Kasson, John. *Civilizing the Machine: Technology and Republican Values in America, 1776–1900*. New York: Penguin Books, 1984.

———. *Rudeness and Civility: Manners in Nineteenth-Century Urban America*. New York: Hill and Wang, 1990.

Kaynor, Edward R. *Dam Policy in Massachusetts*. Amherst.: Water Resources Research Center, University of Massachusetts, 1979.

Keyssar, Alexander. "Social Change in Massachusetts in the Gilded Age." In *Massachusetts in the Gilded Age*, edited by Jack Tager and John W. Ifkovic. Amherst, Mass.: University of Massachusetts Press, 1985.

Kulik, Gary. "Dams, Fish, and Farmers: Defense of Public Rights in Eighteenth-Century Rhode Island." In *The Countryside in the Age of Capitalist Transformation*, edited by Steven Hahn and Jonathan Prude. Chapel Hill: University of North Carolina Press, 1985.

Kutler, Stanley I., ed. *Dictionary of American History*. 3d ed. Vol. 3. New York: Scribners, 2003.

Layton, Edwin T., Jr. "James B. Francis and the Rise of Scientific Technology." In *Technology in America: A History of Individual and Ideas*. 2d ed. Edited by Carroll W. Pursell Jr. Cambridge, Mass.: MIT Press, 1991.

Lewis, Thomas. "The Landscape and Environment of the Connecticut River Valley." In *The Great River: Art and Society of the Connecticut Valley, 1635–1820*. Edited by Gerald W. R. Ward and William N. Hosley Jr. Hartford, Conn.: Wadsworth Atheneum, 1985.

Licht, Walter. *Industrializing America: The Nineteenth Century*. Baltimore: Johns Hopkins University Press, 1995.

Lord, William G. *History of Athol, Massachusetts*. Athol, Mass.: William G. Lord, 1953.

Lynch, Jacqueline T. "The Mills: Skinner—The First Name in Silk." *Chickuppy & Friends* (1987): 14–25.

Lystra, Karen. *Searching the Heart: Women, Men and Romantic Love in Nineteenth-Century America*. New York: Oxford University Press, 1989.

Macaulay, David. *Mill*. Boston: Houghton Mifflin, 1983.

Macurda, Donald Bradford. *Josiah Hayden of Williamsburg, Massachusetts: His*

Antecedents and Descendants. Vols. 1 and 2. Privately published, 1984.

Marzio, Peter C. *The Men and Machines of American Journalism: A Pictorial Essay from the Henry R. Luce Hall of News Reporting.* Washington, D.C.: Smithsonian Institution, 1973.

May, Peter J. *Recovering From Catastrophe: Federal Disaster Relief Policy and Politics.* Westport, Conn.: Greenwood Press, 1985.

Mayer, Henry. *William Lloyd Garrison and the Abolition of Slavery.* New York: St. Martin's Griffin, 1998.

McConnell, Sharon. "The Man: William Skinner, 1824–1902." *Chickuppy & Friends* (1987): 4–13.

McCullough, David. *The Johnstown Flood.* New York: Simon & Schuster, 1968.

McGaw, Judith A. *Most Wonderful Machine: Mechanization and Social Change in Berkshire Paper Making, 1801–1855.* Princeton, N.J.: Princeton University Press, 1987.

Memorial: Alfred Theodore Lilly. Florence, Mass.: Bryant and Brothers, 1890.

Memorial: Charles Delano. Northampton, Mass.: Hampshire Bar, 1883.

Meyer, Donald H. *The Instructed Conscience: The Shaping of the American National Ethic.* Philadelphia: University of Pennsylvania Press, 1972.

Middlebrooks, T. A. "Earth Dam Practice in the United States." *Transactions of the American Society of Civil Engineers.* (1953): 697–703.

Milne, Antony. *Floodshock: The Drowning of Planet Earth.* Gloucester, England: Alan Sutton, 1986.

Modell, John, and Tamara K. Hareven. "Urbanization and the Malleable Household: An Examination of Boarding and Lodging in American Families." *Journal of Marriage and the Family* 35 (1973): 467–79.

Mott, Frank Luther. *American Journalism: A History: 1690–1960.* New York: Macmillan, 1962.

Muir, Diana. *Reflections in Bullough's Pond: Economy and Ecosystem in New England.* Hanover, N.H.: University of New England Press, 2000.

The National Cyclopedia of American Biography. Vol. 23. New York: James T. White Co., 1933.

Northampton and Easthampton Directory, 1882–3. Northampton, Mass.: Price, Lee and Col, 1882.

Northampton and the Northampton Institution for Savings, 1842–1944. Northampton, Mass.: Metcalf, n.d.

"Notable Dam Failures of the Past." *Engineering News-Record* 100, no. 12 (1926): 472–73.

O'Connor, James P. *Williamsburg, Massachusetts: Fact and Fable.* Northampton, Mass: Gazette Printing Office, 1971.

O'Donnell, Edward T. *Ship Ablaze: The Tragedy of the Steamboat General Slocum.* New York: Broadway Books, 2003.

Pabst, Margaret Richards. "Agricultural Trends in the Connecticut Valley Region of Massachusetts, 1800–1900." *Smith College Studies in History* 26, nos. 1–4 (1940–1941): 1–113.

Paneth, Donald, ed. *The Encyclopedia of American Journalism.* New York: Facts on File, 1983.

Parsons, James. *Images of America: Northampton.* Dover, N.H.: Arcadia, 1996.

Perry, Joseph B., Jr., and Meredith David Pugh. *Collective Behavior: Response to Social*

Stress. St. Paul, Minn.: West, 1978.

Pisani, Donald J. "Promotion and Regulation: Constitutionalism and the American Economy." *Journal of American History* 74 (1987): 740–68.

Poirer, Clarisse A. "Aftermath of a Disaster: The Collapse of the Pemberton Mill." In *Labor in Massachusetts: Selected Essays,* edited by Kenneth Fones-Wolf and Martin Kaufman. Westfield, Mass.: Institute for Massachusetts Studies, Westfield State College, 1990, pp. 77–96.

Porter, Glenn. *The Rise of Big Business, 1860–1920.* 2d ed. Wheeling, Ill.: Harlan Davidson, 1992.

Prude, Jonathan. *The Coming of Industrial Order: Town and Factory Life in Rural Massachusetts, 1810–1860.* New York: Cambridge University Press, 1983.

Rae, John B. "Engineers Are People." In *The Engineer in America,* edited by Terry S. Reynolds. Chicago: University of Chicago Press, 1991.

Raphael, Beverley. *When Disaster Strikes: How Individuals and Communities Cope with Catastrophe.* New York: Basic Books, 1986.

Reade, Charles. *Put Yourself in His Place.* New York: Metropolitan, 1895.

Representative Families of Northampton. Vol. 1. Northampton: Picturesque, 1917.

Reynolds, Terry S. "The Engineer in 19th-Century America." In *The Engineer in America,* edited by Terry S. Reynolds. Chicago: University of Chicago Press, 1991.

Ross, Edward Alsworth. *Sin and Society: An Analysis of Latter-Day Iniquity.* 1907. Reprint, New York: Harper and Row, 1973.

Rothman, Ellen K. *Hands and Hearts: A History of Courtship in America.* New York: Basic Books, 1984.

Sandee, Theodore Anton. "The Textile Factory in Pre–Civil War Rhode Island." *Old Time New England* 66, nos. 1–2 (1975): 13–31.

Schlereth, Thomas J. *Victorian America: Transformations in Everyday Life, 1876–1915.* New York: HarperCollins, 1991.

Schuyler, James Dix. *Reservoirs for Irrigation, Water-Power, and Domestic Water-Supply.* New York: John Wiley and Sons, 1901.

Scranton, Philip. "Varieties of Paternalism: Industrial Structures and the Social Relations of Production in American Textiles." *American Quarterly* 36, no. 2 (1984): 235–357.

Sharpe, Elizabeth M. "Capitalism and Calamity: The Mill River Flood of 1874." Ph.D. diss., University of Delaware, 1995.

Sheffeld, Charles A., ed. *The History of Florence, Massachusetts.* Florence, Mass.: Charles A. Sheffeld, 1895.

Shlakman, Vera. *Economic History of a Factory Town: A Study of Chicopee, Massachusetts.* New York: Octagon Books, 1969. Reprint of *Smith College Studies in History* 20, nos. 1–4 (1934–35).

Silk in New England Society, 1730–1930. Exhibition Checklist. Northampton, Mass.: Smith College Museum of Art, 2003.

Siracusa, Carl. *A Mechanical People: Perceptions of the Industrial Order in Massachusetts, 1815–1880.* Middletown, Conn.: Wesleyan University Press, 1979.

Smith, Carl. *Urban Disorder and the Shape of Belief: The Great Chicago Fire, the Haymarket Bomb, and the Model Town of Pullman.* Chicago: University of Chicago Press, 1995.

Smith, Merritt Roe. *Harpers Ferry Armory and the New Technology: The Challenge of Change.* Ithaca, N.Y.: Cornell University Press, 1977.

Smith, Norman. *A History of Dams.* London: Peter Davies, 1971.

Steinberg, Theodore. *Nature Incorporated: Industrialization and the Waters of New England.* New York: Cambridge University Press, 1991.

———. *Acts of God: The Unnatural History of Natural Disaster in America.* New York: Oxford University Press, 2000.

Stern, Gerald M. *The Buffalo Creek Disaster.* New York: Vintage Books, 1976.

Sternagle, Mary E., and Henry S. C. Cummings Jr. *Middlefield History.* N.p. Privately printed, 1985.

Stevenson, David. *Sketch of the Civil Engineering of North America.* London: John Weale, 1859.

Strasser, Susan. *Never Done: A History of American Housework.* New York: Pantheon, 1982.

Sutherland, Daniel E. *The Expansion of Everyday Life, 1860–1876.* New York: Harper and Row, 1989.

Sweeney, Kevin M. "From Wilderness to Arcadian Vale: Material Life in the Connecticut River Valley." In *The Great River: Art and Society of the Connecticut Valley, 1635–1820,* edited by Gerald W. R. Ward and William N. Hosley Jr. Hartford, Conn.: Wadsworth Atheneum, 1985.

Tager, Jack. "Massachusetts and the Age of Economic Revolution." In *Massachusetts in the Gilded Age: Selected Essays,* edited by Jack Tager and John W. Ifkovic. Amherst: University of Massachusetts Press, 1985, pp. 3–30.

Technological Innovation and the Decorative Arts: An Exhibition at the Hagley Museum. Wilmington, Del.: Eleutherian Mills–Hagley Foundation, 1973.

Tierney, Kathleen J. "The Social and Community Contexts of Disaster." In *Psychological Aspects of Disaster,* edited by Richard Gist and Bernard Lubin. New York: John Wiley and Sons, 1989.

Trachtenberg, Alan. *Reading American Photographs: Images as History.* New York: Hill and Wang, 1989.

Trumbull, James Russell. *History of Northampton, Massachusetts.* Vol. 1. Northampton, Mass.: Press of Gazette Printing Co., 1898.

Twain, Mark, and Charles Dudley Warner. *The Gilded Age: A Tale of Today.* New York: Penguin Books, 1994.

Van Voris, Jacqueline. *The Look of Paradise: A Pictorial History of Northampton, Massachusetts, 1654–1984.* New Canaan, N.H.: Phoenix, 1984.

Von Drehle, David. *Triangle: The Fire That Changed America.* New York: Atlantic Monthly Press, 2003.

Wallace, Anthony F. C. "The Industrialist as Hero: An Emerging Educational Theme in Nineteenth-Century America." *Educational Studies* 12, no. 1 (1981): 69–83.

———. *Rockdale: The Growth of an American Village in the Early Industrial Revolution.* New York: Norton, 1972.

———. *Tornado in Worcester: An Exploratory Study of Individual and Community Behavior in an Extreme Situation, Disaster Study Number 3.* Prepared for the Committee on Disaster Studies, National Academy of Sciences—National Research Council. Washington, D.C.: National Academy of Sciences—National Research Council, 1956.

Ward, Peter. *Courtship, Love, and Marriage in Nineteenth-Century English Canada.* Montreal: McGill-Queen's University Press, 1990.

Wegmann, Edward. *The Design and Construction of Dams.* New York: John Wiley and Sons, 1927.

Weisner, Stephen G. *Embattled Editor: The Life of Samuel Bowles.* Lanham, Md.:
    University Press of America, 1986.

Whittelsey, Sarah Scovill. "Massachusetts Labor Legislation: An Historical and Critical
    Study." *Annals of the American Academy of Political and Social Science,* supple-
    ment to vol. 15 (1901): 9–34.

Wisely, William H. *The American Civil Engineer, 1852–1974.* New York: American
    Society of Civil Engineers, 1974.

The World's Charity to the Conemaugh Valley Sufferers and Who Received It.
    Johnstown, Penn: Harry M. Benshoff, 1890.

Photographs of Williamsburg Reservoir dam on cover, Quigley house on frontispiece, the Leeds button mill after the flood on insert page 6, Collins Graves and George Cheney on insert page 7, Cheney's house and the dam from the west side on insert page 8 used by permission from the Williamsburg Historical Society, Williamsburg, Massachusetts.

Photographs of Haydenville boardinghouse on back cover, the devastation at Skinnerville on insert page 4, and Florence Meadows on insert page 5 courtesy of the Meekins Library Local History Collection, Williamsburg, Massachusetts.

Map of Massachusetts and affected area on page xiii copyright © 2004 Jeffrey L. Ward.

Diagram of the Williamsburg dam on page xv by John Del Gaizo, adapted from a sketch by the author.

Maps of Haydenville, Williamsburg, Skinnerville, and Leeds on pages 12, 18, 22, and 27 adapted from County Atlas of Hampshire, Massachusetts. New York: F.W. Beers and Co., 1873.

Images of Haydenville on insert page 1, Joel Hayden Sr., Joel Hayden Jr., Isabell Hayden, and Robbie Hayden on insert page 2, and Haydenville Company card on insert page 3 courtesy of the Forbes Library, Northampton, Massachusetts.

Photograph of Skinner family on insert page 4 courtesy of Wistariahurst Museum, Holyoke, Massachusetts.

Photographs of the Nonotuck Silk Company directors on insert page 5 and the Mill River Button Company before the flood on insert page 6 courtesy of Historic Northampton, Northampton, Massachusetts.

INDEX

Page numbers in *italics* refer to maps.